PAINTING IN ABSTRACT

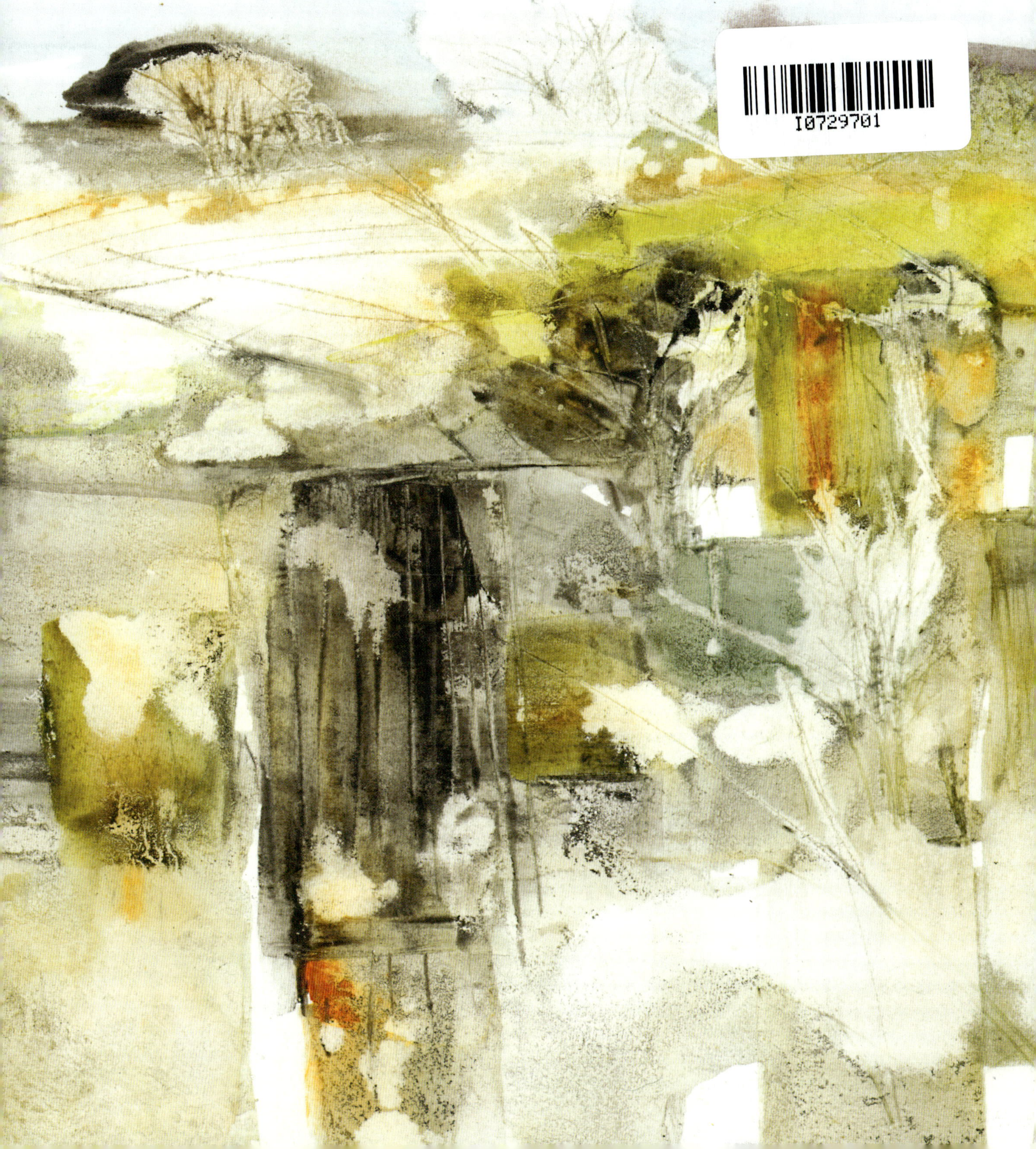

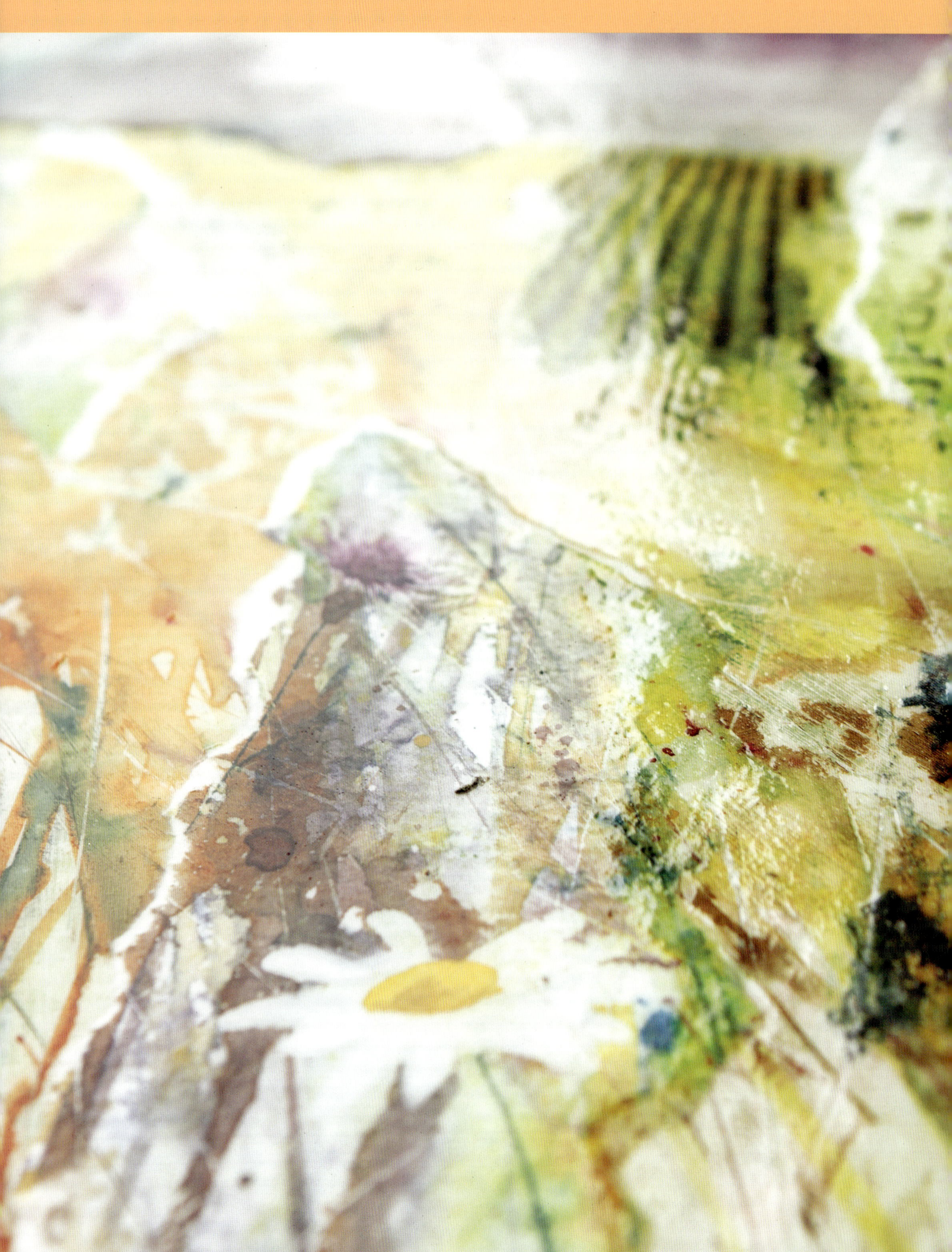

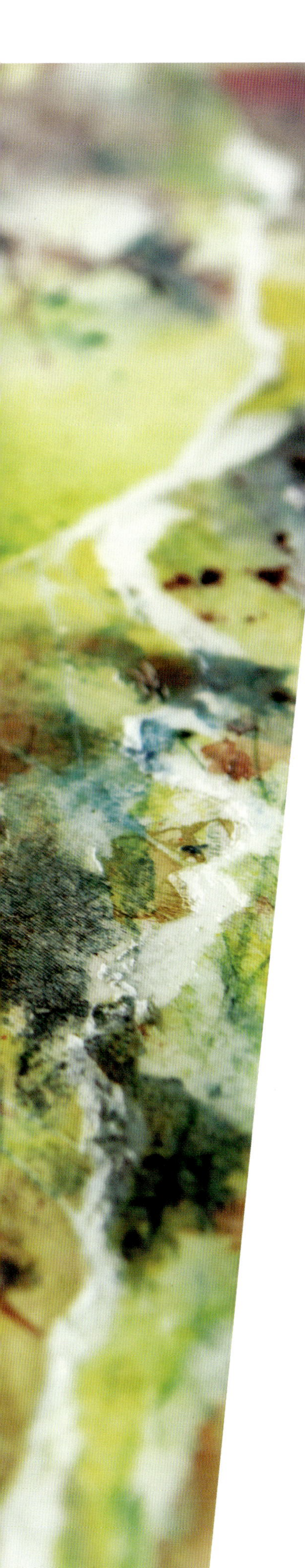

PAINTING IN ABSTRACT

MIXED MEDIA ARTWORK INSPIRED BY THE NATURAL WORLD

Carole Robson

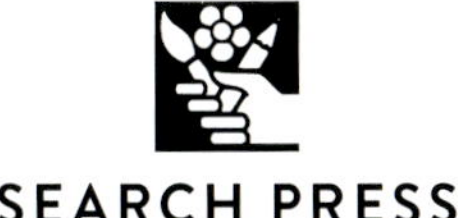

SEARCH PRESS

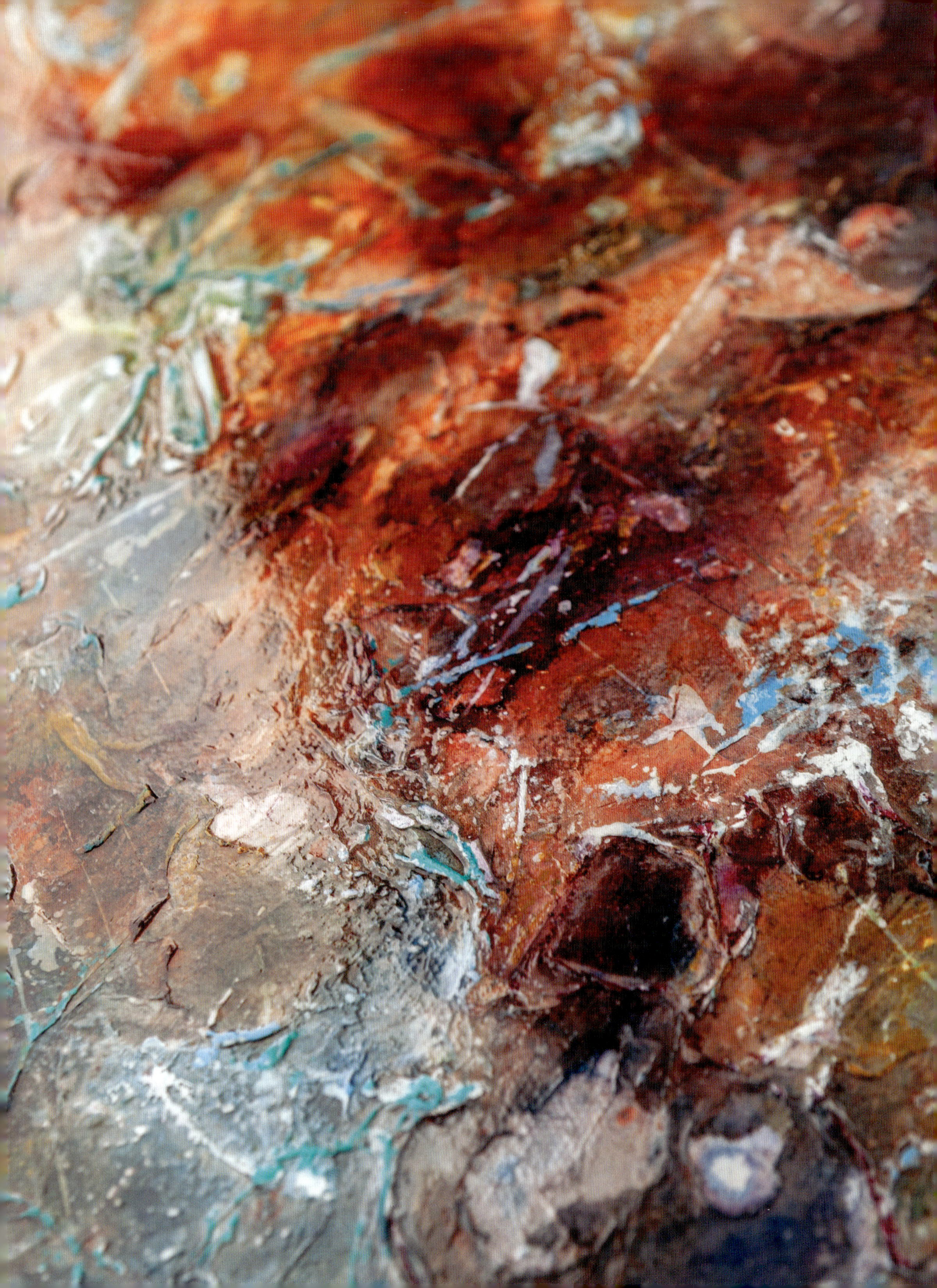

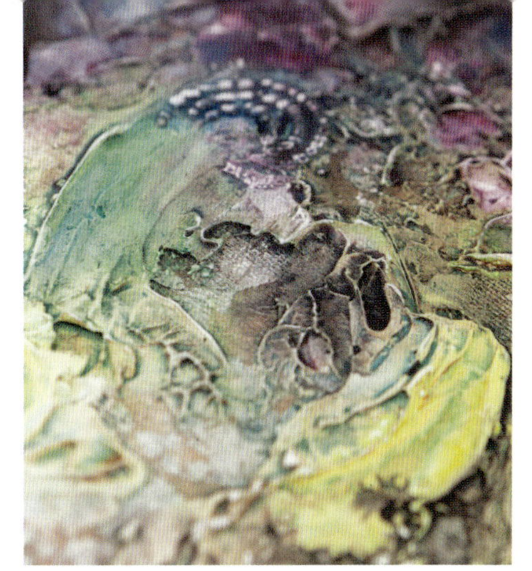
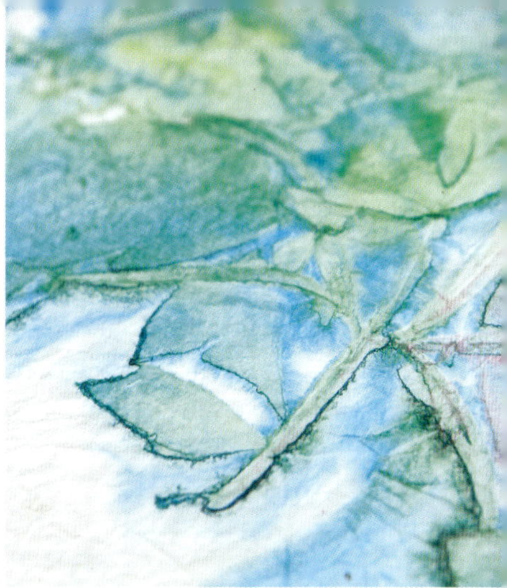

CONTENTS

INTRODUCTION

Art that takes its inspiration from the natural world – its landscape, flora and fauna – is arguably more relevant than ever before. It reinforces the importance of nature in our lives and deepens our connection with it. The paintings in this book all have their beginnings rooted in nature and move in varying degrees towards the abstract. They frequently hold on to some figurative elements and occupy that very wide, middle ground between representational and purely abstract art.

Over the years, I have enjoyed exploring the area of semi-abstraction, both in my paintings and my digital mixed media. The natural landscape, in all its aspects, has remained my inspiration and my personal preference is for art that maintains a visual relationship with its subject.

This is very much a mixed media book, illustrated with my own paintings in a loose and fluid style. It includes a range of both traditional and experimental materials and techniques. It also examines a variety of influences from other artists and genres.

Painters who follow a path of pure abstraction develop their paintings solely from elements such as line, shape, form, texture and so forth. These formal elements are the building blocks of all art, and understanding them is key to increasing our appreciation of abstract art. The first part of this book deals with the formal elements in some detail; it examines their individual roles in picture making and suggests ways to use them in our own art.

Abstract art can be a challenge to both understand and create. Moving away from representational art demands a certain amount of self-belief and confidence; so my aim with this book is to help you break down any self-imposed barriers and overcome any doubts.

We can choose whether our art is completely abstract, combines elements of representation and abstraction, or dips in and out of each at will. The mantra 'Art for art's sake' declares our right to do so. Though originally coined in nineteenth-century France, the phrase still sounds remarkably modern. It confirms our right to freedom of expression and never needing to justify our art.

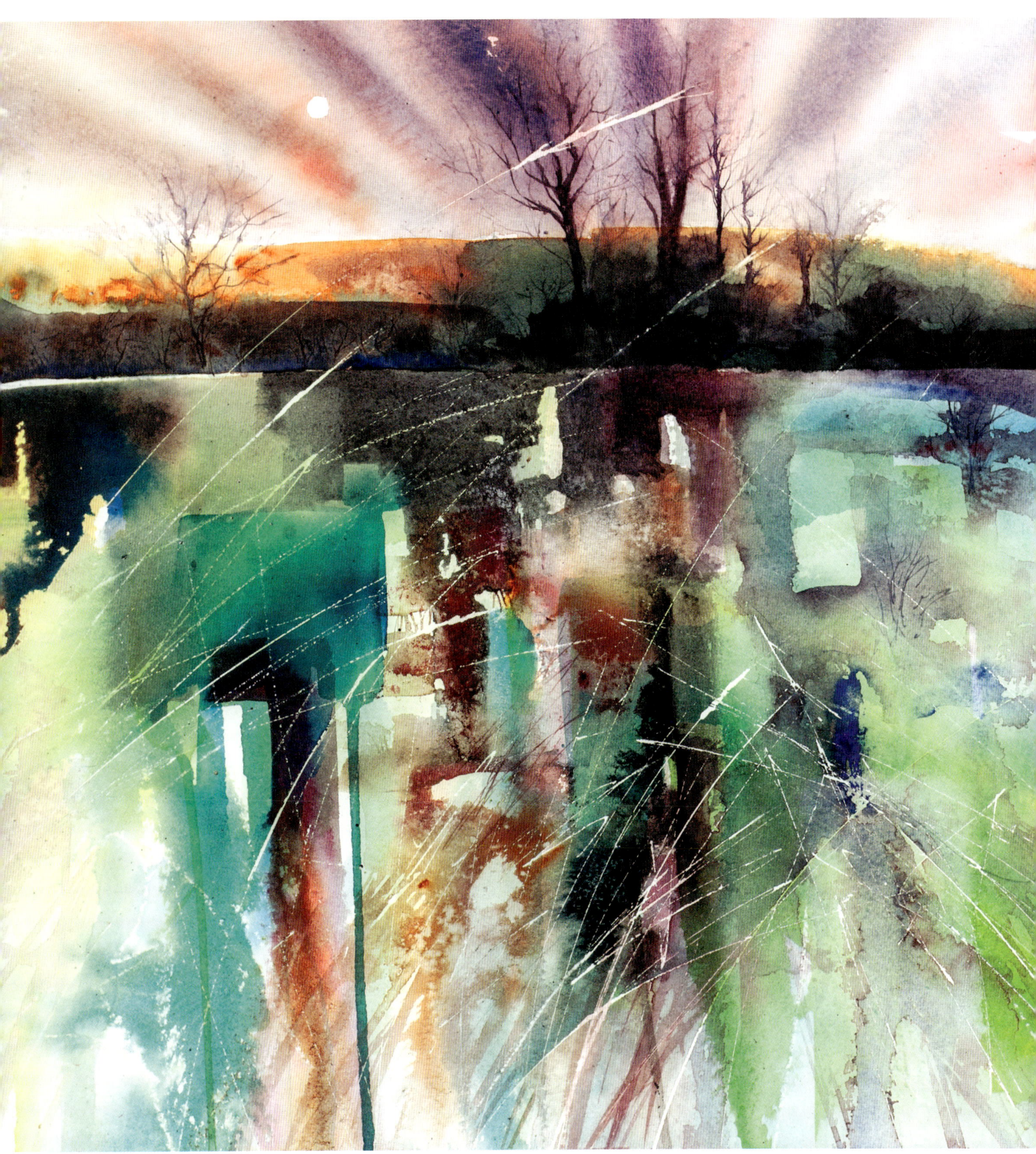

Shapes of the Night
35 × 35cm (13¾ × 13¾in)

FRAMING THE MIND

How do we get into the right mindset to begin our journey towards abstract art? Representational art often has a clear narrative or message. Abstract art can be far more nuanced, and it includes any art that intentionally moves away from reality. Abstract art allows for many different interpretations and takes on a variety of guises. It may be formalized and geometric or flowing and organic; it may be methodically planned over time or created in the moment and guided to a greater or lesser degree by intuition. Abstraction may begin with a subject, which it represents to some degree or other, or it may be purely abstract and based on elements such as line, shape or colour.

As artists, we quite rightly claim to express ourselves as we choose and have imaginative and creative freedom. 'Art for art's sake', as I mentioned in the introduction, is our battle cry. All this freedom, however, can be a double-edged sword. We may feel at a loss and left to wonder, 'Where to start?'

For me, the natural world is always my starting point. It is an infinite source of invention and a limitless fund of inspiration. I live in a rural area and for me it is not the breathtakingly grand vistas that attract me, but my everyday views over fields and woodland, watery meadows, and weedy and neglected places. Wherever we live, whether rural or urban, we don't need to go far to find inspiration. It is often whatever surrounds us; the things that we have the closest connection to, that give most meaning to our art.

The value of experiment

Experiment, as any scientist will tell us, is key to discovering new
ideas; and we frequently learn the most from trying something new.
Often the most exciting artworks are born from experiment and this is
especially true when working in mixed media.

If you want to be successful, you need to be brave and bold. We all learn and
make new discoveries by trying things out – and learning from our mistakes.

When we are working in mixed media, we are often combining
materials, like a scientist might, just to see what happens. We might
expect one result but get something completely different. Serendipity
takes charge and we discover something new and exciting!

Leonardo da Vinci, as we know, was an inveterate experimenter with
an insatiable curiosity. In his *Treatise on Painting*, he advised artists to
look 'attentively at old, smeared walls and veined marble of various
colours'. Leonardo called these ideas 'apparently trifling, and almost
laughable', but 'out of this confused mass of objects, the mind will be
furnished with an abundance of designs and subjects perfectly new'.

Leonardo and his contemporaries used these accidental marks and
textures to inspire and discover interesting compositions for their
realistic paintings. Experimental ideas like these seem modern and
before their time. They are, in fact, still relevant and used by artists
today, although it wasn't until the early part of the twentieth century
that their value to abstract art was recognized.

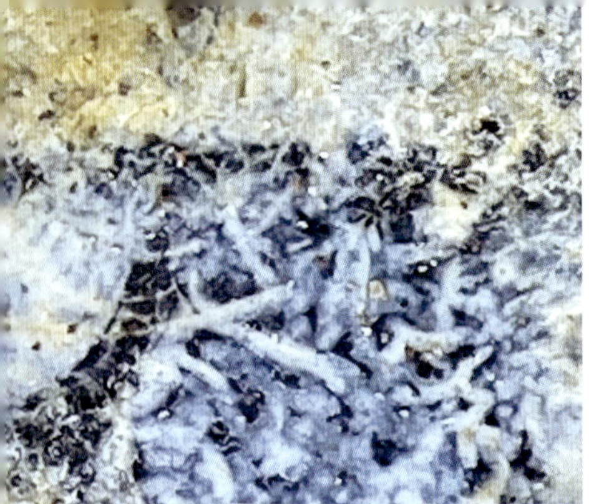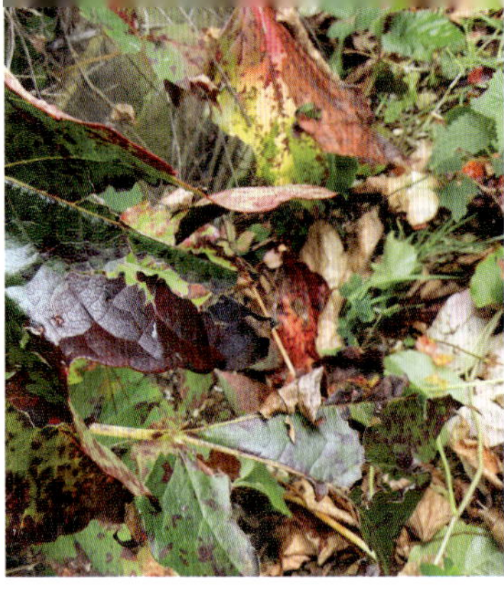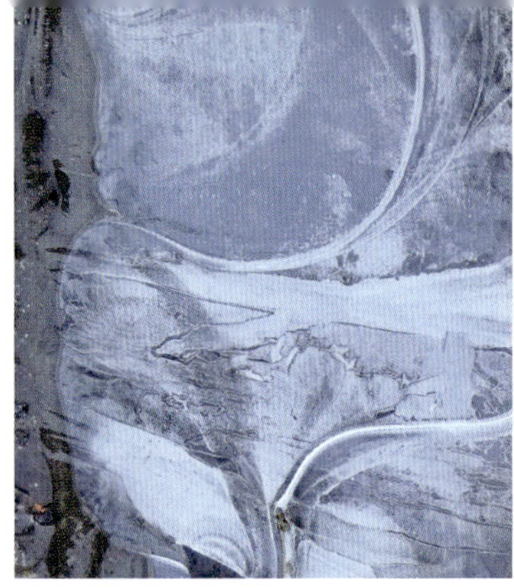

Collecting source material from nature

Abstract patterns and textures are all around us. Once you begin to look, you'll see them everywhere: in tree bark, shells, leaves, fur and feathers. In the sky, cloud formations can be particularly textural, such as cirrus or a mackerel sky. Ripples on water are also fascinating, their patterns and shapes changing so rapidly. Frost and winter snow transform and camouflage familiar objects, allowing us to appreciate them anew – the surface of puddles, for example, can become ready-made abstractions as they ice over.

Why not use your camera to start recording these everyday abstracts, and begin to build up a stock of source material for reference? You can see some of mine here. Likewise, taking short videos of moving subjects like sea or sky will allow you to study them at your leisure. The act of searching out and collecting these fascinating images will improve your observation and fire your imagination.

Responding to nature

Humans have always been inspired by the abstract patterns and textures found in nature, and in the landscape around them. Deep in prehistory, artists painted richly illustrated scenes on cave walls and sacred sites, some of which survive today. The uneven stone, blackened with carbon from their fires, was far from a blank canvas; its varied colours, shapes and textures doubtless proved fertile ground for these artists' imaginations.

We are no different today. When we see shapes, we look for meaning and try to make sense of them – we see the man in the moon and readily conjure up animal forms and human faces in the clouds (or even our morning toast)! We have always been drawn to pattern and texture, and our brains are wired in such a way that these random shapes and marks serve to kickstart our imaginations.

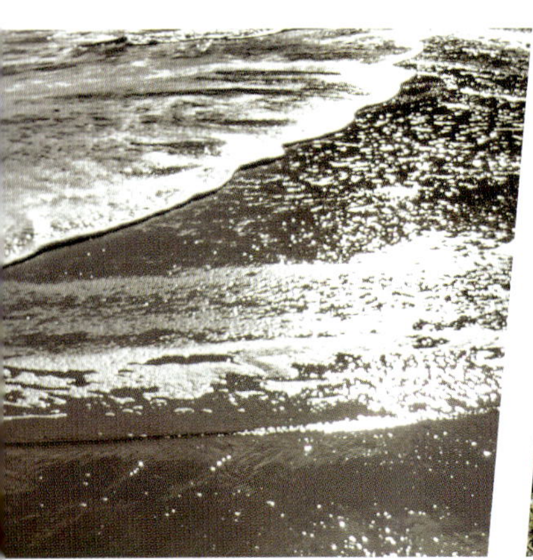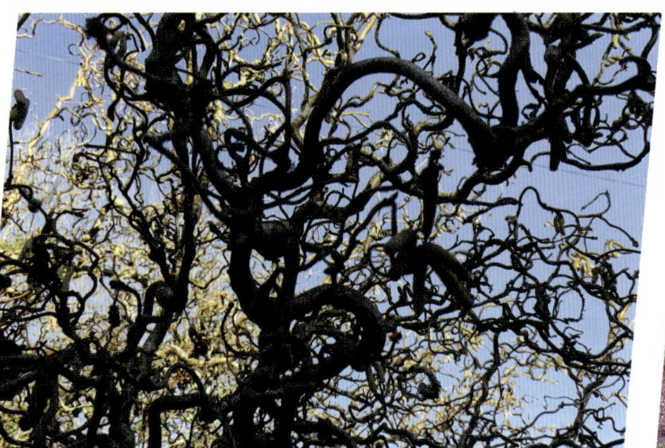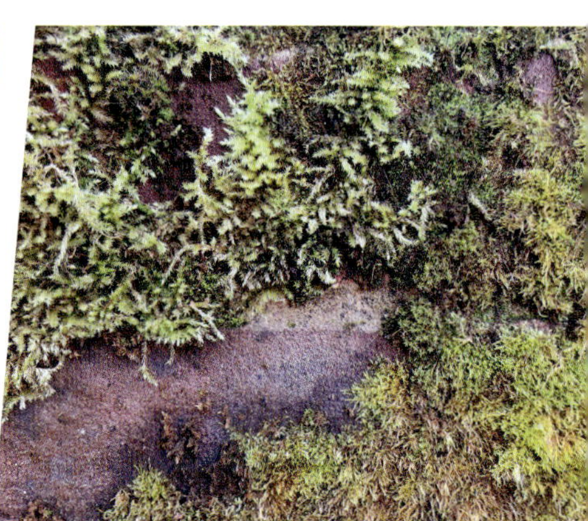

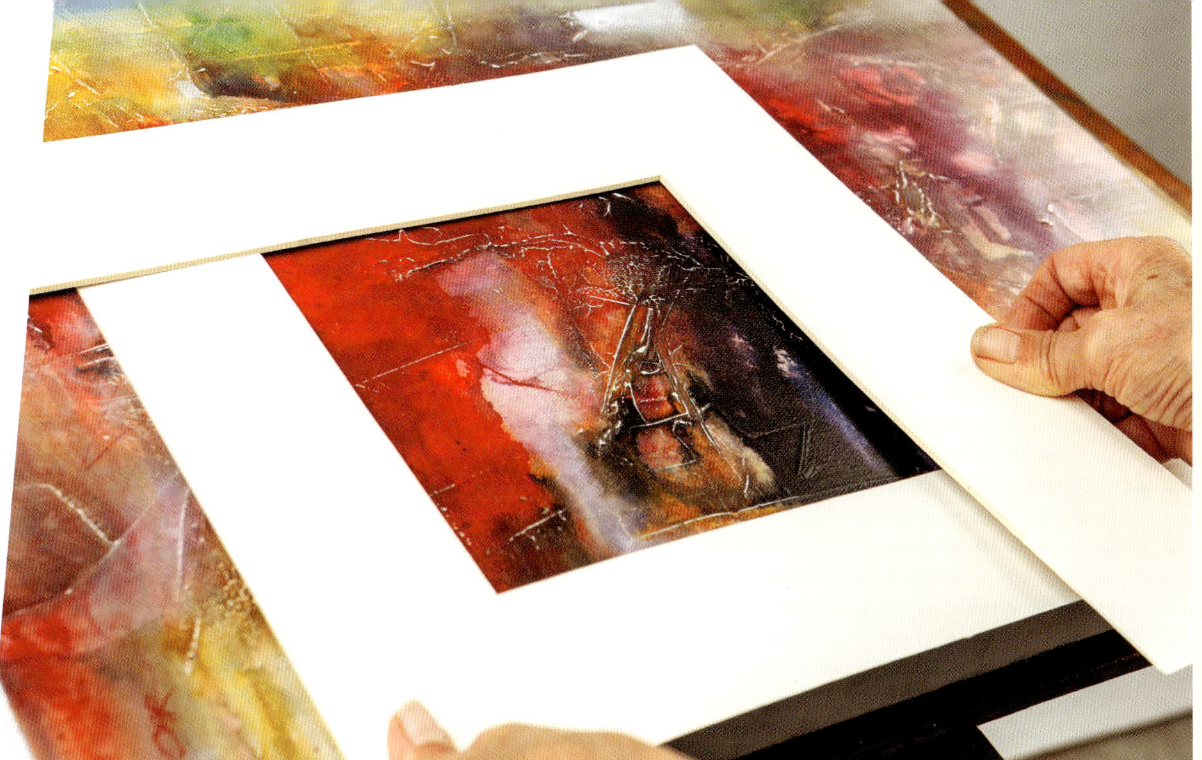

A different way of looking

Try using a viewfinder over one of your paintings to find smaller abstracts – you may find more than one!

Looking closely at a subject, using a camera or some other kind of viewfinder, allows us to isolate an image from its surroundings, in order to sketch or record it.

A card viewfinder is a versatile tool; little more than two L-shaped pieces of card that are moved to provide a temporary frame. A viewfinder of this kind is easy to make and very useful for visualizing potential compositions by cropping out the surroundings or extraneous areas.

Viewfinders are useful both in the home or out in nature to isolate textures and patterns. You can also use them to see a finished painting without the messiness around it, or move them around over pictures in magazines to help find interesting compositions.

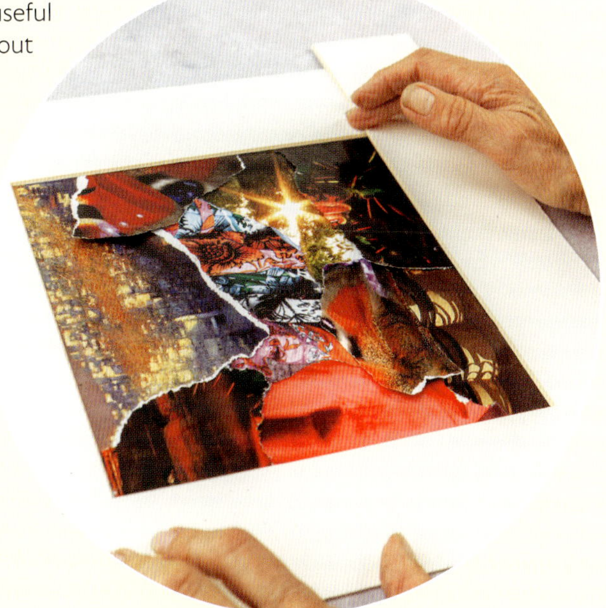

Tear up pieces of collage, arrange them and use the viewfinder to isolate a potential abstract.

EXERCISE Develop a simple abstract

The source material that you have collected may well include some photographs that need little alteration to develop them into ready-made abstracts. This exercise will show you how to move your source material further from reality and to create an altogether new image that works as a piece of art.

Try making an abstract painting from one of your reference photographs. Here are some ideas to try as potential starting points.

- Simplify or remove some of the image.

- Change a full colour image to monochrome, or vice versa.

- Reverse colours to their complementary opposites (see page 43).

- Reproduce the image in line only, changing the weight of the lines so that they are either very even or more uneven than they were before.

- Simplify or exaggerate tonal differences.

- Add marks, texture or pattern.

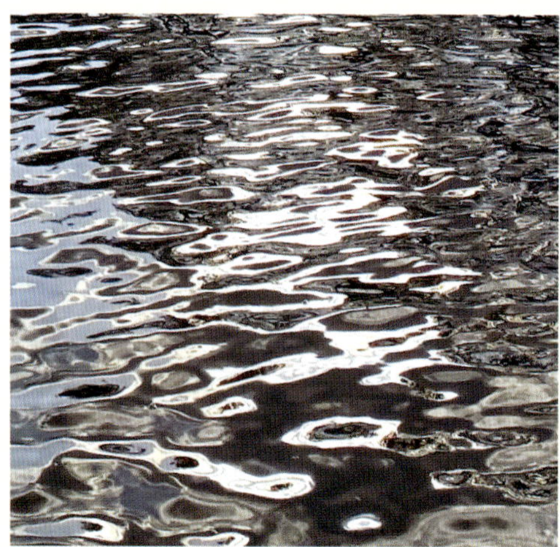
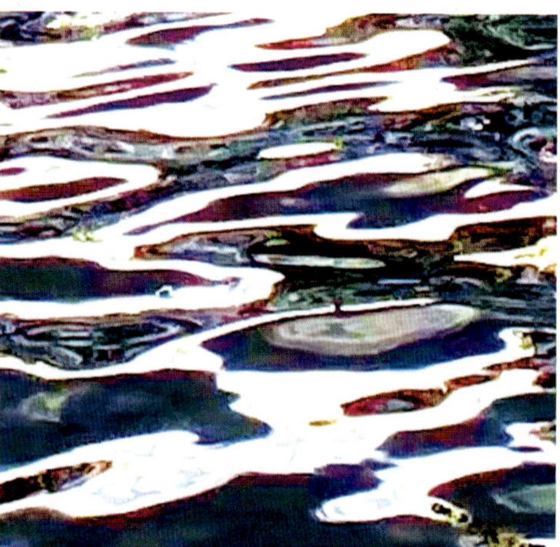

Using technology

If you are able to, why not use the software in your camera or tablet to make further alterations to an image? As well as zooming in and cropping the photograph, I also intensified the colours with an image-editing app on my tablet. This is described opposite.

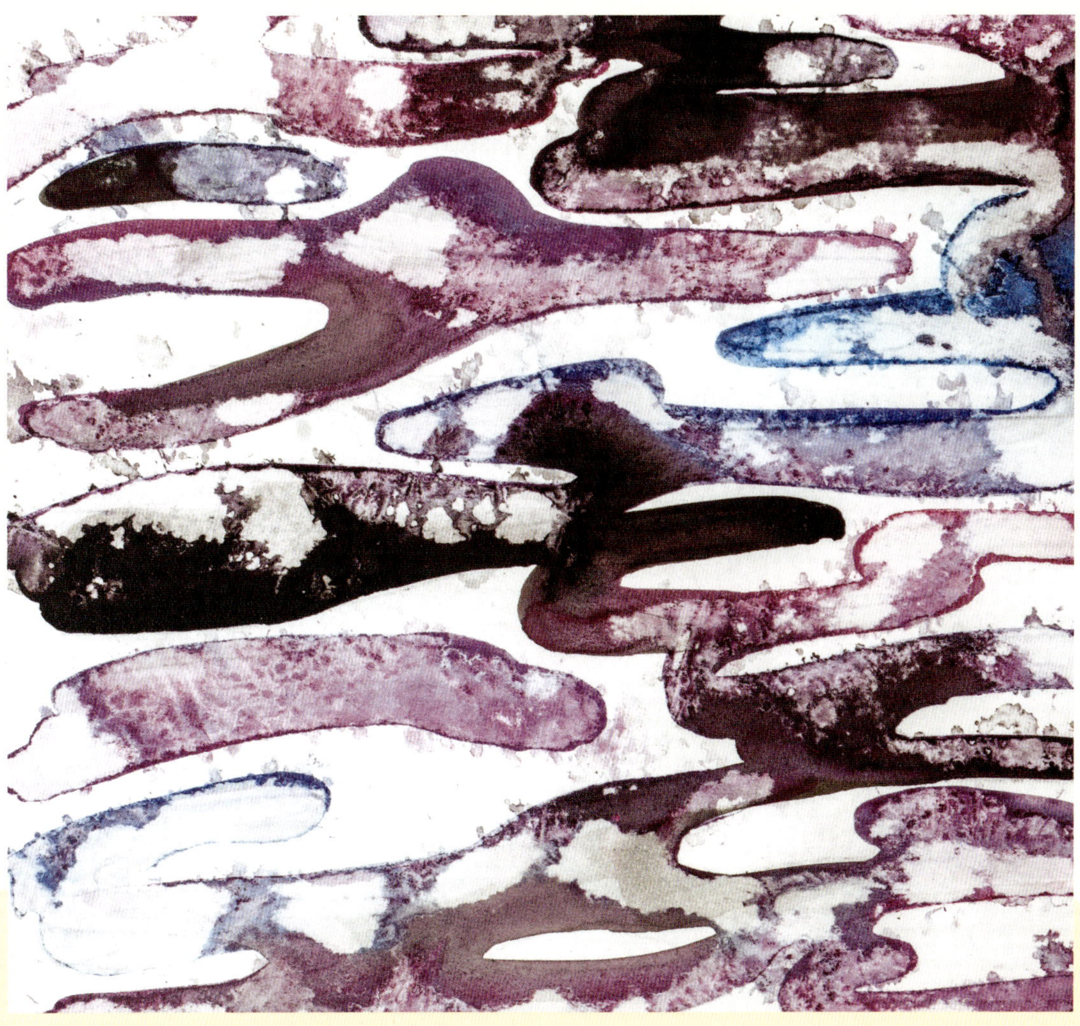

Sea Creatures
20 × 20cm (8 × 8in)

Painting *Sea Creatures*

The photograph of ripples on water on the opposite page was my starting point. I used the basic image-editing software on my tablet to crop the image to the central section and push the saturation slider to maximum in order to intensify the colours – you can see the results of this process opposite. You could, of course, simply use your eye and imagination, but digital tools will help you to avoid any unconscious preconceptions of what you expect to see.

Taking a piece of white mount card as my support, I then sketched on the design and mixed up wells of quinacridone magenta and Winsor blue watercolour, together with a purple mixture of the two. All were mixed to a milk-like consistency. I also put out a small amount of black acrylic ink.

I began painting with a size 12 round brush, freely interpreting the shapes and simplifying them even more. I used the watercolours first, adding a drop or two of black ink in places. Some of the shapes began reminding me of sea creatures, which I quite liked.

As the paint was drying, I couldn't resist adding a little spray of water, to give some texture and to see what would happen. As the piece started to dry, I decided to wash the image off in order to add yet more texture – the technique is explained on page 77.

THE FORMAL
ELEMENTS

A wholly abstract painting is just as likely to stop you in your tracks as one that is representational – but what makes an artwork so eye-catching, if it isn't the subject? It may be that varied and interesting shapes are arranged into an attention-grabbing composition, there may be dramatic tonal values, perhaps a striking colour palette with zinging complementaries, or gestural lines that create a strong sense of movement.

Line, shape and form, tone, colour and texture are known as the formal or basic elements. They are the building blocks of all art, whether representational or abstract. Beyond this, they are fundamental to our lives in general – the vocabulary of the formal elements is commonplace in our everyday lives. We talk about 'a line of music' or 'getting in line', 'body shape', 'tone of voice', 'the shape of things to come' and so on.

Pure abstract art (also known as non-objective or non-representational) describes art that has no intention of depicting physical things. Instead, it uses the visual language of the formal elements to create its compositions.

In this chapter, we will look at the main formal elements and the role that they play in abstract painting, so that we can use them more effectively in our own art.

Exploring the exercises: what to use?

For the exercises in this chapter, you are free to enjoy exploring the formal elements with the tools and materials with which you are already familiar and comfortable – whether this is paint and brush, pencil and paper, or something entirely different.

We look in detail at tools and materials on pages 52–61, and go on to explore other techniques and ways of working in later chapters.

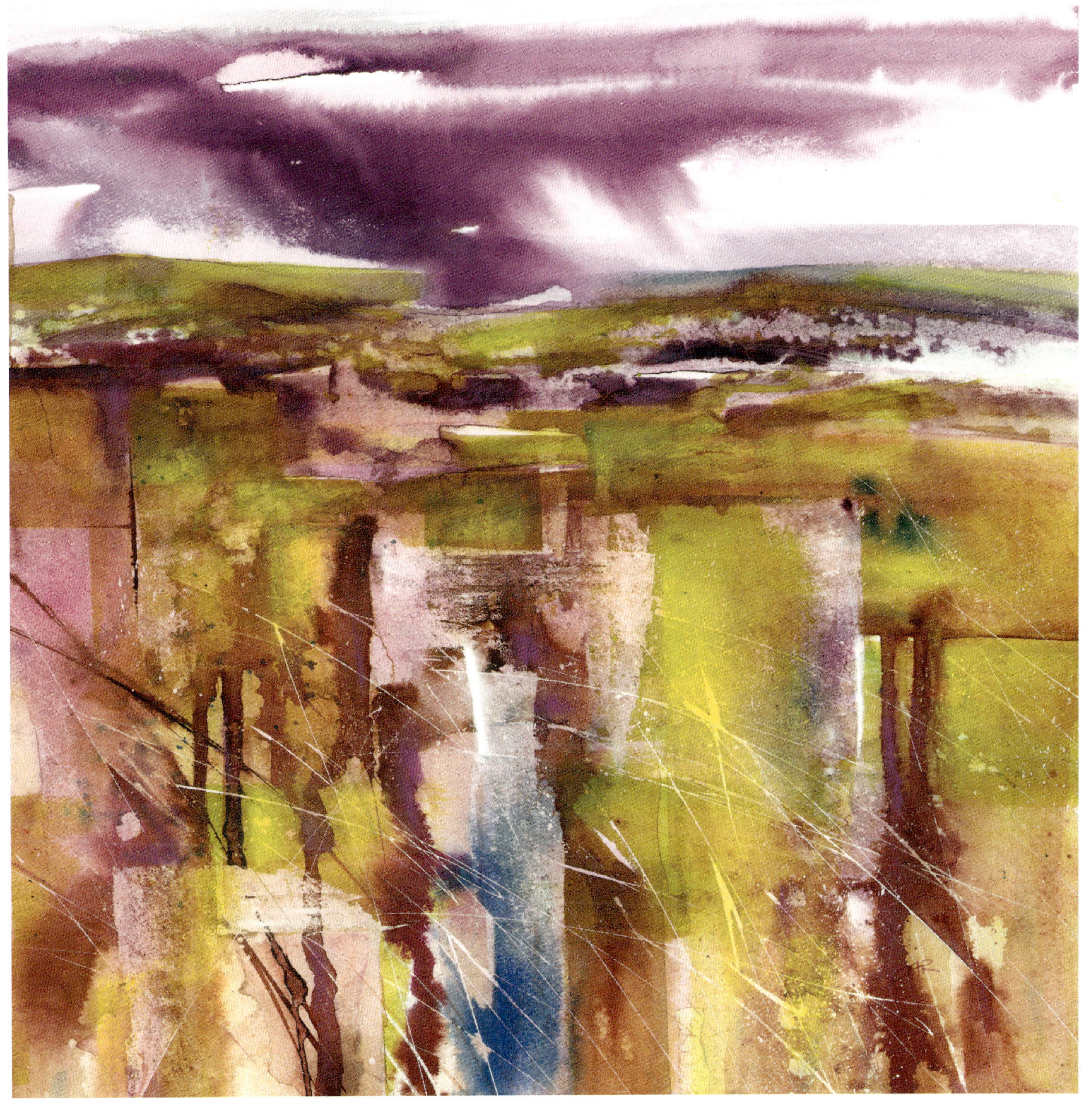

Purple Rain

35 × 35cm (13¾ × 13¾in)

*All of the formal elements are at work in this imaginative landscape.
The colour scheme, based on the complementary pairing of yellow and
purple, is simple and non-realistic. The combination of rounded and
geometric shapes adds to the painting's abstract feel. Line is used in the
foreground, to add a sense of movement, while varying tones and textures
are balanced throughout the painting, unifying the composition.*

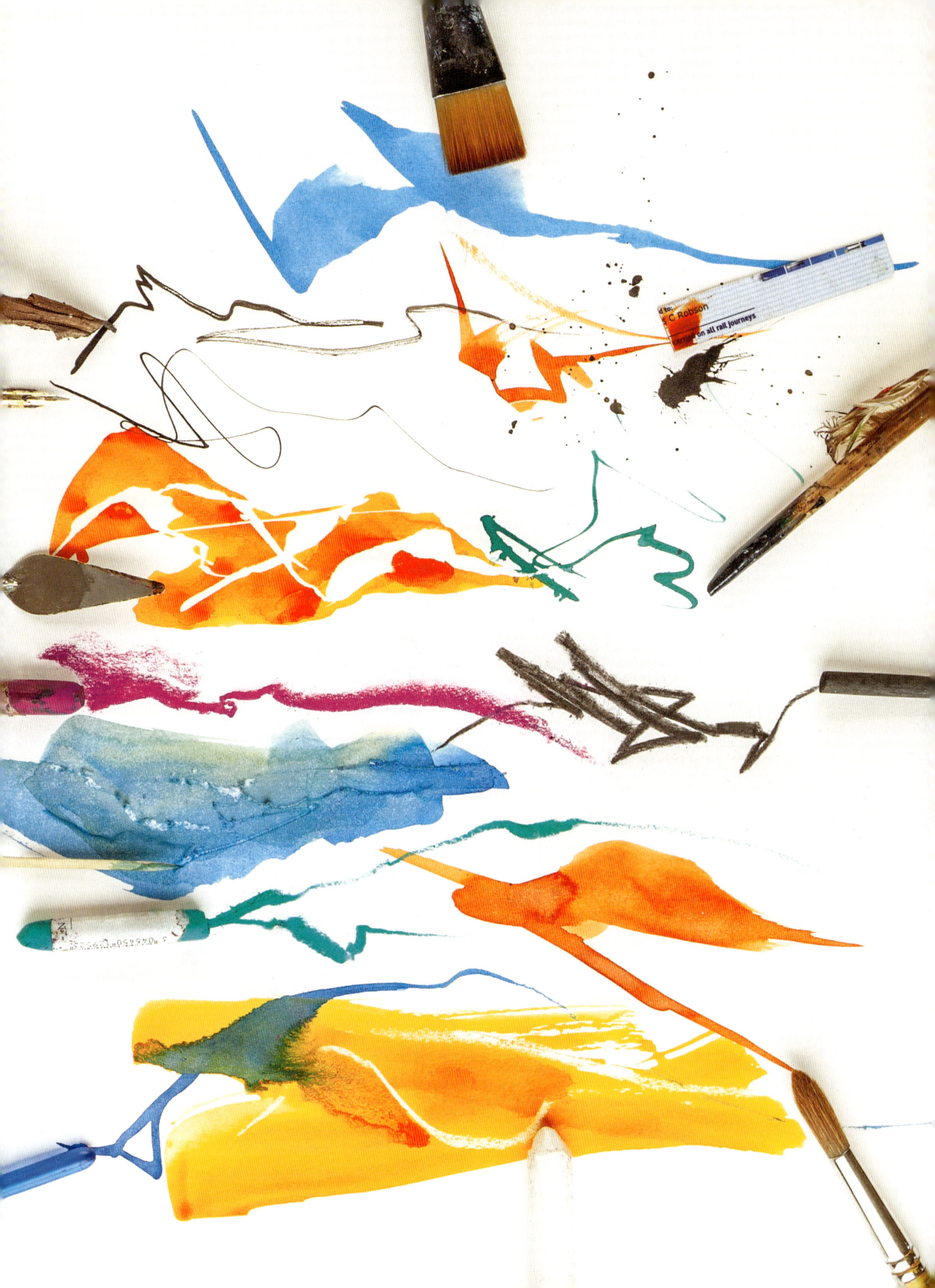
d to:
C Robson
on all rail journeys

Line

A line is defined as a continuous mark, longer than it is wide, but there are many different types and ways of producing a line. A line can be thick or thin, broken or solid, positive or negative (that is, reversed out of a background).

We can use line in our art to create mood: a calm line could be straight or gently undulating – imagine the difference between the contour lines of a flat plain and those of gently rolling hills. Lines that are spiral or jagged create tension, or can express agitation or anger.

Lines are also like paths: they lead us in different directions and can help to guide the eye around a painting. A meandering line takes us on a slow wander, while a straight line can lead you, lightning fast, from one point to another.

Experiments with line

Discovering the variety of line that you can make with a range of tools, whether found or man made, can improve both your skills and fluency in their use. Not only that, but the marks that you make are as unique as your signature. You should aim to build a vocabulary of marks that you can dip into as needed. By using tools and marks repeatedly in your paintings, they contribute to your own personal style.

Whatever drawing tools you are used to, cast around and try something different: a palette knife, ruling pen or piece of plastic card, for example, can create fine, graphic lines. You can draw fluid lines with the dropper from an ink bottle, while the open neck of a paint tube or a piece of twig will give more tonal or broken marks. Just about anything can become a tool when dipped into paint or ink.

Marks and scribble

'Mark making' is a term that describes the range of lines, strokes, dots, daubs, drips, splashes, scratches and so on that we use in our art. Every tool that we use, even a finger, will make a different set of marks. Mark making is at its best when it is experimental; it is about exploring as many different marks that we can think of, with one idea leading to another.

From early childhood we use line to explore our world and to communicate our thoughts in ever more complex ways. It begins with abstraction: crayon scribble and finger painting; lines drawn in the sand or the condensation on a window. When youngsters draw, they have no preconceptions or inhibitions; small hands experiment and explore, while as adult artists we try to regain their creative mindset! Adults prefer the word doodling to scribbling, but it's only a name-change for marks, shapes and patterns that are produced semi-consciously, when the mind is dwelling on other things.

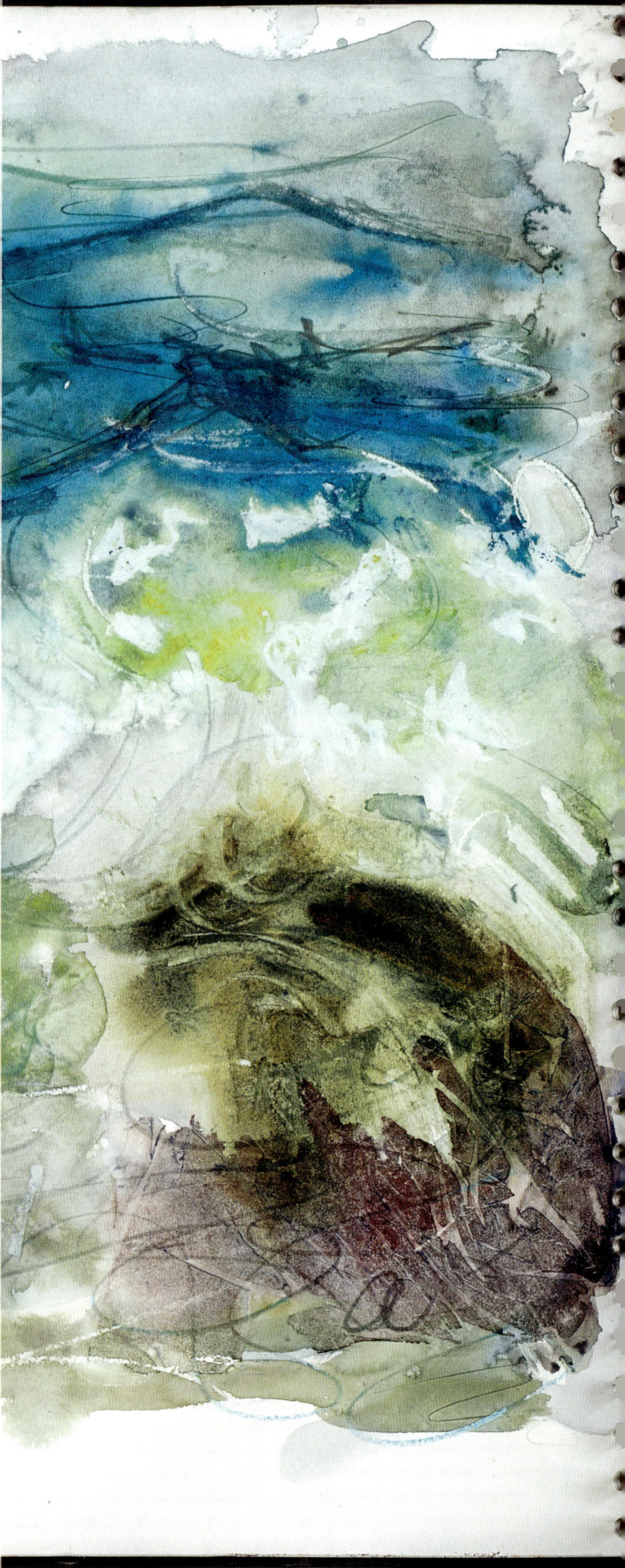

Sketchbook study

This sketch uses a lively drawn and scribbled line to very loosely define its subject of sea and rocks. First of all, I used a wax crayon to scribble lines that would resist the watercolour painting to follow. I then painted freely using the wet in wet technique (see page 64), adding some stronger paint dry in wet to suggest the rocky areas, while keeping all the edges soft. Next, I scribbled into the wet paint, making horizontal and swirled lines and marks in all directions. The last step was to use my finger nails to incise lines and a pencil to add some stronger marks.

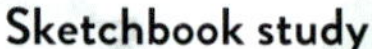

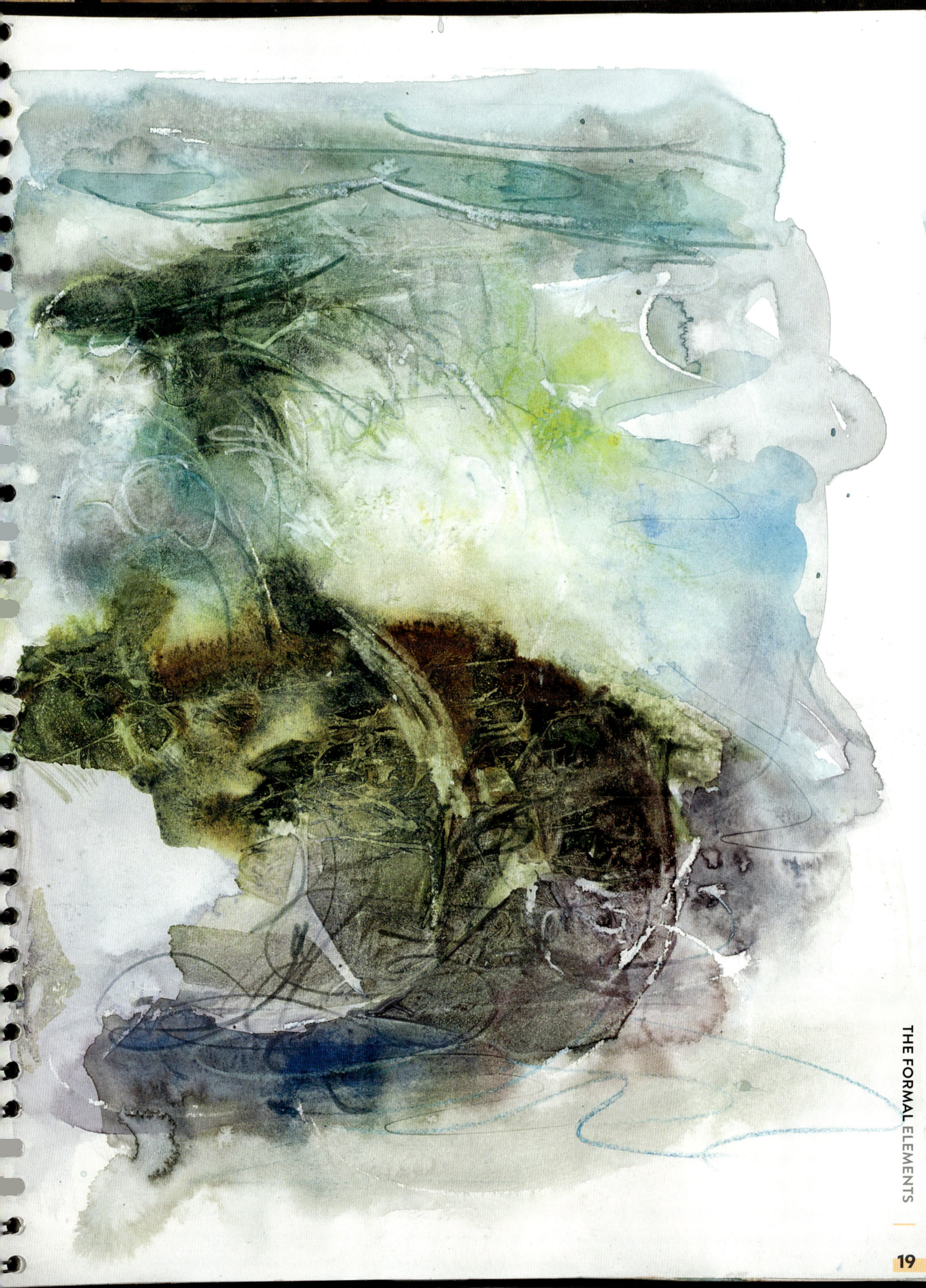

'Take a line for a walk.' **Paul Klee**

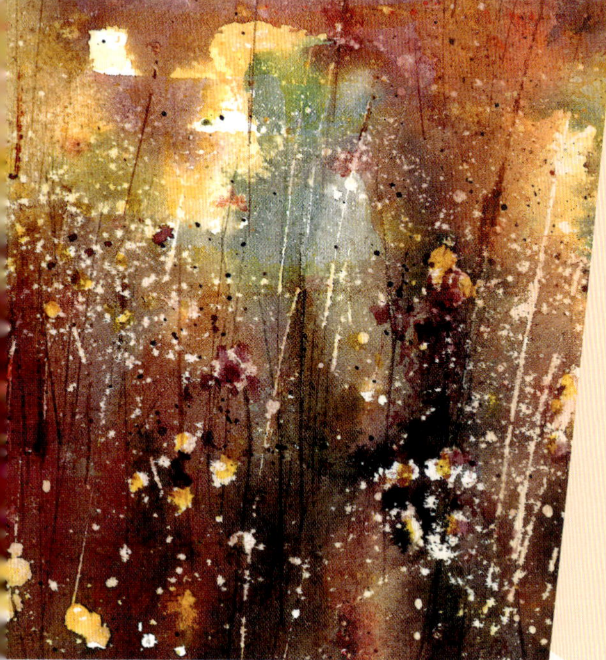

Painting *Grass Movements*

I enjoy sketching and photographing grasses in the landscape and their gestural, arching lines feature in many of my paintings. In the painting *Grass Movements*, I used a combination of line, marks and wet in wet painting to create the rhythmic movement of the grasses.

The first step was to reserve lines and flicks with masking fluid. I usually use a palette knife for a loose gestural line and add flicks with the tip. A ruling pen or quill pen can also give a good result, and a toothbrush can be used for the flicks.

The painting progressed with wet in wet washes of watercolour that followed the movement of the grasses; I continued to add lines, flicks and drips with paint to add to the sense of movement. Further lines were incised into the wet paint where needed using my thumbnail, and more were scratched out with a craft knife or scalpel once the painting was completely dry.

Gestural abstraction

Gestural art, also known as 'action painting', flourished between the 1940s and 1960s. This movement used line in a completely new and spontaneous fashion. Gestural artists painted intuitively, conveying their emotions through their bodies with vigorous, sweeping arm movements.

The American artist Jackson Pollock (1912–1956) is famous as a gestural painter and most well known for the 'drip' technique of his abstract expressionist paintings. His method of painting was directly influenced by the Surrealists' automatism technique and involved leaning over his canvas, laid out on the floor. He dripped, poured and splashed the paint rhythmically and expressively. His swirled, linear marks were charged with emotion and appear to build up fractal-like structures that some studies have suggested mimic nature's complex, underlying geometry.

Hans Hartung (1904–1989) was another exciting gestural painter who emerged as a leading figure of twentieth-century abstraction. He was an experimental artist who developed a dynamic and emotional use of line as his unique means of self-expression.

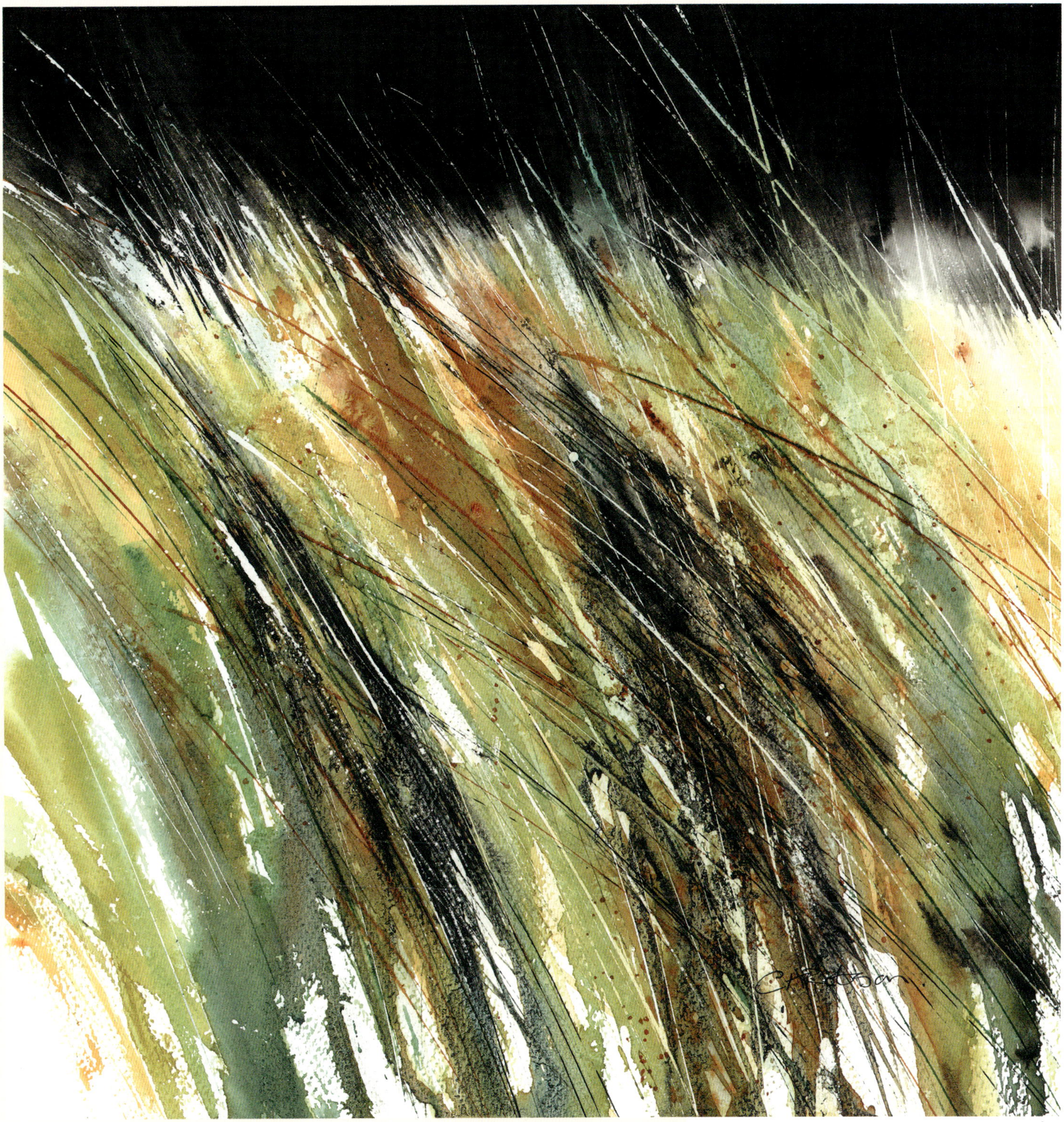

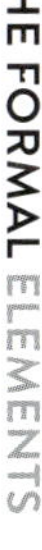

Grass Movements
35 × 35cm (13¾ × 13¾in)

Painting *Meadow Flora*

The semi-abstract painting opposite shows the linear qualities of umbellifer seed heads, with their curved sun ray-like heads and ridged stems, together with meadow plants and grasses.

The composition uses a variety of line and textures, including lines drawn freely with a brush, more controlled fine lines made with a ruling pen, finely drawn pen and ink drawings which are collaged onto the surface, loose scribble and gestural lines made with a palette knife.

Some lines are positive: black lines on a white background, while others are white against a darkly-toned background. There are fine lines, broad lines; some that are washed off and others that use the gouache resist technique. These techniques are described in more detail in the chapter 'Irresistible Resists' on pages 70–87, and also explored in the project *River Birds*.

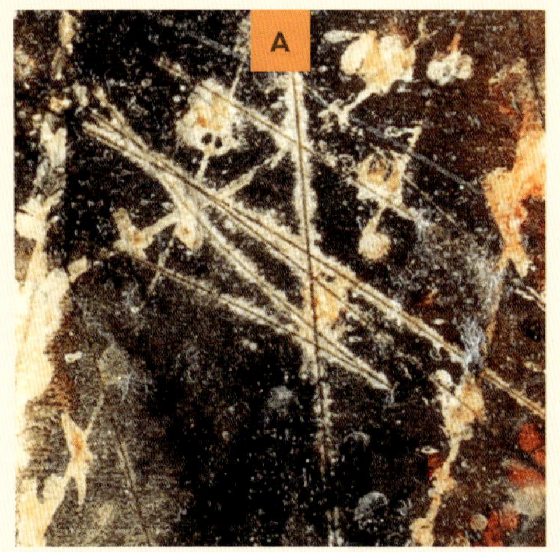
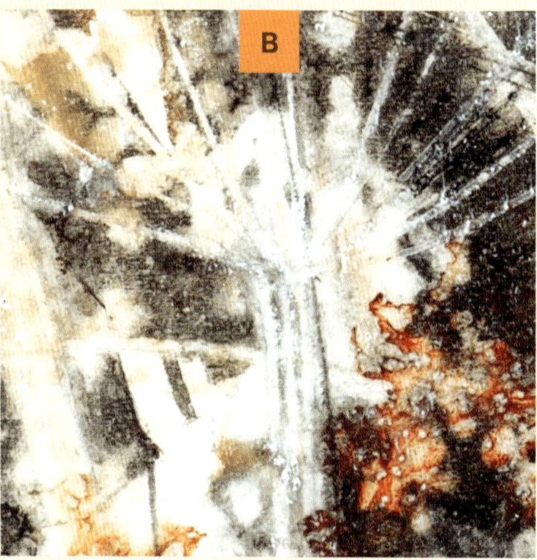
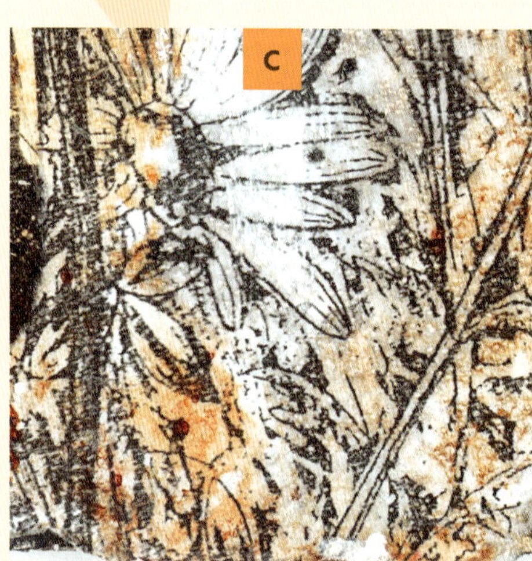

A This detail shows some lines freely scribbled using a palette knife and ink. They were painted over and then washed off when almost dry, which created the interesting edges to the marks.

B This shows details of lines and shapes made with the gouache lift technique (see pages 78–79). Gouache was painted on, allowed to dry and washed over with ink, which was later washed off.

C This is a piece of collage, taken from a print of one of my old etchings that I wanted to recycle. The meadow flowers are drawn in a fine graphic line, which contrasts well with the free washes around it.

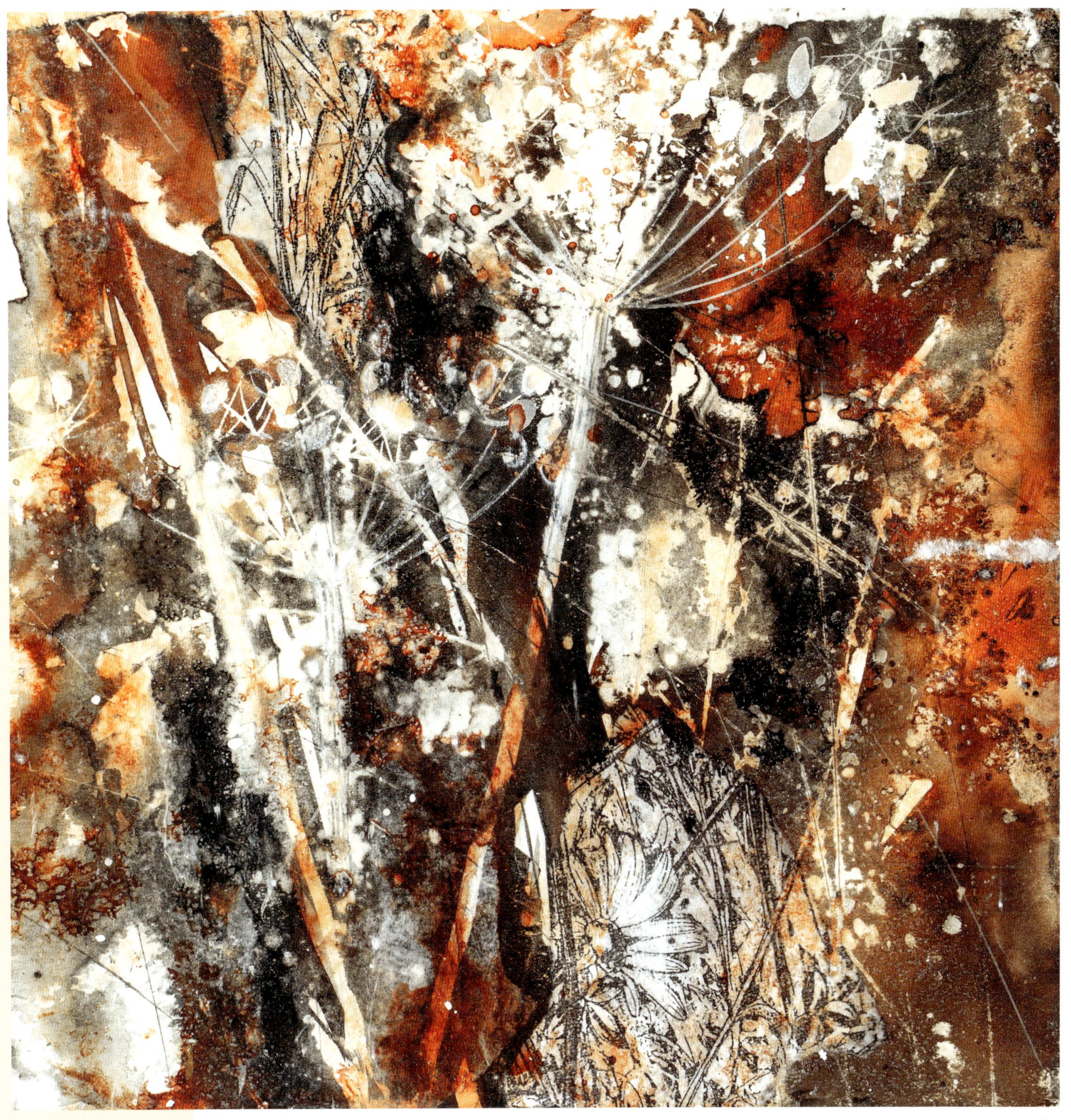

Meadow Flora

30 × 30cm (11¾ × 11¾in)

Shape and form

'Shape' describes two-dimensional areas, while 'form' describes three-dimensional areas. For example, a circle is a shape, while a ball is a form. Shapes can be natural and organic or hard-edged and geometric. Curved or swirled forms are energetic, like racing clouds on a windy day; diagonals introduce movement to a painting and help to lead the eye. Geometric shapes bring solidity and strength, remind us of manmade structures or even nature's underlying geometry.

We also use the words 'shape' and 'form' to describe the structure of an artwork, talking about how a painting is 'shaping up' or the 'form' it is taking.

Shape, form and composition

Shape and form are integral to how we 'see' and compose our paintings. When you begin to see the world in front of you in terms of shape or form, you are on the right track to successful painting!

Composing shouldn't be a rigid exercise that you work through laboriously – and certainly not at the expense of spontaneity. There is always scope for intuition and developing a painting as it progresses. A bit of forethought, however, is always a good plan. The tried and tested guidelines on the following pages will give us a helping hand.

The rule of thirds

The rule of thirds is perhaps the most well known compositional tool and is a simplification of the Golden Section; a seemingly magical ratio that is found throughout nature: in the spiral of a snail shell, the centres of flowers and even in the galaxies. Artists have long used the Golden Section to achieve pleasing, harmonious proportions in their works.

Nowadays, the rule of thirds is generally accepted as a rule of thumb; a 'near enough' approximation of the Golden Section. The lines of the thirds can be used to place elements of interest, such as a horizon, a tree, a building or an abstract movement or shape.

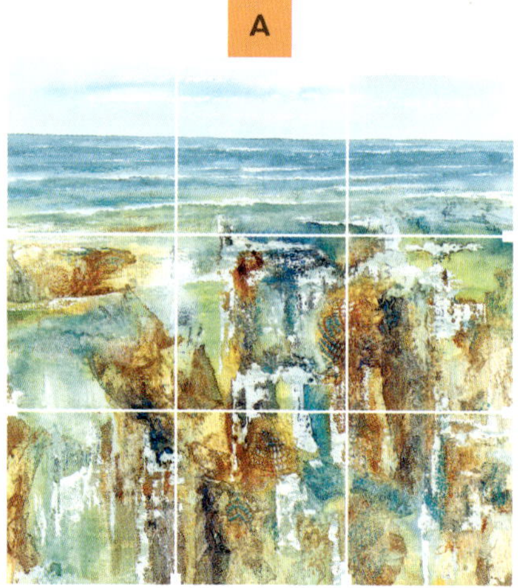

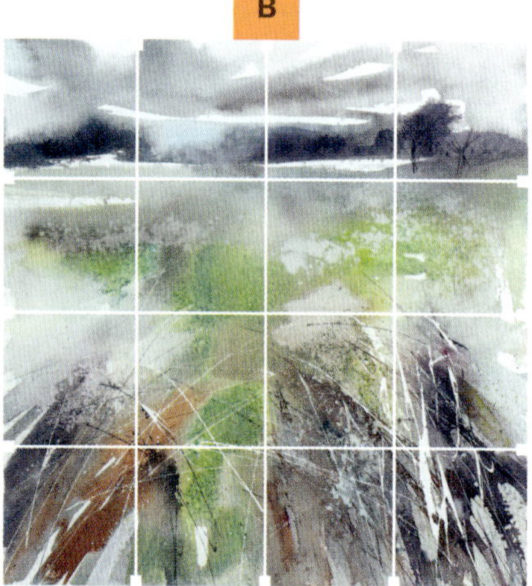

A The rule of thirds in action. The gridded frame laid over the painting highlights how the composition is split into thirds. Note how the top third appears serene and simple, with horizontal strokes; while the remainder of the painting is more complex and textural.

B Just as the rule of thirds is a generalization of the Golden Section, there is a case for even more variation. While we can use the rule of thirds to achieve pleasing proportions in our paintings, by using quarter divisions instead of thirds, we can create a more dramatic effect.

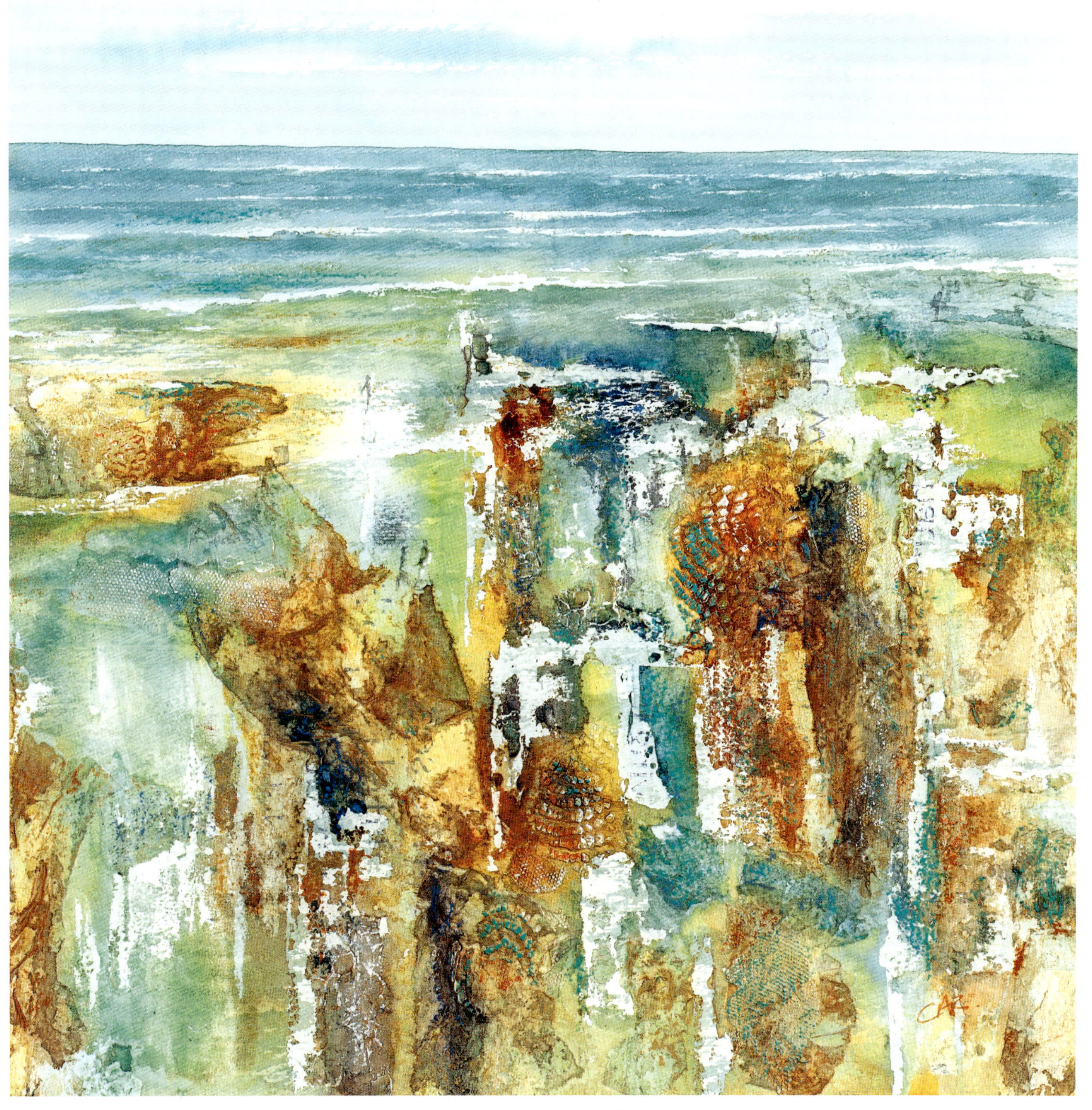

Last One on the Beach

35 × 35cm (13¾ × 13¾in)

*The sky and sea take up just the top third of this painting, in order to
allow the abstract shapes and textures of the beach area to dominate the
composition. The rule of thirds is used to place various focal points, with the
major area of texture placed a third from the right. To balance this there is a
large rocky shape, more muted in colour, placed roughly a third from the left.
There is also a small figure within a patch of light on this third division.*

Composing with shape

Shape is one of the key design elements in composition. When learning to draw, we begin by sketching out the basic shapes of our subject. Composing our paintings is about arranging and rearranging these shapes and other important elements until the design is working, taking into account the principles of design, which you can read more about on page 28.

When you are sitting in a field looking at a mass of swirling, linear grasses and wildflowers, it can be difficult to see it in terms of shape and form. Thumbnail sketches made on the spot can really help to reduce the mass of vegetation, light and shade into simpler and stronger shapes – as you can see in the examples here.

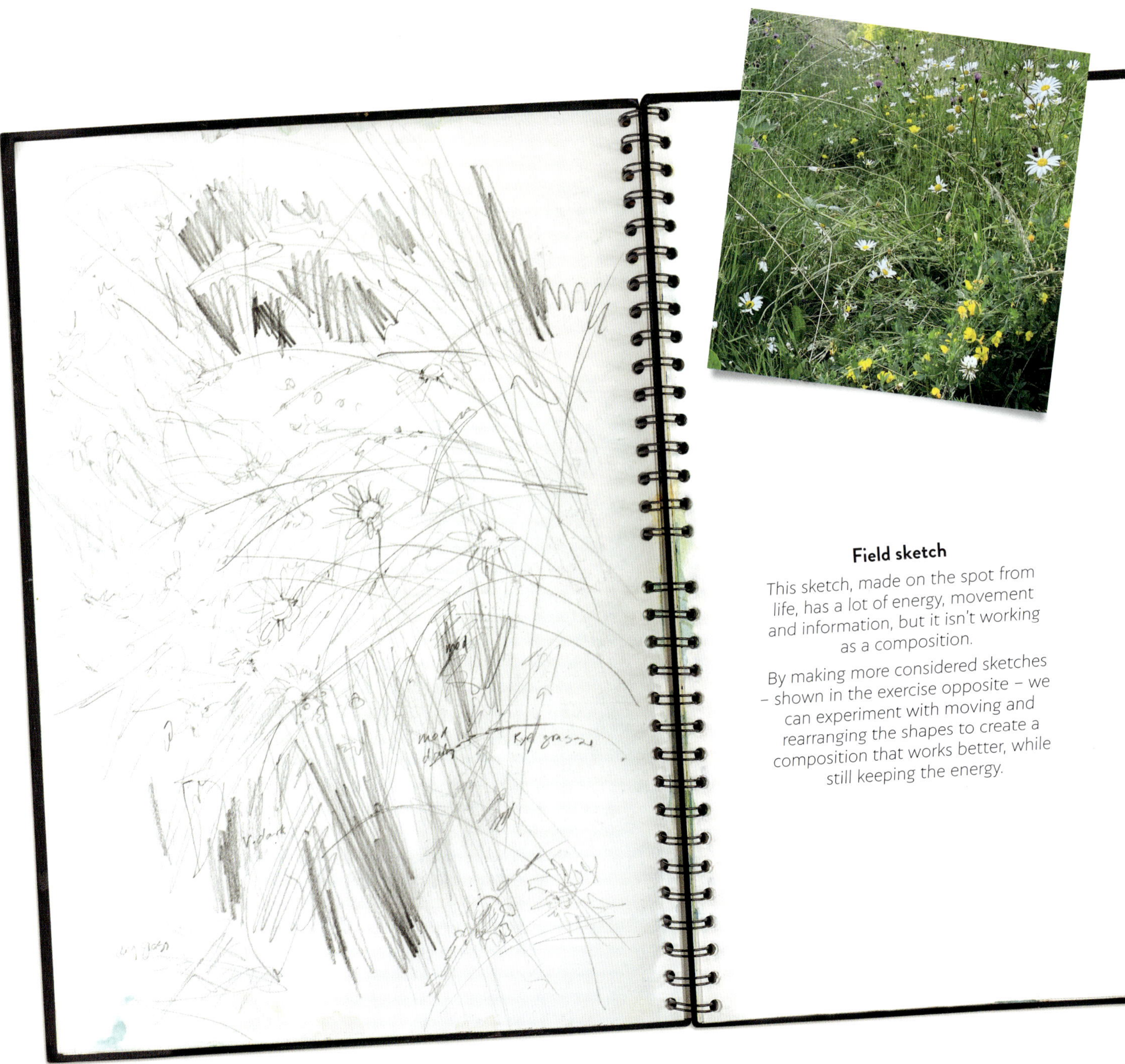

Field sketch

This sketch, made on the spot from life, has a lot of energy, movement and information, but it isn't working as a composition.

By making more considered sketches – shown in the exercise opposite – we can experiment with moving and rearranging the shapes to create a composition that works better, while still keeping the energy.

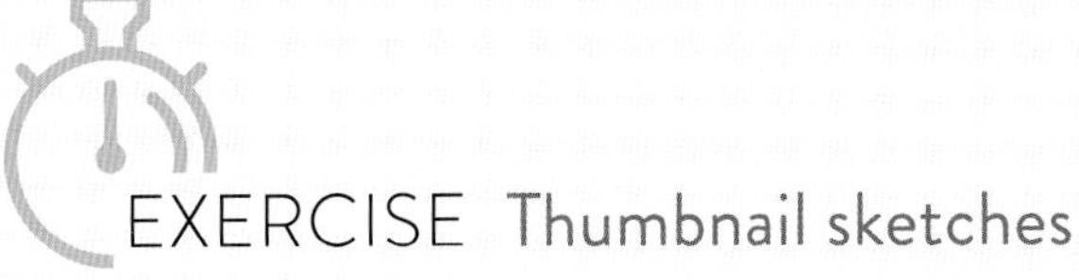

EXERCISE Thumbnail sketches

Use ideas of your own to practise some thumbnail sketches. Try small landscapes or simple abstractions made up of scribble texture, gestural marks or even ripped collage pieces.

Alternatively, you could look at one of your own paintings where the composition is not working as well as it could, and rearrange its elements using the rule of thirds.

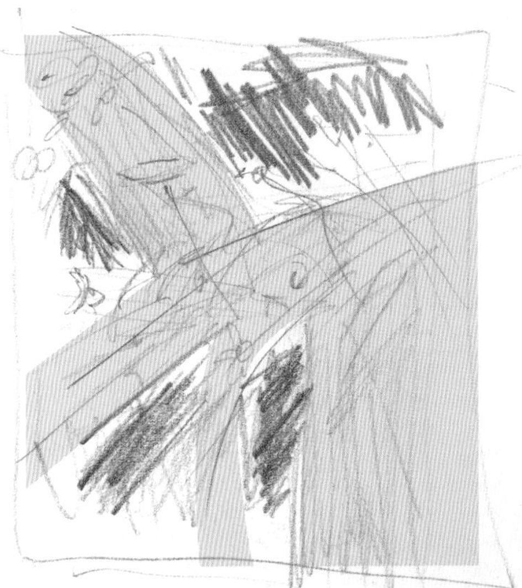

Square composition

In this square format, the corners and the middle are used much more than in the rectangular thumbnail, which relies more on the rule of thirds. 'Diagonals are dramatic!' I always say, and they work to create lots of movement in this design.

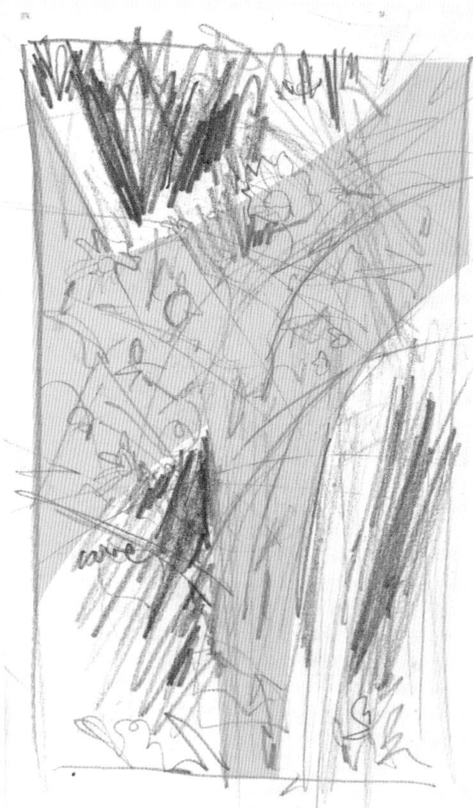

Design in a rectangle

This thumbnail, made in a portrait format, uses the rule of thirds to emphasize the vertical growth a third from the right, while also retaining the important diagonal shape in the middle section.

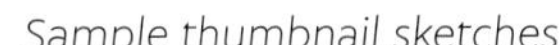

What is a thumbnail sketch?

The job of a thumbnail sketch is to work out the main elements of the composition, where the shapes and tones will be placed from the whitest highlights to the darkest of darks. They can be any size that you choose but around 5–10cm (2–4in) is usual. They can be in any media, in monochrome or colour, and be as simple or complex as you choose. It's a good idea – and certainly good practice – to try out your design in each of the main picture formats: square, landscape and portrait.

The more that you put into your thumbnails and other trial pieces, the more confident you will be when it comes to a finished painting.

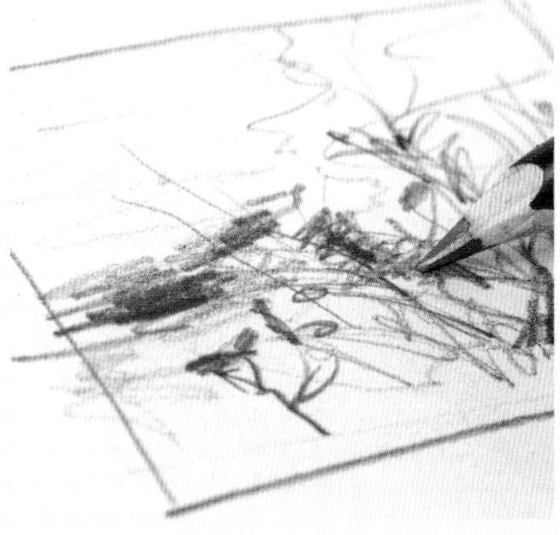

Sample thumbnail sketches.

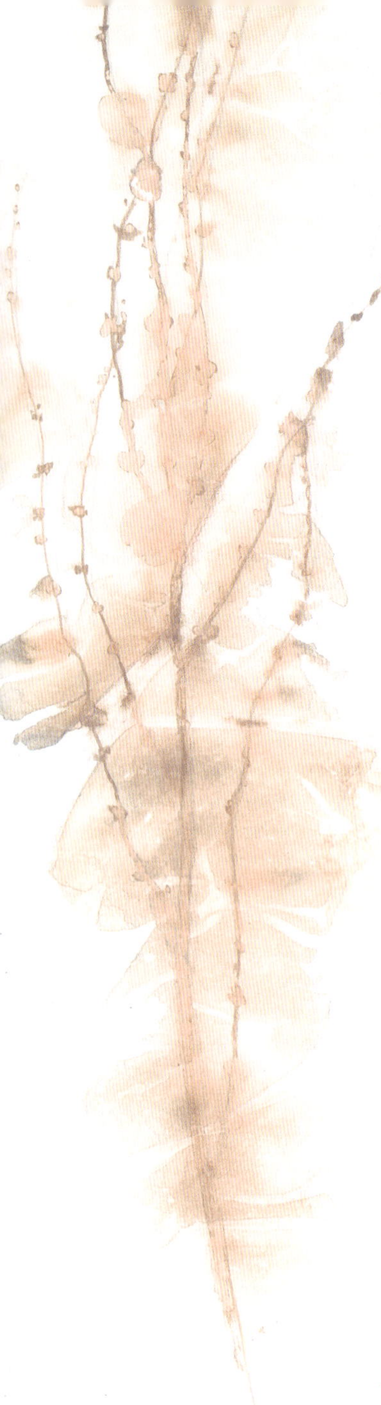

Principles of design

There are a number of commonly recognized design principles that can really help us when composing our paintings with a focus on shapes.

Variety Life would be boring if every day was the same, with no variety! Using a mixture of shapes and forms in a composition – some rounded, some geometric, some softer-edged and some harder-edged – adds interest and sets up a kind of conversation or interplay between them.

Negative shapes The spaces in between objects are called 'negative shapes', and are just as important as the shapes themselves. An idea for an abstract artwork might be one that focuses on the negative spaces and emphasizes these over the positive ones.

Scale Scale is the relative size of one element compared with another; the larger that the shape or form is within a composition, the more important and dominant it is. We can use scale to create distance or depth in an artwork just as we use perspective in a landscape – as in *Fragmented Landscape* on page 105.

Scale also relates to the physical size of a work. Abstract paintings often work well on a large scale, especially those with a pattern-like, all-over design. Painting on a large scale can encourage a looser, gestural and more abstract style.

Balance Balance is about the way that shapes are distributed in a painting. A well-balanced composition, where there is an even spread of elements, can produce an appealing and harmonious effect. The opposite to this is when more weight is deliberately left on one side of the painting than the other, creating imbalance and tension.

Pattern and repetition By repeating shapes, or other elements such as colours, line or texture in a design, we can set up a rhythm across the picture space. A pattern of repetitions creates movement and can be used to lead the eye, either to specific focal points or around the painting.

Unity and harmony A successful painting needs a good balance between variety and unity: while the various elements might be different and interesting, they still need to work together. Simplifying and repeating shapes, colours and textures, and using a limited colour scheme throughout, are easy ways to help to achieve a unified design.

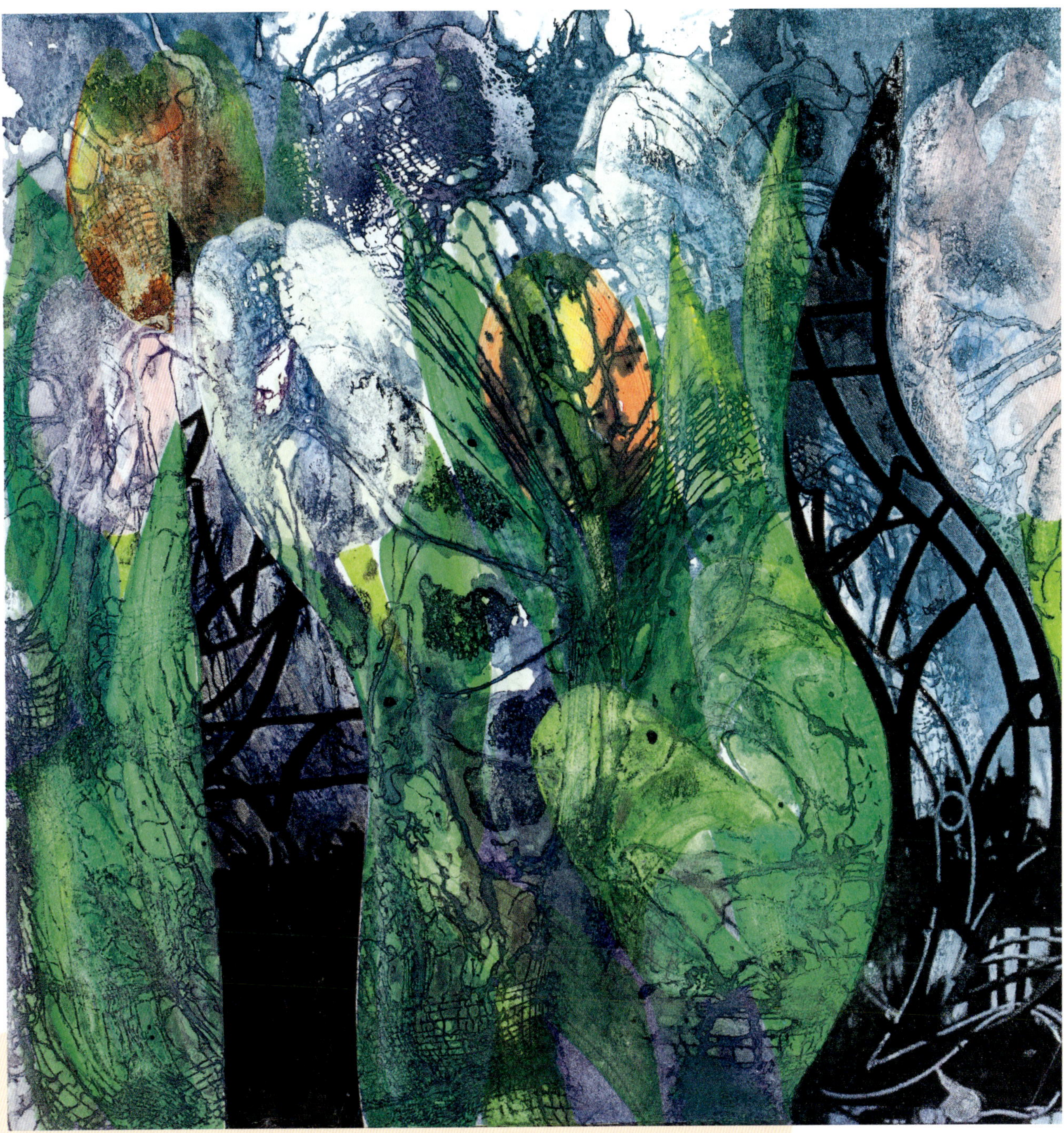

Painting *Tulips in a Wild Garden*

This painting is made up of a variety of shapes, colours and tones. The rounded, softly toned tulips contrast with both the rough texture of the printed scrim and the dark and geometric foreground structures. These collaged pieces add scale and solidity, grounding the design. All the formal elements are repeated and balanced, bringing harmony as well as unity to the composition.

Tulips in a Wild Garden
30 × 30cm (11¾ × 11¾in)

Tone or value

A grey and cloudy day can be uninspiring at the best of times, as the lack of light makes the world look flat and midtoned. When the sun does burst through, everything springs to life, bringing out highlights and deepening shadows. It changes the tonal values of a scene completely, as bright light allows us to pick out objects more clearly, transforming dull, almost flat shapes into three-dimensional forms.

Tone and value are terms that are often used interchangeably in art; both refer to the lightness or darkness of a colour. We also put them together and talk about tonal values when assessing the degrees of tone in an artwork, from white at one end of the scale to black at the other, as explained opposite.

A painting that contains the complete tonal range from black to white can pack quite a punch, but this amount of contrast isn't always needed. It depends on whether you are trying to achieve a full range of values, from bright whites to deep darks, or whether the effect you're after is softer, with narrower modulations of tone.

A lack of tonal contrast is a common reason for a painting not to work. The tones may be too close, or there may be too few darks and lights to make the painting pop. In order to check this in your own paintings, stand back from your work and squint or half close your eyes. This will immediately allow you to see tonal values more clearly.

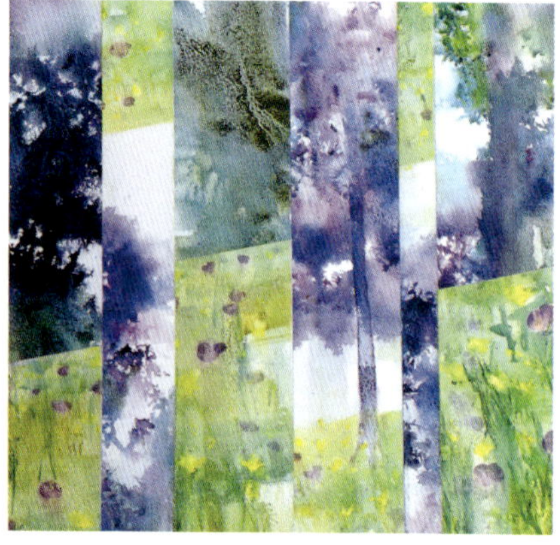

Tone and technology

Another good way to check the tonal variations in your work is to take a photograph of your artwork (above) using a smartphone or tablet and then convert it to black and white, as shown below, using its basic photo-editing software.

Look for sufficient contrast and a good pattern of light, medium and dark tones across the piece.

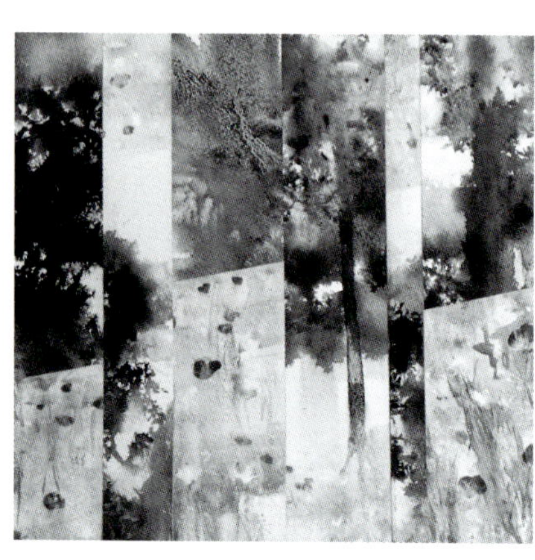

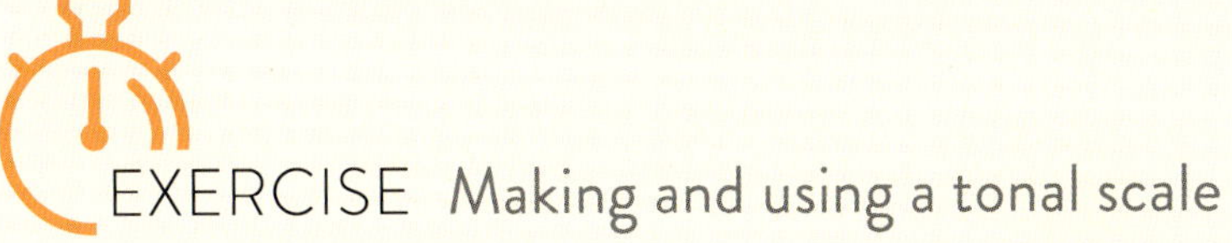

EXERCISE Making and using a tonal scale

A tonal scale is a useful tool that can be held up to a painting to check the tonal balance. To have good tonal contrast, most paintings need to have an even spread from white to very dark tones.

Making your own tonal scale is simple. Take a strip of paper or card, about 4 x 20cm (1½ x 8in) long and any drawing media that allows you to make smooth gradations of tone – a 2B or 4B pencil is ideal. Simply draw a long rectangular box within the strip and shade evenly from one end to the other, gradating from the white of the paper at one end to as dark as you can get at the other.

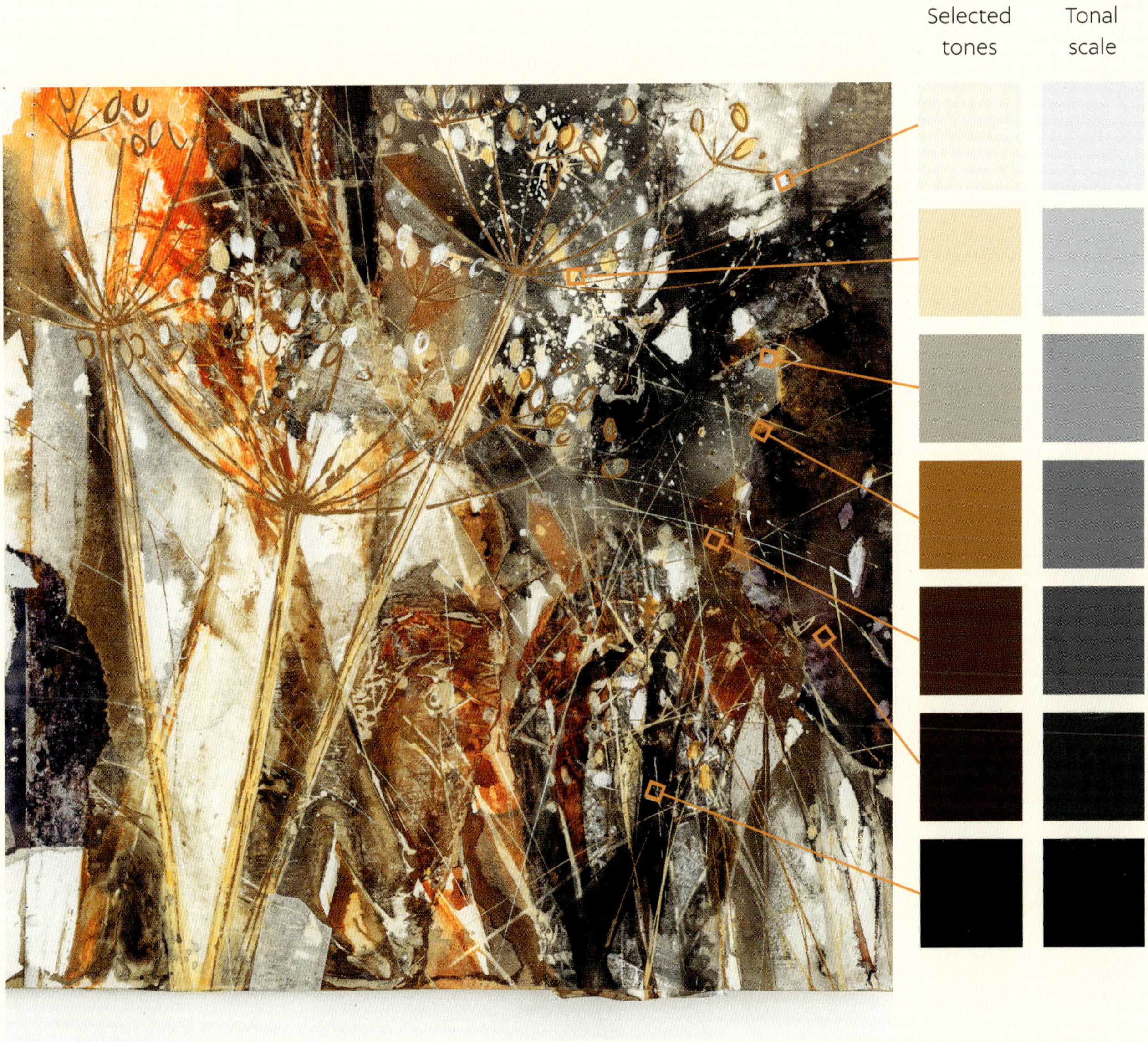

Selected tones   Tonal scale

Using the tonal scale

Here I've picked out a range of tones in a finished painting and compared them with a range of greys. Note how the range of tones present in the painting ranges from the lightest tint to the deepest shade on the tonal scale.

Composing with tone

Tone, like shape, is another of the fundamental building blocks of a
design and should be addressed early in the planning stage of a painting.
Thought should be given to where the various tones will appear – I tend
to plan for the pure whites, the next lightest passages, the darker tones
and the very darkest darks. Making a small thumbnail sketch of the
tones, as shown in the example below, is often all that is needed to work
through your options.

Shape The horizontal shapes of the rocks and the breakwaters are like
stepping stones, drawing the eye down from the top of the painting. The
figures are placed on the right-hand side using the rule of thirds.

Tones There are roughly four tones in all: the white light, lighter mid-grey
and darker mid-grey tones all over the composition, and the very dark
tones of the rocks, figures and foreground foliage.

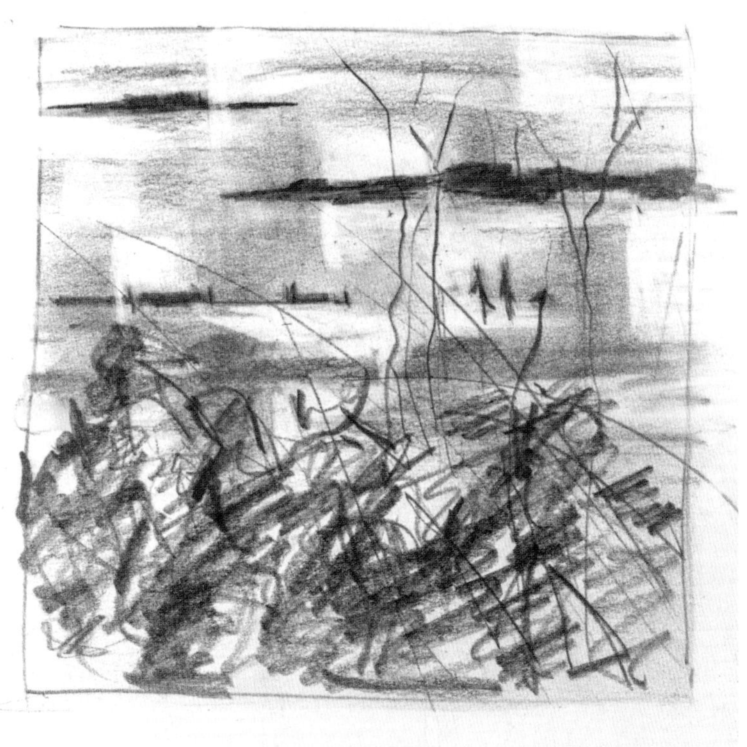

Thumbnail sketch for *A Thanet Morning*

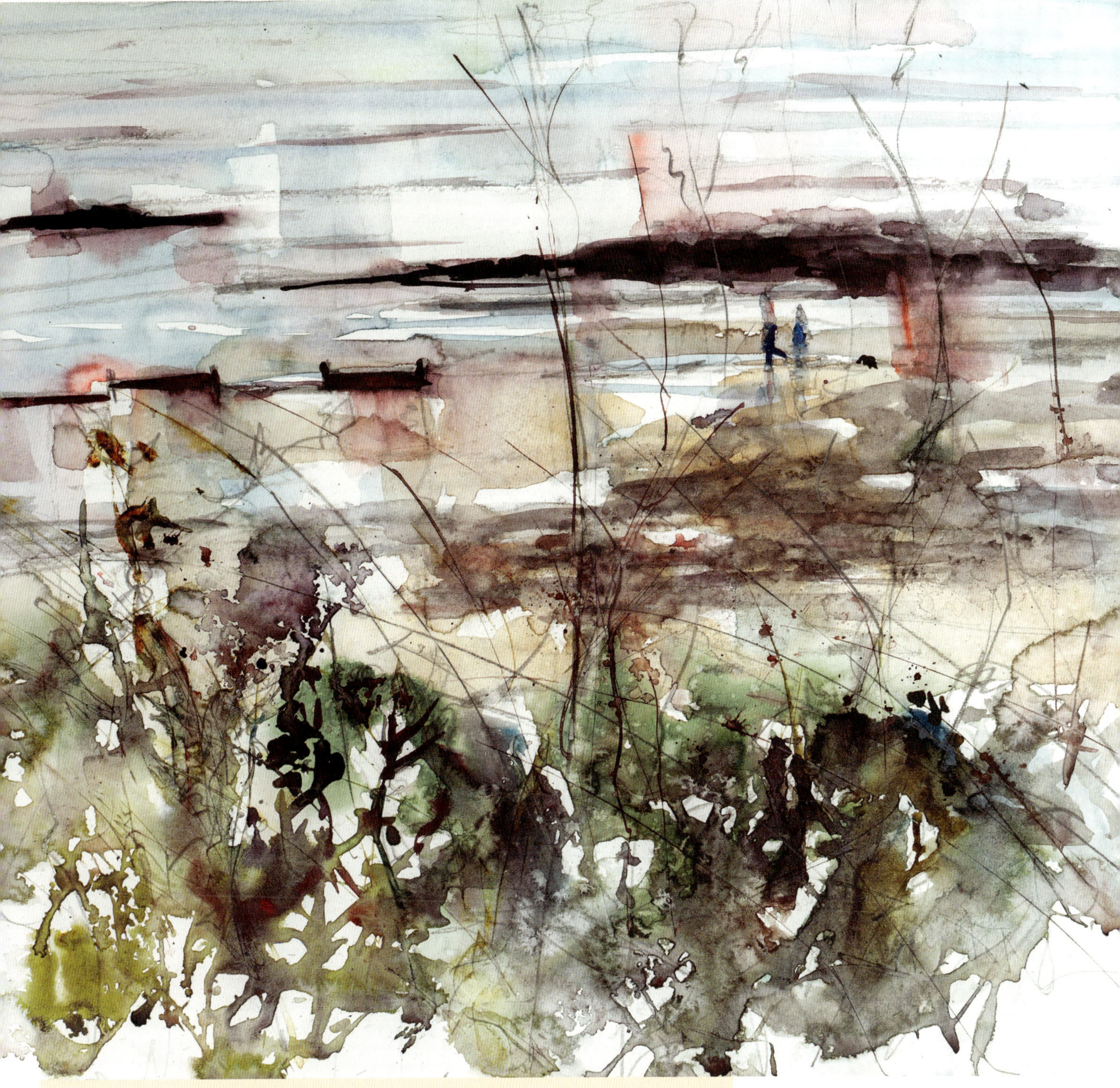

A Thanet Morning
31 × 26cm (12 × 10¼in)

Painting *A Thanet Morning*

Having used the thumbnail opposite to check that my idea would work,
I made a loose pencil and watercolour sketch on cartridge paper. Referring
to the thumbnail, I made sure to retain the strong variations in tone in the
finished piece – from the pale layered tones in the sky and the sea, to dark,
silhouetted rocks and foreground foliage.

Notan

Notan (pronounced 'No-tan') is a Japanese term that literally translates as 'light–dark harmony' and is thought to combine beauty with strength. A traditional Notan painting is typically a monochromatic brush painting where ink is watered down to supply the grey tones, but any painting or drawing medium can be used. The idea of a Notan painting is to limit the number of tones that you are using to as few as possible – to two, three or four tones.

Practising Notan sketches is a very useful way to improve how we see and design with tone by focussing on the underlying value structure. A two-toned Notan is perhaps the trickiest to achieve: when you only have black and white to play with, you need to think carefully about how many of your light tones you will make white and how many black. In a three-tone painting, the very light tones would become white, the darker lights and the lighter darks would become mid grey and the darker greys join the blacks.

An important lesson that a Notan can teach us is to focus on the abstract shapes of the overall tonal design and the balance between them. We are not aiming for symmetry in this tonal balance, but instead the natural unevenness that we find in nature.

'Notan-beauty means the harmony resulting from the combination of dark and light spaces – whether coloured or not – whether in buildings, in pictures, or in nature.' **Arthur Wesley Dow**

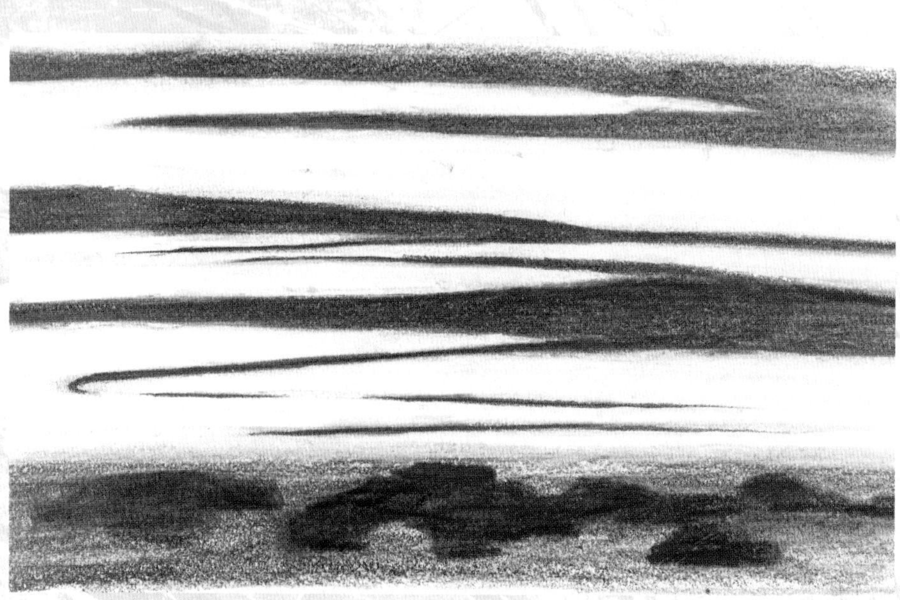

Notan sketch in pencil

In this simple Notan sketch, the subject is simplified and abstracted by reducing the tonal variations to a minimum. It was drawn with a very soft 6B pencil and enhanced with a white chalk pastel.

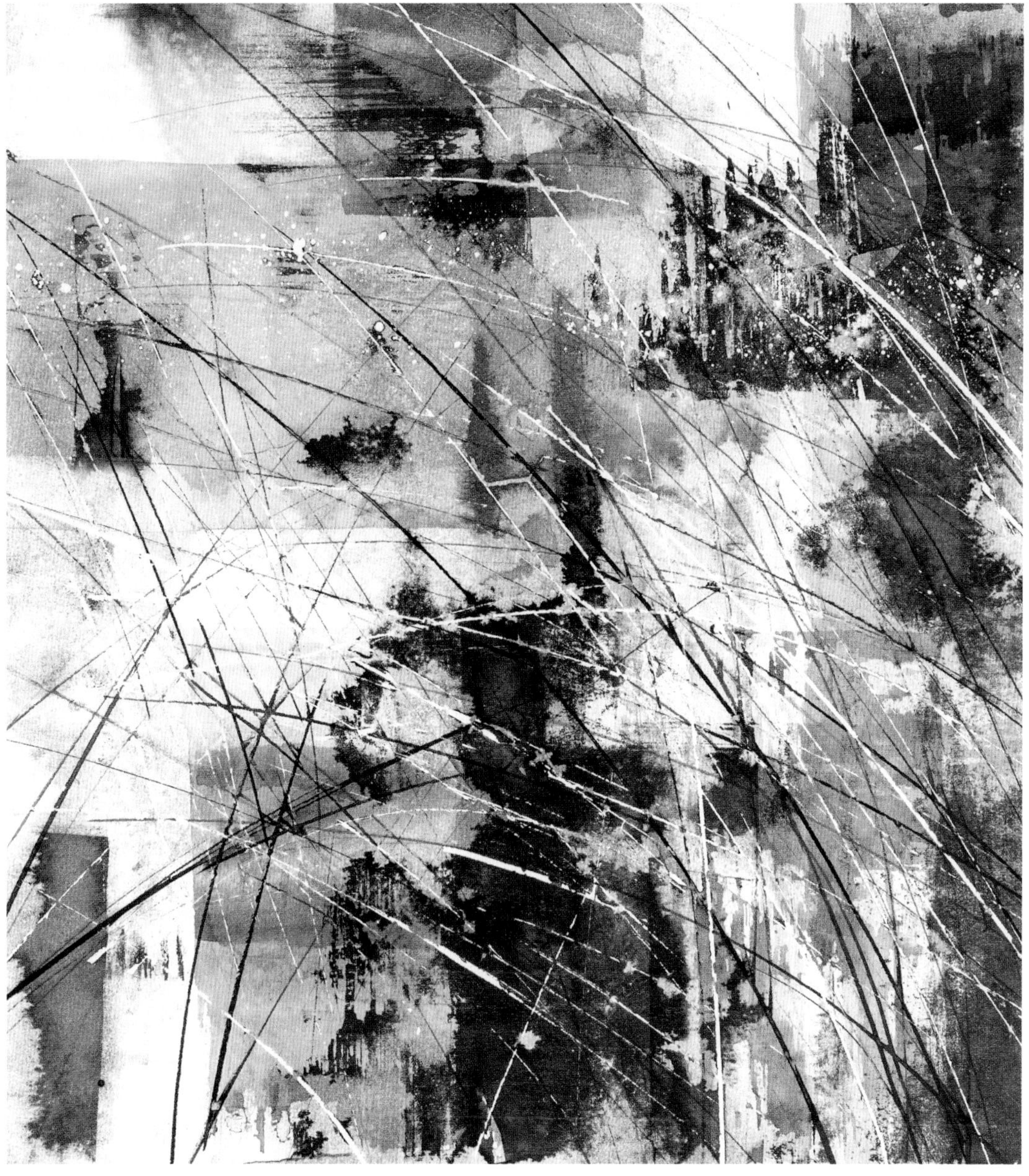

Notan sketch in black acrylic ink

19 × 19cm (7½ × 7½in)

This small Notan sketch was the result of some play and experiment. Restricting myself to five tones, I also limited the tools that I used to just a 50mm (2in) wide flat brush and a palette knife.

I began by reserving some white lines in masking fluid and then added some broad horizontal and vertical strokes from light to dark. The dark tree-like shapes in the top right-hand segment were made with the tip of the flat brush, while the fine black lines were made with the edge of the palette knife. Finally, when all was dry, I rubbed away the masking fluid to reveal the clean surface beneath.

Colour

The importance of colour in our lives can't be underestimated. Personally, I love colour,
the more vibrant the better. On the other hand, I'm also drawn to monochromatic
schemes of greys and blues, evocative of dull, misty days. Perhaps it has something to
do with the very changeable climate in the UK, where I live!

Our relationship to colour is personal, complex and completely individual. We often
have favourite colours and some with which we have strong associations for one reason
or another. I love a cool blue or green colour, but magenta comes a close second – and
I have absolutely no idea why I like them so much. This instinctive rather than reasoned
response may be familiar to you, too. Colours become part of our lives; they creep into
our art and become integral to our personal style.

Colour symbolism

Colours have a huge amount of both personal and cultural symbolism and significance
attached to them. Artists, designers and advertisers work with these various attributes:
to attract the eye, create a mood, tell a story, express a feeling or evoke an emotion. You
can see this in the painting opposite, *Landscape in Red*, where colour is used very literally
to describe the earth heating up, as a result of climate change.

In recent years, science has shown that colour can even have a physical effect on us.
Seeing red can even raise one's blood pressure – we 'see red' – while cool colours have
an opposite, calming effect.

Reds and yellows In nature, red denotes danger or aggression: it has strong cultural associations and also describes physical and emotional attributes, such as excitement, passion and a fiery temperament.

Colours are not limited to a single interpretation, of course. The hot colours of a sunset have been shown to have a therapeutic effect, filling us with wonder and leaving us with a feeling of wellbeing that lasts long after the display has passed.

Blues and greens These are restful colours. Walking in nature is recognized to improve our wellbeing. The natural greens and blues of plant life, the sky and sea are associated with feelings of tranquillity and balance in our lives.

Brilliant and electric blues, on the other hand, can be stimulating and dynamic. Deep blues symbolize importance and confidence – which is where we get the idea for blue corporate suits and police uniforms.

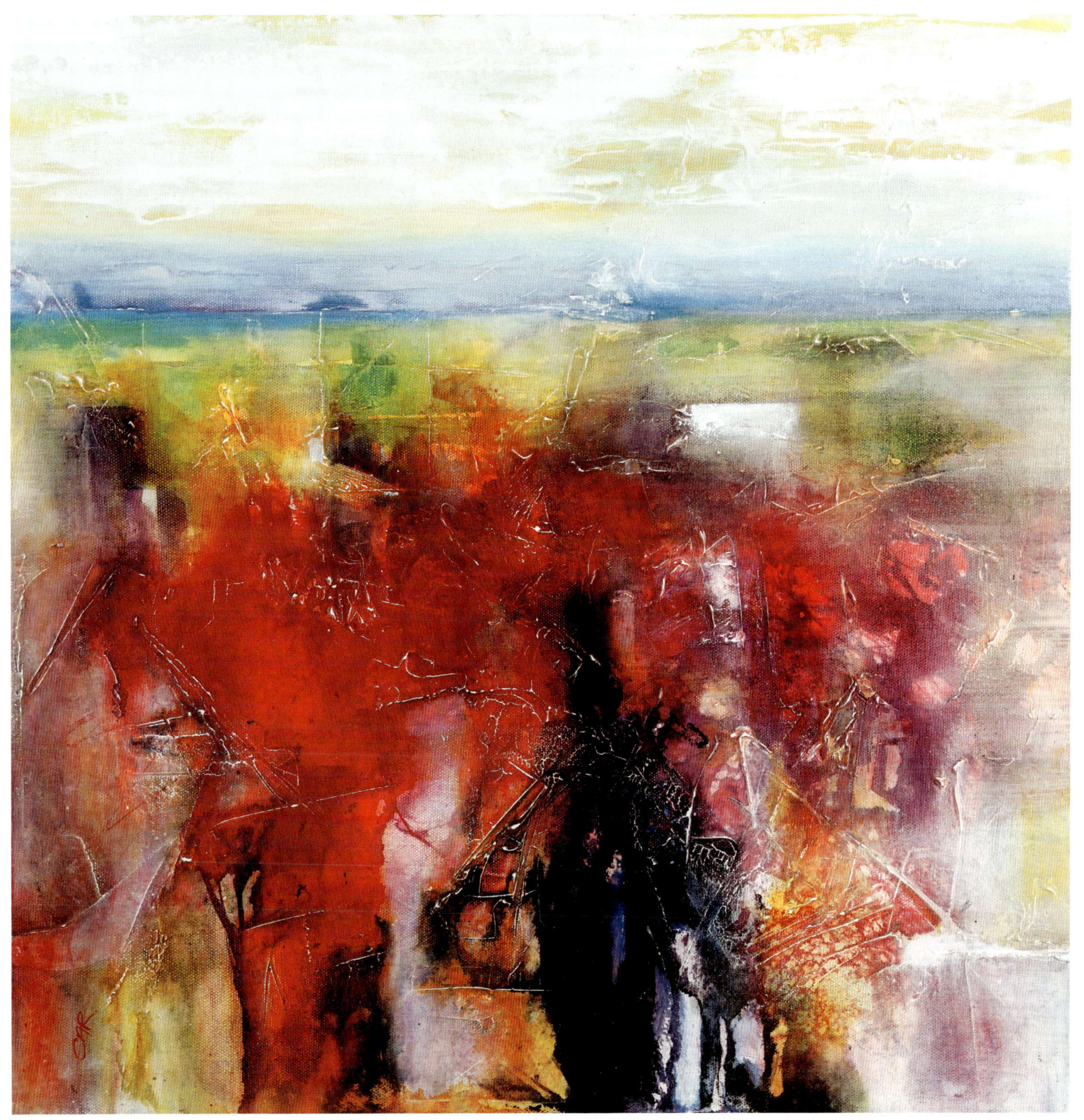

Landscape in Red
51 × 51cm (20 × 20in)

'If you are only moved by colour relationships, you are
missing the point. I am interested in expressing the big
emotions – tragedy, ecstasy, doom.' **Mark Rothko**

Local colour versus emotional colour

When our artwork begins with observations of nature, it can be difficult to divorce ourselves from simply using local colour. This term refers to the colour that things actually appear: green grass, red poppies, blue sky and so on. Abstract art aims to do more than just describe; it involves our emotions and imaginations and allows for the viewer to interpret a piece in their own individual way.

The colour scheme for a painting or series of paintings should emerge naturally and organically from the thoughts and feelings behind it; so, before we reach for our paintbox, we should think our idea through and be quite clear about what we are trying to put across.

Suppose that you want to describe seasonal change, the freshness of new spring growth or the vibrancy of high summer – if you want your painting to be about the mood and emotions that the subject evokes, the colour scheme needs to reinforce this theme for the idea to work.

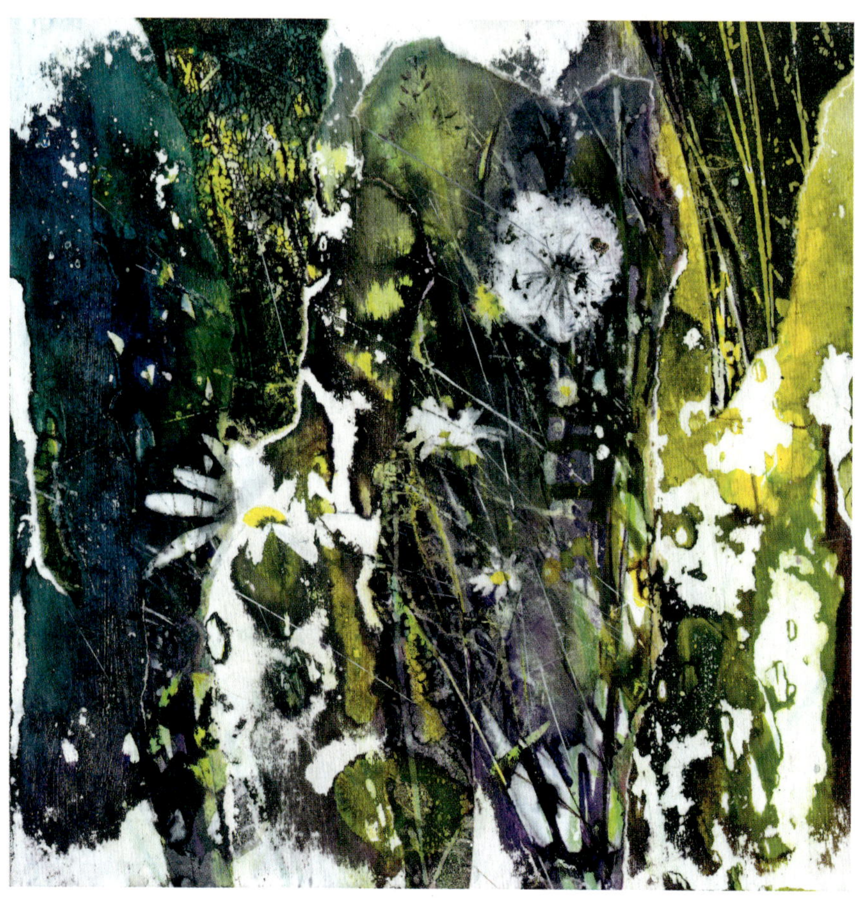

In the Night Meadow
30 × 30cm (11¾ × 11¾in)
This painting uses a simple local colour scheme of lime and dark green colours to draw the viewer in and express the mystery of the nocturnal scene. The fragments of collage, together with washing off some of the colour, help to give it an abstract feel.

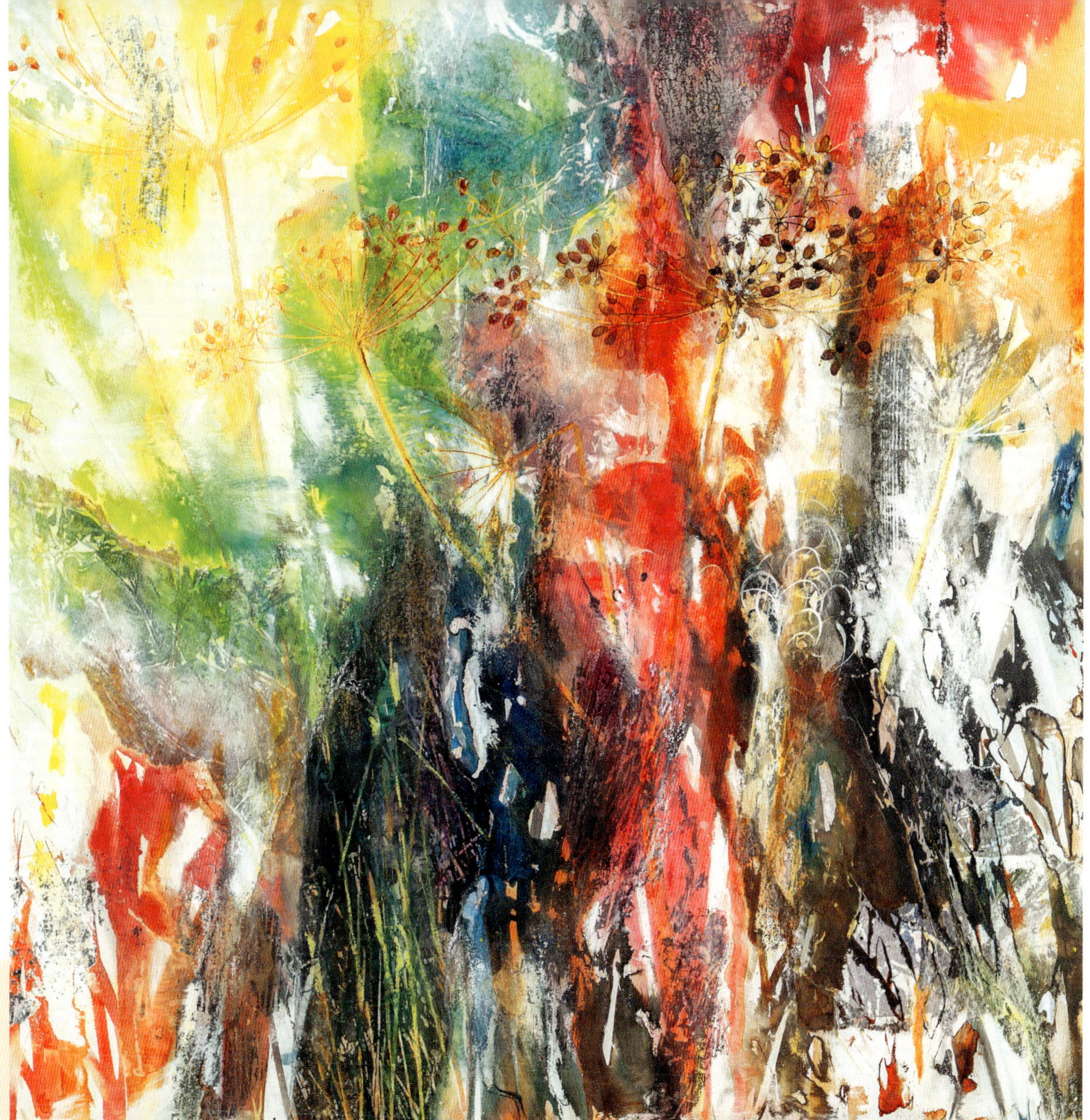

Cornucopia
60 × 60cm (23½ × 23½in)

Painting *Cornucopia*

This painting contains a cornucopia of local and emotional colour. The local colour begins in the top left-hand section with the yellow of sunshine, golden seed heads and blue-green of flowing water. Moving to the top right of the painting, the colours deepen. Do they represent late summer colours, fiery heat, or even passions raised? In the bottom half of the painting the images become more confused and fragmented. Are those shapes, or perhaps people? The colours deepen and darken further. Is this local colour, describing darkness, or does it suggest destruction, sadness or grief?

Colour here is used to prompt such questions. Informed by their own personal colour associations, each viewer will likely interpret the painting differently.

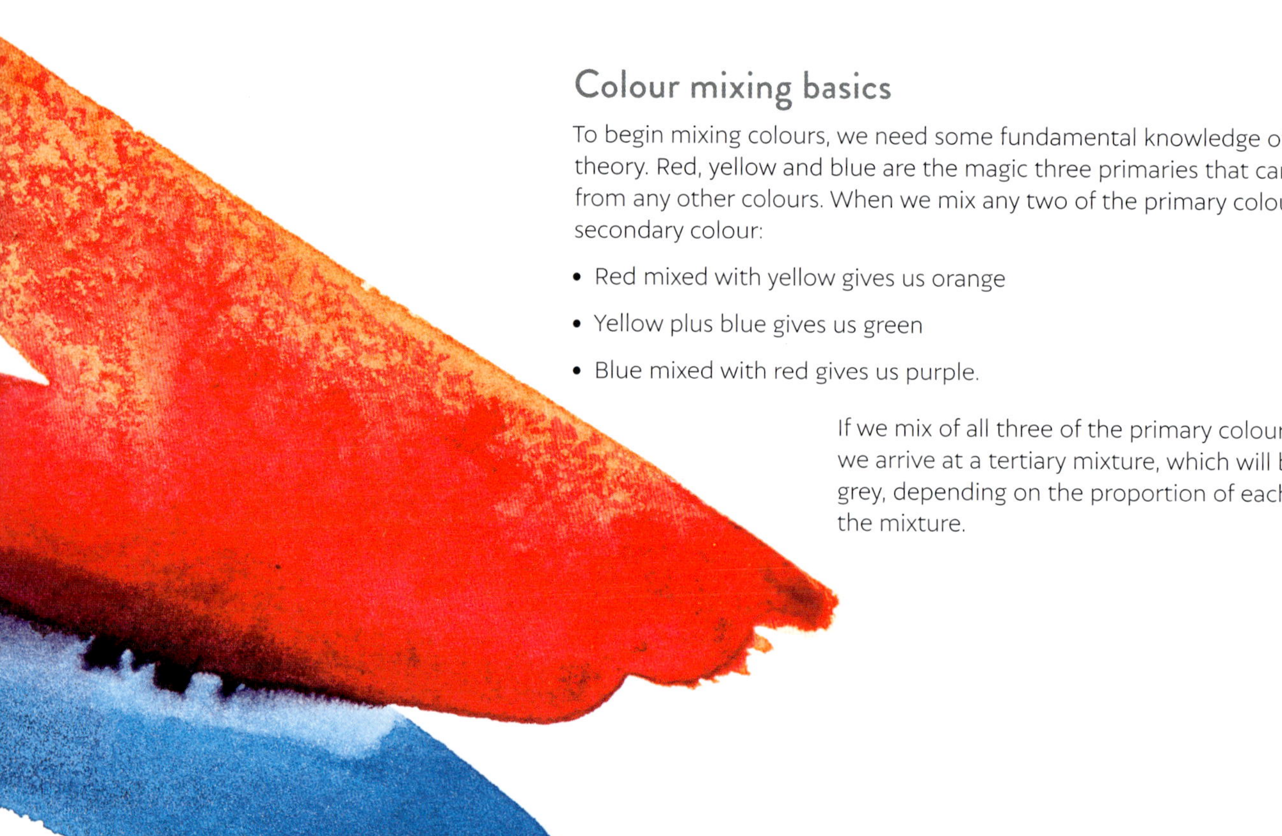

Colour mixing basics

To begin mixing colours, we need some fundamental knowledge of colour theory. Red, yellow and blue are the magic three primaries that can't be mixed from any other colours. When we mix any two of the primary colours, we get a secondary colour:

- Red mixed with yellow gives us orange
- Yellow plus blue gives us green
- Blue mixed with red gives us purple.

If we mix of all three of the primary colours together we arrive at a tertiary mixture, which will be brown or grey, depending on the proportion of each colour in the mixture.

Which paints to choose?

The basics of colour mixing are simple, but as artists we need to understand which of the many reds, yellows and blues in our paintbox are closest to the true primary colours, as this will give us the ability to make the purest mixes. A clue to this conundrum can be found in the printing industry. Printers use combinations of just three primary-coloured inks to achieve prints with a full colour range. The primary colours used in printing are cyan, which is a greenish-blue; magenta, which is a cool red; and lemon yellow, a cool yellow. (A fourth ink, black, is also used to strengthen the tones.)

Knowing what the primary colours look like is half the battle, but finding these colours in paints that derive from a wide range of pigments is not easy. Artists sometimes have different opinions about which of our paints are closest to the primaries, but here are my suggested choices:

Cyan The closest pigment to cyan that I use is phthalocyanine blue, shortened to phthalo blue. Some artists use cobalt blue instead.

Magenta I use either quinacridone magenta or permanent rose for my magenta hues.

Yellow The easiest choice, lemon yellow, is readily available as a paint. However, nearly all lemon yellows are opaque or semi-opaque. For that reason, I choose Winsor lemon or aureolin yellow, which are transparent.

Colour purity

Paint manufacturers aim to provide us with as much choice as possible. Their paint ranges are made up of both pure single pigment and multi-pigment paints. The latter are already partly mixed and only need to be mixed with water to the strength that you need. You may combine them further, of course, but in order to keep your mixes as pure as possible, err towards a palette of single pigment colours.

See pages 54–55 for more on pigments and paints.

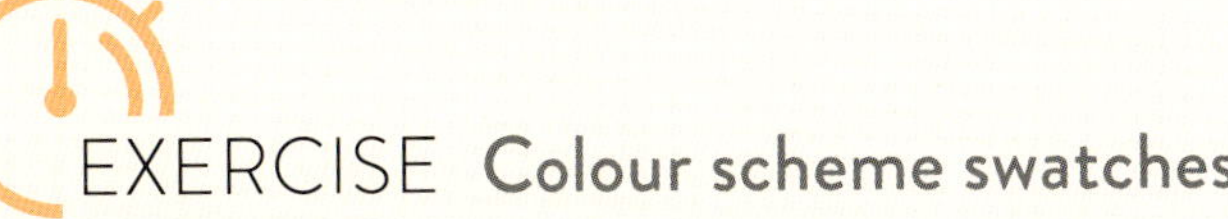

EXERCISE Colour scheme swatches

Making swatches of various combinations of colours is a way of discovering new, interesting colour schemes that work for your paintings. It is also both very good training in colour mixing and a very practical way of learning colour theory.

Note down the colours that you are using as you go. There is no need for these swatches to be neat and formal. Use watercolour, a loaded brush and gestural brushstrokes so that the colours flow and mix easily.

The three swatches below are examples of alternative primaries being used.

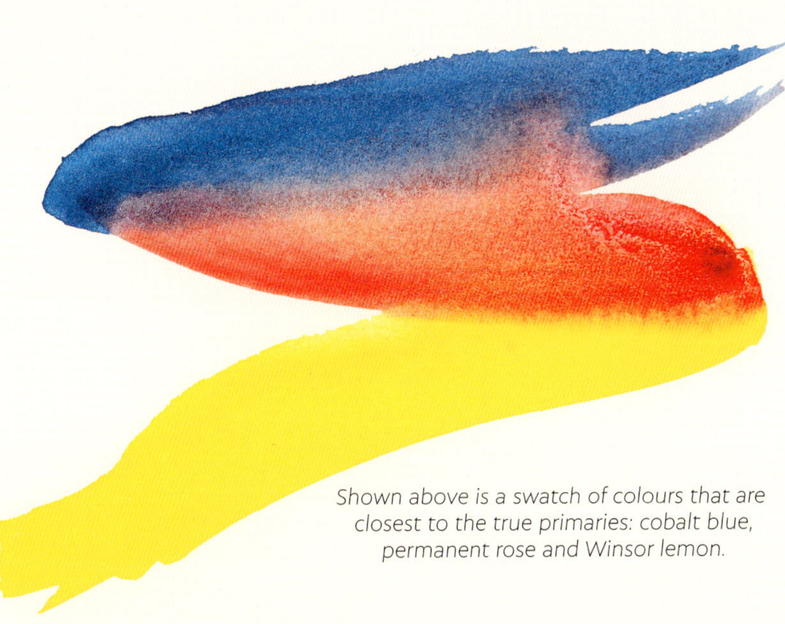

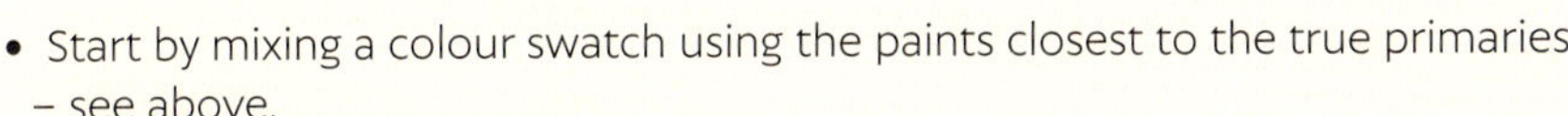

Shown above is a swatch of colours that are closest to the true primaries: cobalt blue, permanent rose and Winsor lemon.

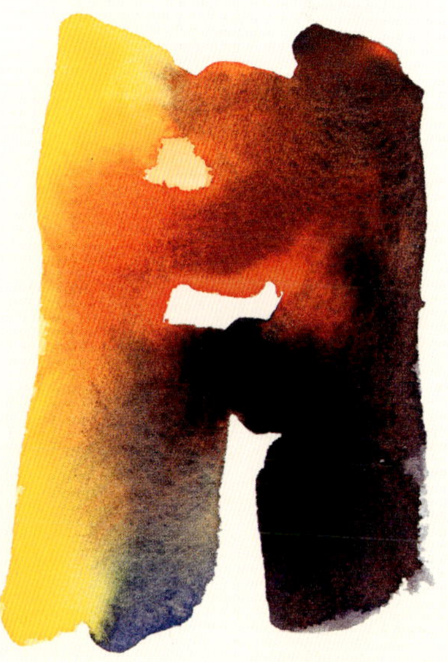

- Start by mixing a colour swatch using the paints closest to the true primaries – see above.

- Next, take some time to experiment freely by making a second set of colour swatches that substitute other reds, yellows or blues for the 'true' primaries.

- Try using multi-pigment colours that are even further from the primaries to make a third set. For example, use green gold or quinacridone gold in place of yellow; burnt sienna or perylene maroon instead of red; and phthalo turquoise or indigo for blue.

Compare these three sets of swatches and think about their uses. Have you discovered any interesting colour combinations? Do some of them suggest a particular mood or emotion? Do you think some would make better colour schemes than others?

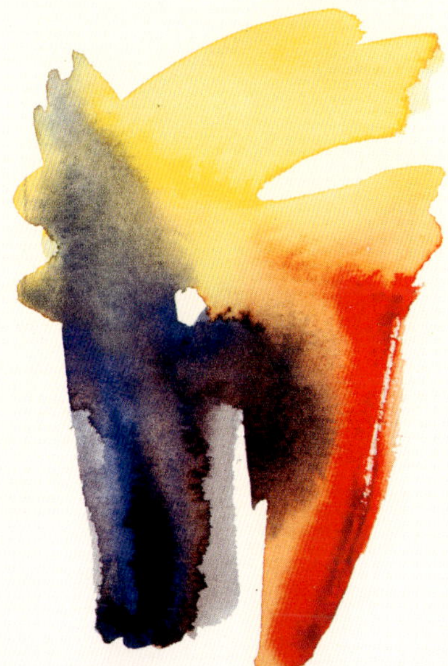

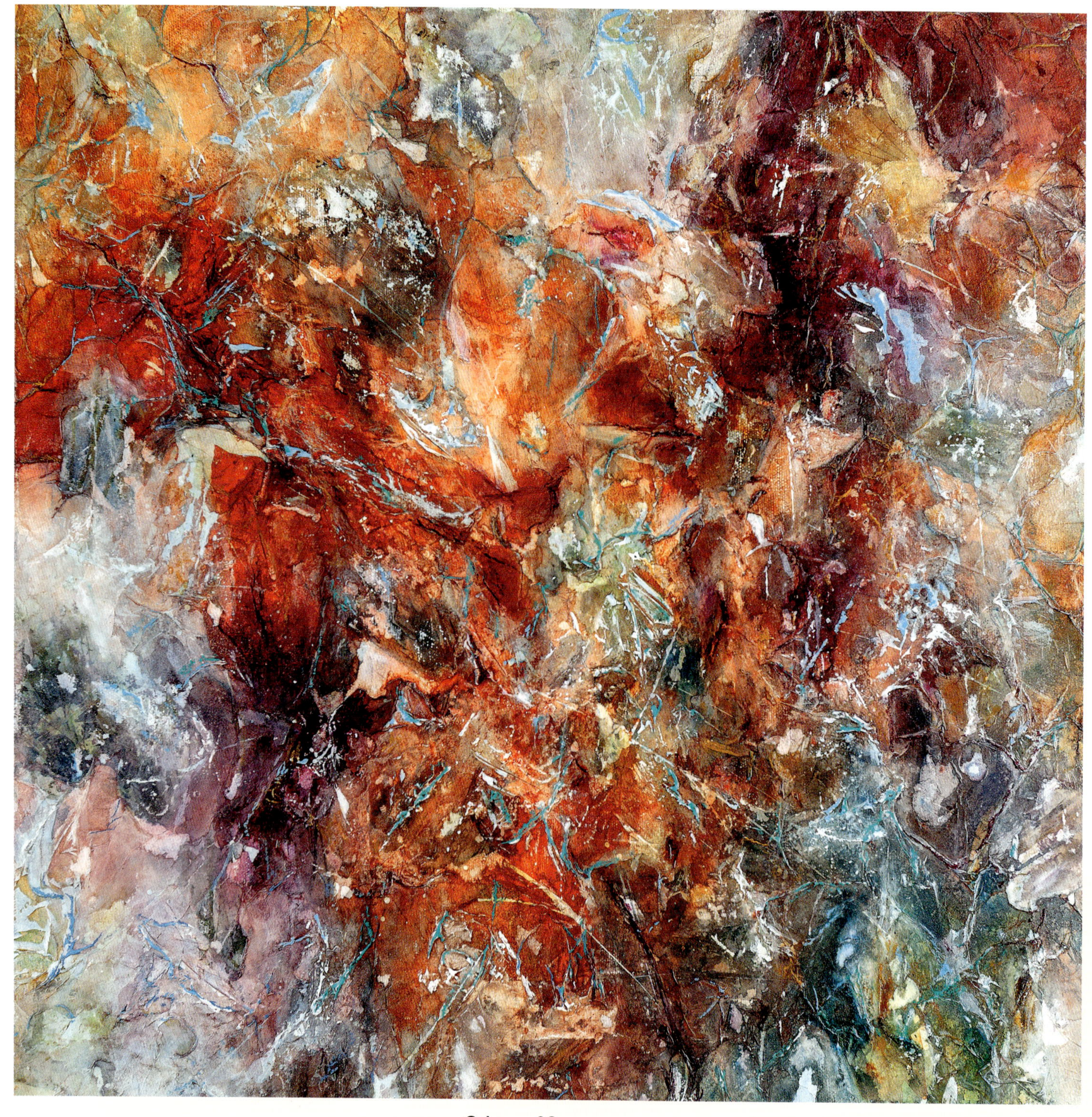

Colours of Summer
51 × 51cm (20 × 20in)

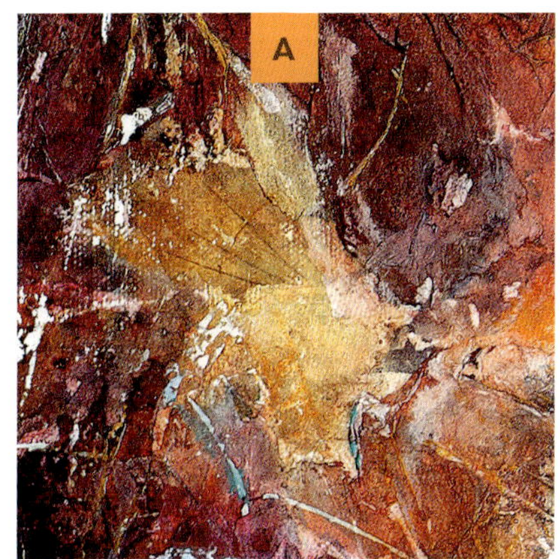

A

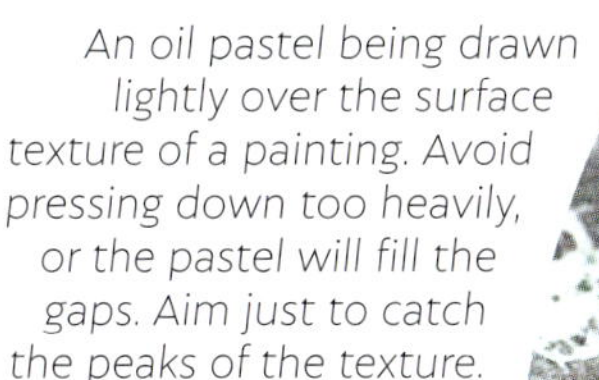
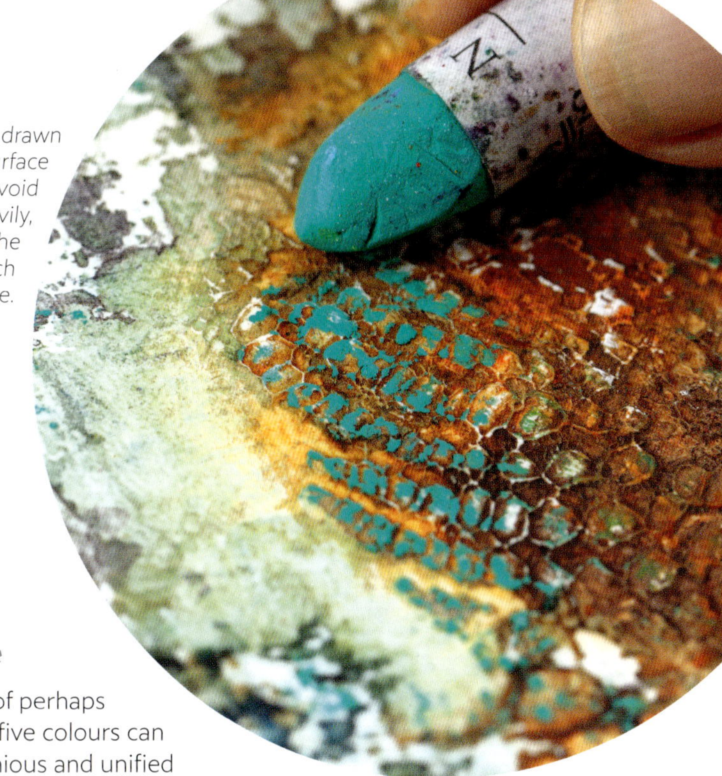

An oil pastel being drawn lightly over the surface texture of a painting. Avoid pressing down too heavily, or the pastel will fill the gaps. Aim just to catch the peaks of the texture.

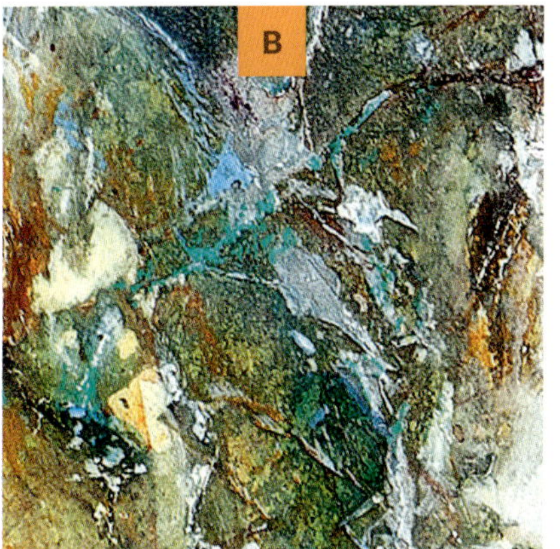

B

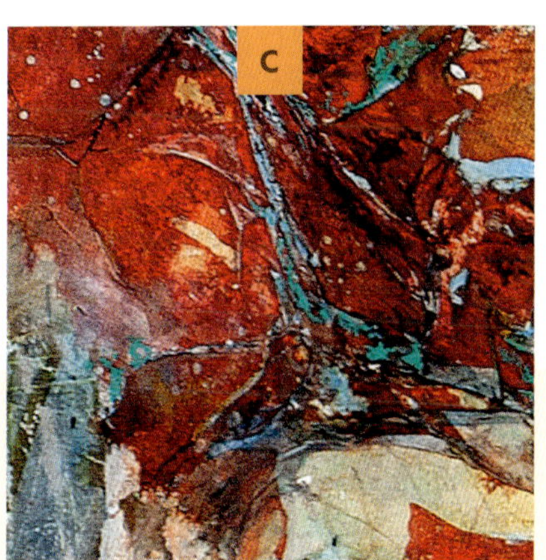

C

A limited palette

Using a limited palette of perhaps three to a maximum of five colours can result in a more harmonious and unified artwork. It also improves your knowledge of paints, as well as being very good colour mixing practice. Another advantage is that over time your paintings will harmonize as a collection, so that they sit well together when shown alongside one another and contribute to your signature style.

The mixed media canvas shown opposite, *Colours of Summer*, is an example of a colourful painting achieved with a limited palette. It is painted mainly in acrylic inks, using quinacridone magenta, quinacridone gold, phthalo blue and burnt sienna. This is a warm and harmonious colour scheme with accents of blue and green that fits the summer theme. I have also used complementary pairings throughout the painting.

A A patch of gold surrounded by its complement, a mix of magenta and purple.

B Blue and green oil pastels, drawn lightly over the raised texture, contrast and complement the underlying colours.

C This is a vibrant complementary pairing of red paint with blue and green oil pastels.

Complementary pairs

Complementary colours are the pairs of primary and secondary colours that are opposite to each other on the colour circle. These pairings are red–green, yellow–purple and blue–orange. When used next to each other in a painting, these pairs bring out the best in each other by enhancing each other's hue, brightness and vibrancy.

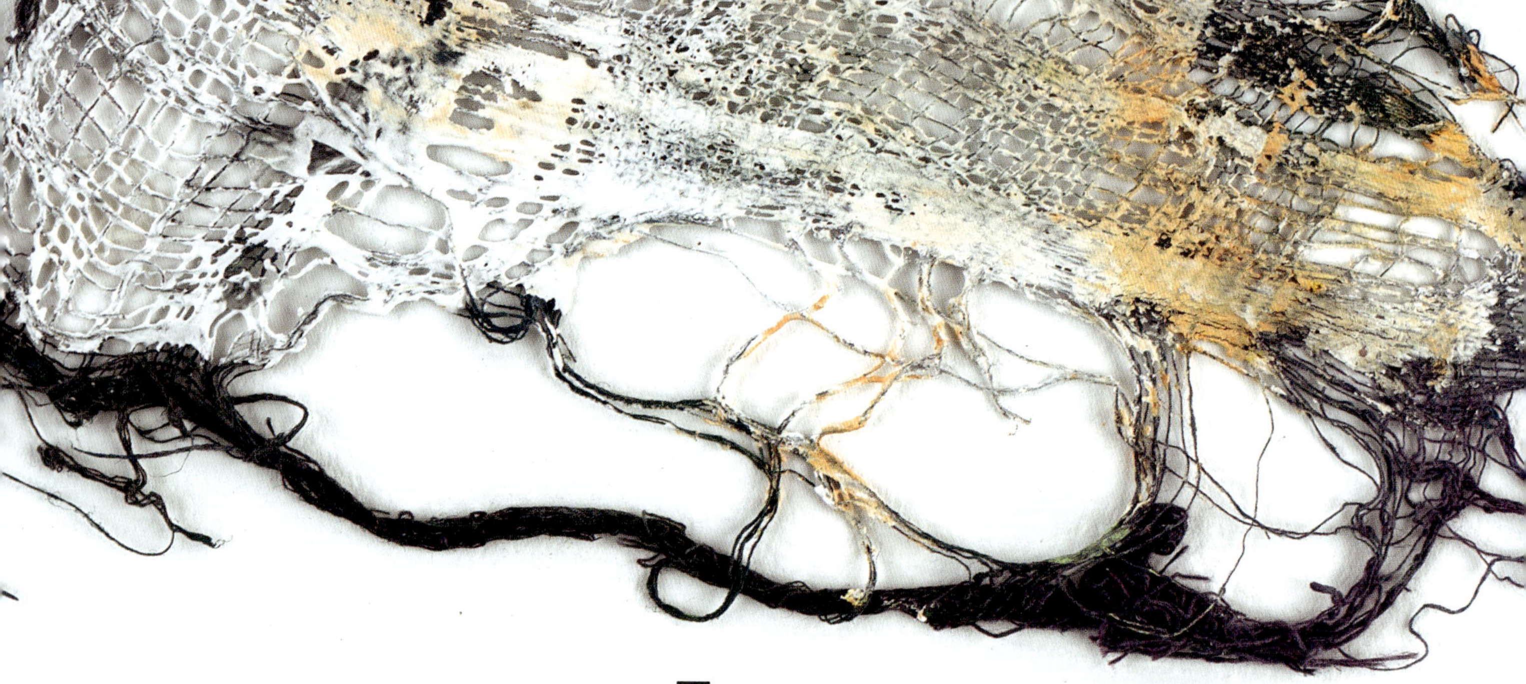

Texture

Have you ever wondered why texture is so very satisfying to gaze at? Texture has the effect of working on our imaginations, evoking memories, associations and sensations. It allows us to look for meaning where none is offered.

Texture refers to the surface quality of a piece, whether it is tactile and has actual depth (physical texture) or is just a visual illusion (visual texture). In either case, texture serves the same purpose; it activates the surface of an artwork, adds interest and contrasts with smoother, quieter areas.

Texture plays an important part in a painting by drawing the eye and tempting the viewer to linger for longer. In exhibitions you will see people move in for a closer examination of a painting with heavy texture. It begs to be explored from every angle, as the light plays across its surface and highlights its three-dimensional qualities. As artists, we need to look closer, to get an insight into how it was made!

Painting *Sea of Waves*

The title and inspiration for this painting is a translation of *Mare Undarum*, a track on the album *Imagined Oceans* by Karl Jenkins, one of my favourite composers.

The painting began with a 'start' (see page 90) of texture paste, freely applied with a plastic card. The paste was applied expressively, with diagonal marks in the sky and in the sea to describe the movement and energy of foamy wave tops. These rough textures contrast with the gentler wavelets that ripple out onto the sand.

The techniques for developing particular areas of the painting are noted below.

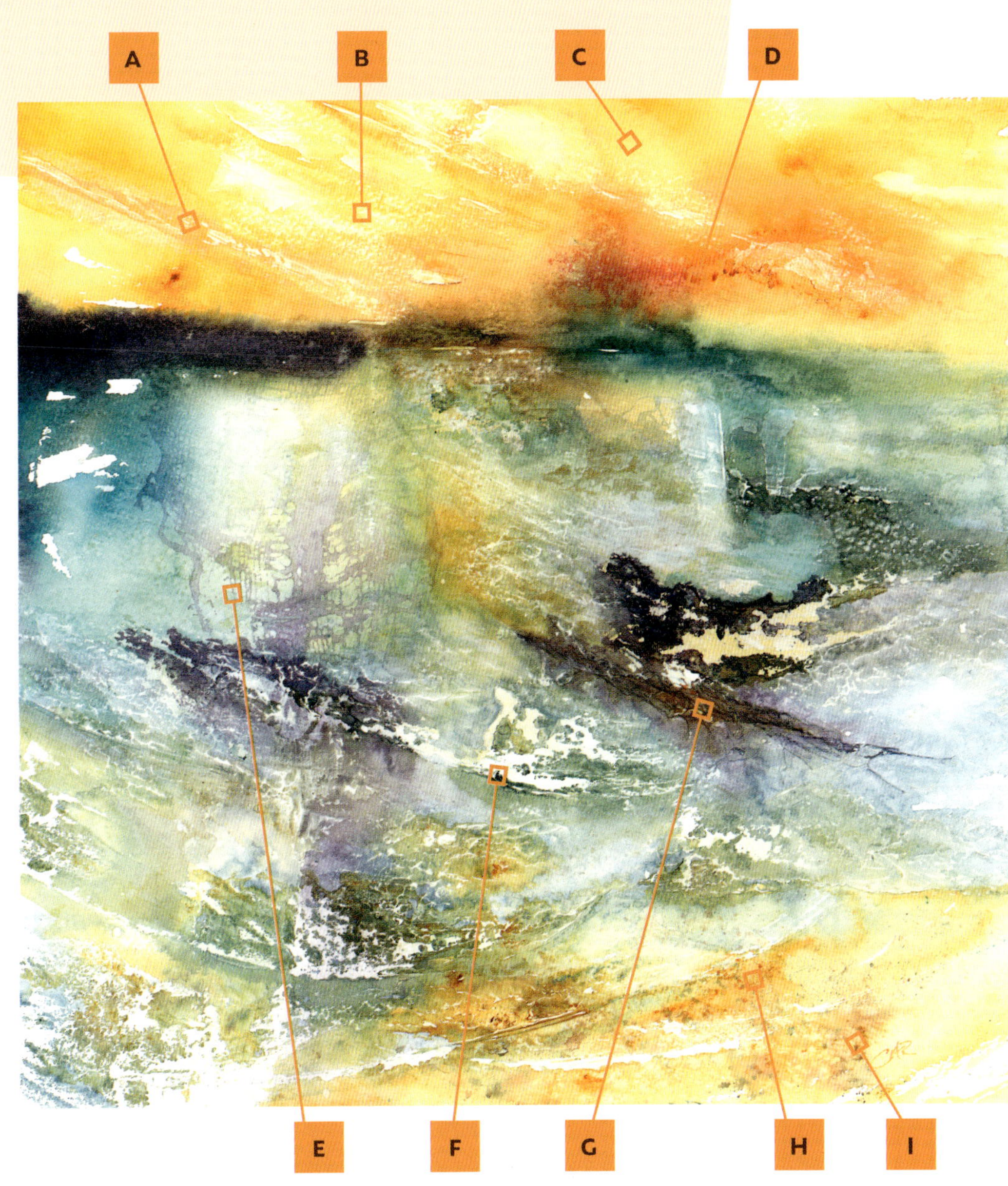

Sea of Waves
35 × 35cm (13¾ × 13¾in)

A Texture paste applied diagonally.

B Marks made with a dry brush.

C Marks left when a very wet wash dries.

D Strong paint mix.

E Scrim print.

F Texture paste applied with a palette knife.

G Scrim collaged on.

H Paint flicks.

I Salt.

EXERCISE Swift texture studies

Texture is enjoyable to create, as there are so many possible techniques
to try that need only your basic art kit and everyday materials. Producing
small texture studies allows us to explore a range of possibilities and to
discover ideas of our own. Making studies like this can be valuable practice,
so that when a painting needs that extra something, the technique is at your
fingertips. They can also make successful abstracts in their own right.

Before you start, prepare a support. Here I am using Not surface
watercolour paper, taped all the way round onto a board. This example
combines some of the techniques from later in the book, so I have given page
references so you can copy along – but the specific techniques you choose for
this exercise are less important than simply exploring texture.

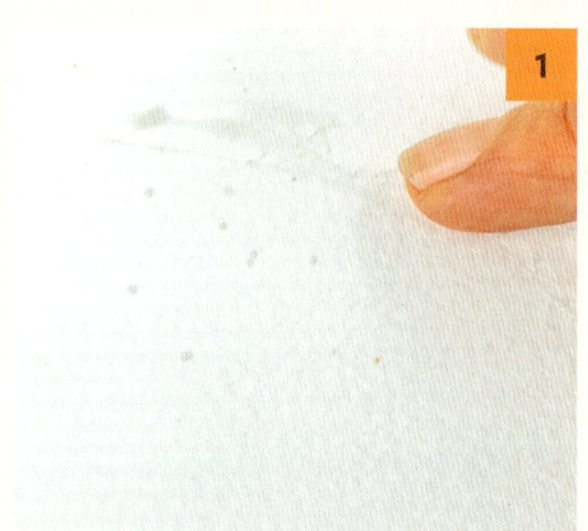
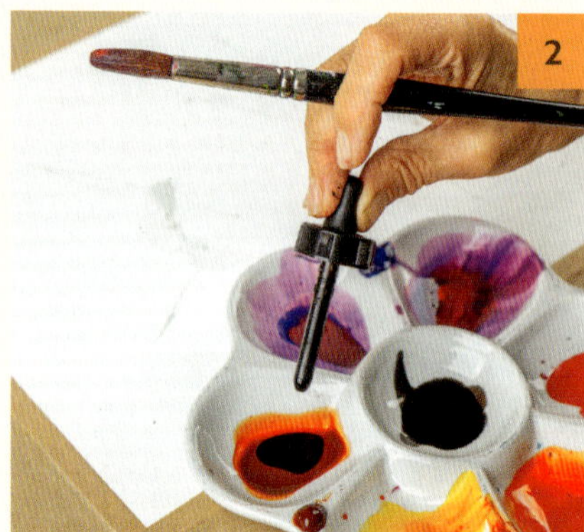
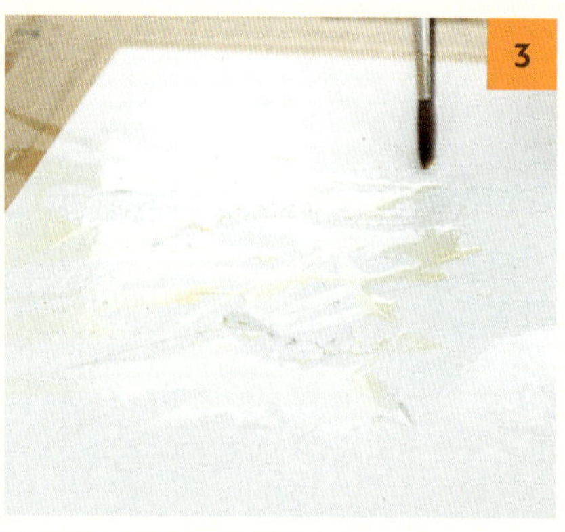

1 Reserve a few lines and flat areas with masking fluid (see
page 74). When the masking fluid has dried completely,
lightly rub some of the flat areas to open them out and
create a foam-like texture as shown.

2 Mix up wells of fluid watercolour and/or acrylic inks.
Adding a granulating colour or two will increase the
texture that you can achieve, and by adding a drop or
two of Indian ink to your darks, you will easily be able to
achieve a separation effect (see right) without the use
of texture mediums.

3 Wet the paper ahead of applying the first wet in wet
wash (see page 64). When wetting the paper, aim to
make interesting marks: you might use a water sprayer,
make flicks with your brush and move it about from
its tip to its side. The way that you wet the paper is
important, as the paint will follow the water and spread
into any patterns of droplets or wet marks that you
make. Wet it lightly in places and make it much wetter
in others. Try picking up the board and tipping it in
order to encourage the water to flow.

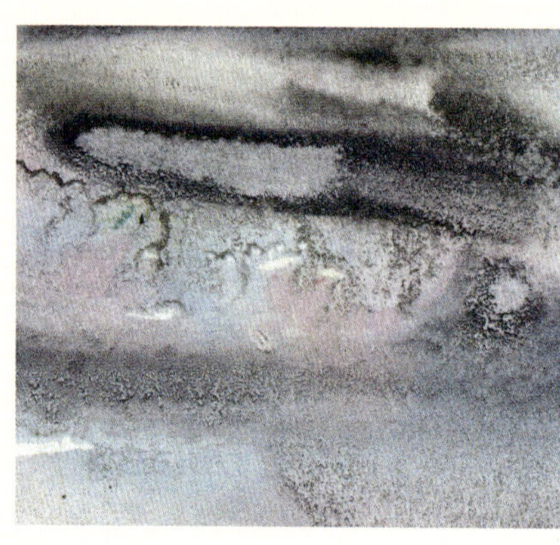

*Example of separation, from
Spring Greens the Winter Gloom
on page 125. The effect is caused
as pigment particles from the ink
settle unevenly within the wet wash.*

Be distinct

While the paper is still wet, materials like skeletal leaves, petals,
threads, torn pieces of food wrap or other soft plastic wrapping
can be pressed into the surface. If the surface is still damp, impress
some drawn or scribbled lines with a palette knife or pointed stick.
Once dry, continue to add texture by spattering colour with a tooth
brush, impressing leaves, threads or textured fabrics.

The texture that food wrap makes (just like the salt effect) is very
recognizable and shouldn't be overdone.

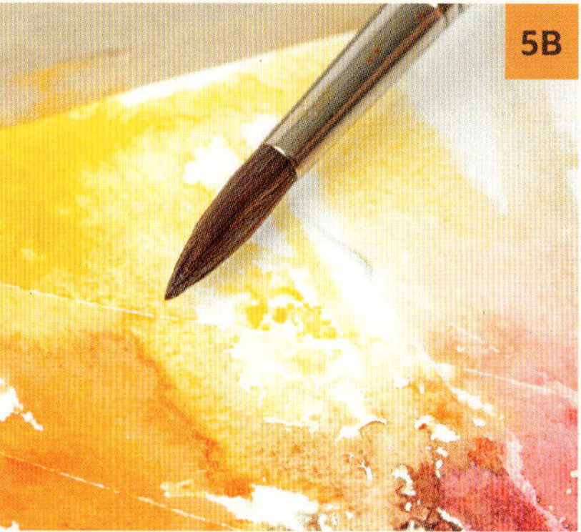
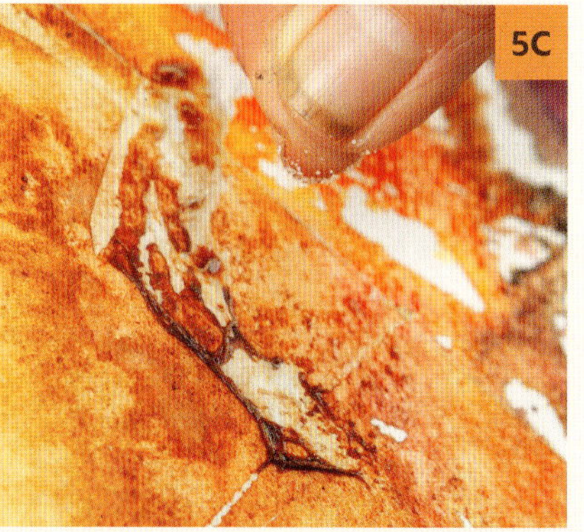
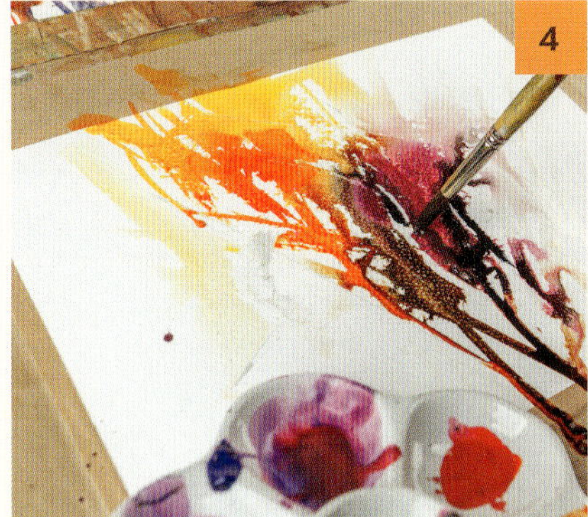
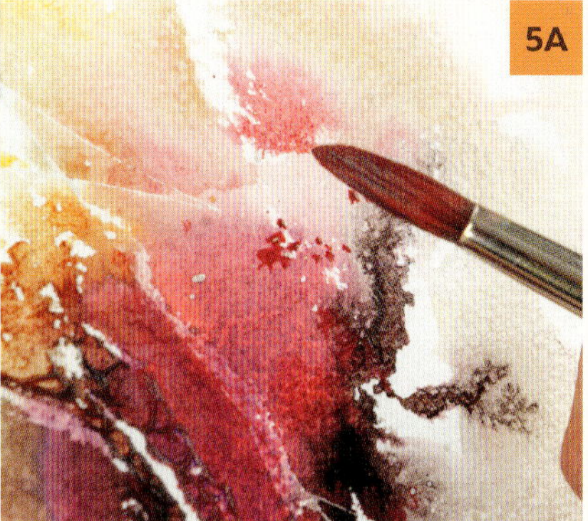

4 Apply brush loads of your prepared
colours to the wet surface. If the
paint and ink is fluid enough, it will
find its own way through the wet
areas. Add stronger colour in places
and vary the marks that you make:
draw and stipple with the tip; flick
droplets of colour and make dry
brush marks.

5 While the wash is still wet, you
can develop the texture further
by flicking spatters of paint from
a loaded brush onto the surface
(A); by drawing the side of a brush
lightly, loaded with paint, across
the paper surface (B) or by adding
a sprinkling of salt to open up the
star-like shapes this creates (C).

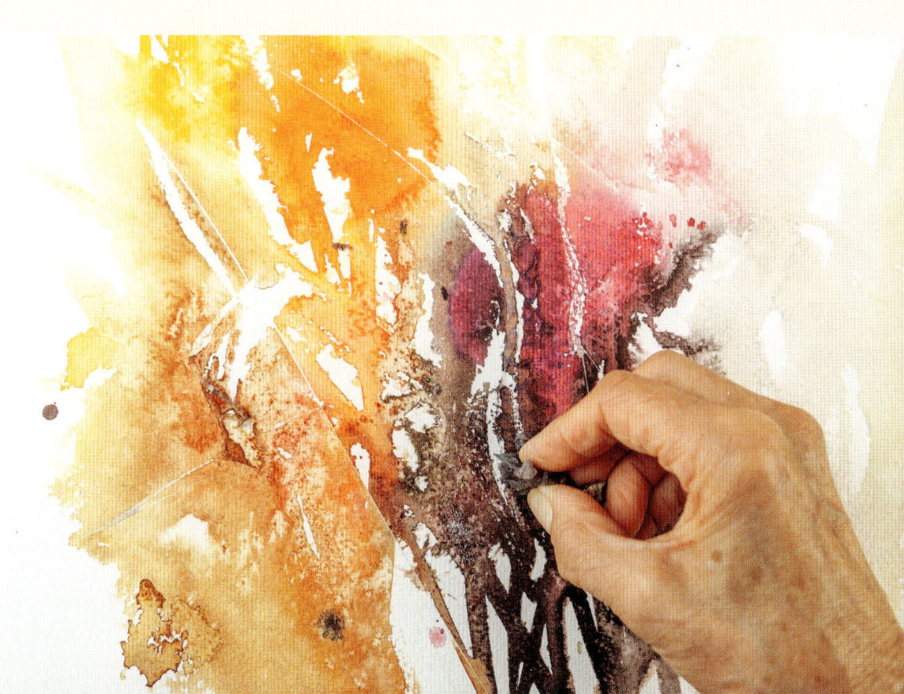

*Once dry, you may want to add surface
texture by spattering colour with a
toothbrush, or adding drawn, shaded or
scribbled marks with any kind of drawing
materials such as a pencil, crayon, charcoal,
chalk or oil pastel.*

*Once completely dry, the salt and masking
fluid can be removed with a clean fingertip
or a masking fluid eraser to reveal the
marks that were being reserved.*

Physical depth

Artists who use impasto techniques in acrylics or oil paints can create deep layers of texture using thick layers of paint and sometimes with the use of mediums and additives. Thankfully, those of us who prefer to paint with thin, fluid media need not miss out on deep texture. We can achieve the same effects by preparing and texturing our supports before going on to apply paint.

Gesso A primer, available readily in white, and in other colours too. You can also buy transparent gesso, which allows the support to remain visible. Gesso's main function is to prepare the surface of a support to accept paint, but it also has a bit of a 'tooth' (surface texture) and can be used to create a moderately deep texture. Gesso can be applied with a brush, squeegee, palette knife, or any number of other tools.

Texture pastes There are a huge range of different texture pastes and gels available. The majority are thicker than gesso, which allows them to hold more defined shapes and create deeper texture. For more information on using texture pastes and gels, see pages 90 and 91.

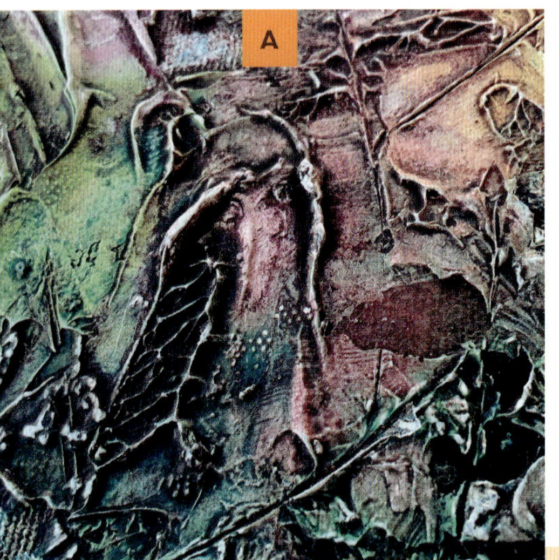

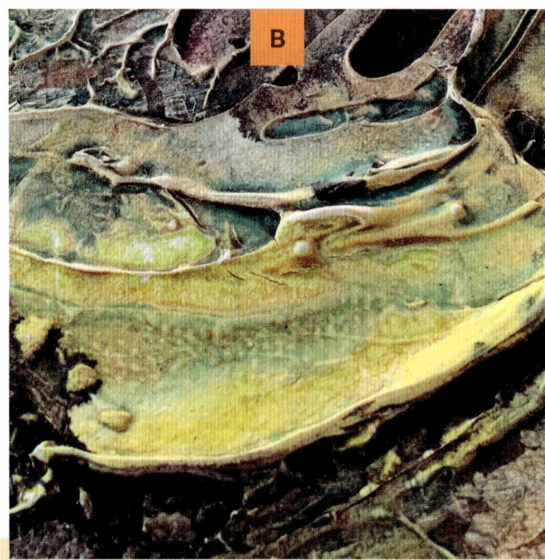

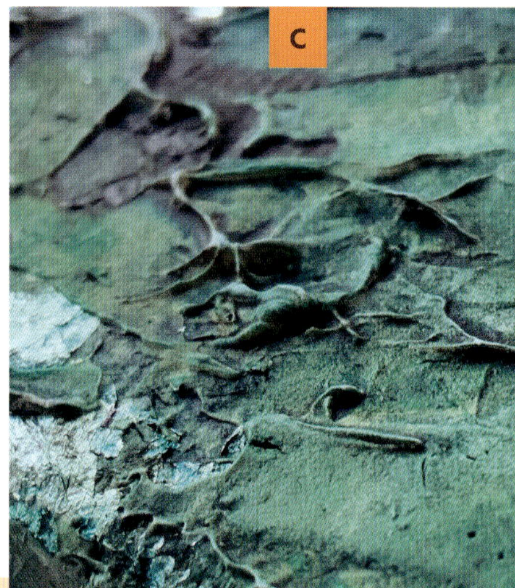

Marks in texture paste

These details, taken from *Nocturne* on page 89, show a canvas textured with paste (applied using a palette knife) and painted with acrylic inks once dry.

A Here the face of the palette knife was used to create leaf shapes, and its edge to create lines and the point to incise lines.

B Pressing the flat of the palette knife down and drawing the long edge up will create broad shapes like this.

C Pressing the face of the palette knife into the paste and then lifting it away will form peaks like this.

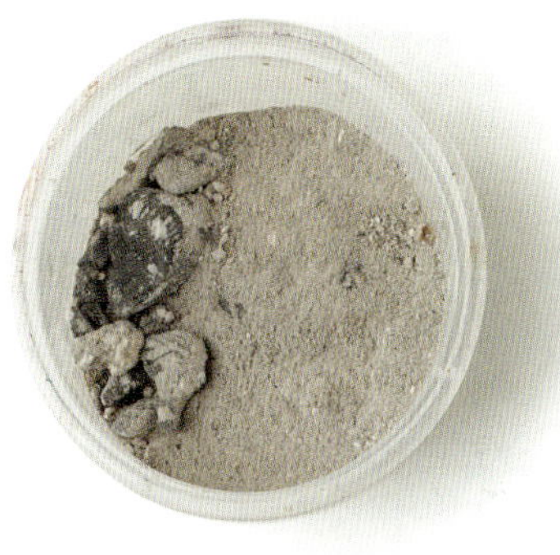
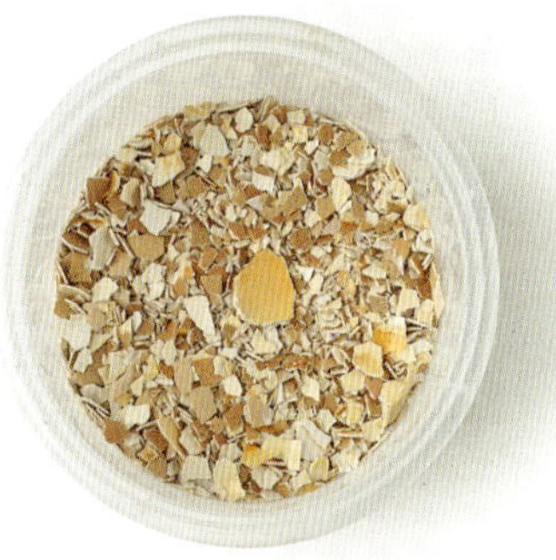

Customizing pastes and gels

All acrylic media, whether paint, gesso, texture paste, mediums or gels are strongly adhesive. This means that you can incorporate all sorts of materials into them. You can buy bottles of dry media from art suppliers or add your own for free: sand, pencil shavings, ground-up eggshells, scraps of paper, fabric, beads, threads, plant detritus are all possibilities. Shown to the left are just some of the various grits, gravels, sands and eggshells that I use.

These can be stirred into the medium before being applied to the surface – this allows you to make the additions more evenly distributed – or you can apply the medium to the surface and then add the materials more selectively.

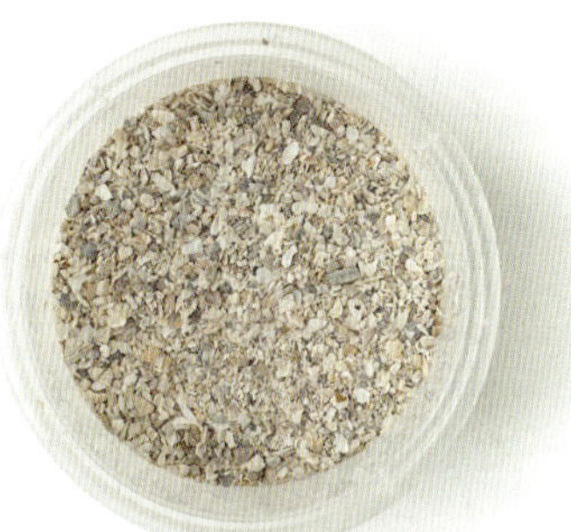
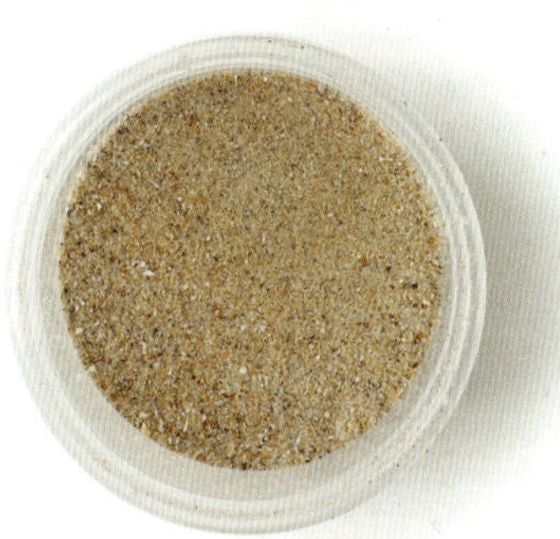

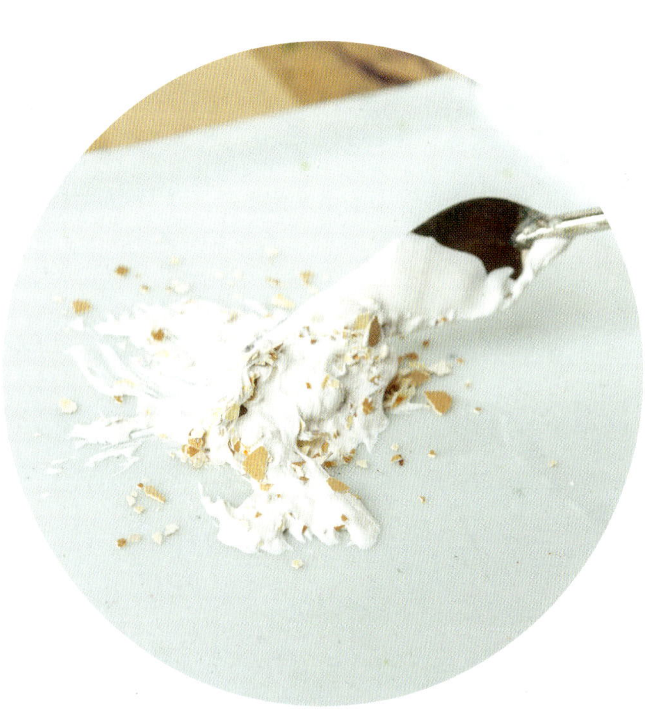

Eggshells being added to texture paste on the palette, prior to being applied to the painting surface. You can instead apply the gel or paste to the surface and work the material in directly.

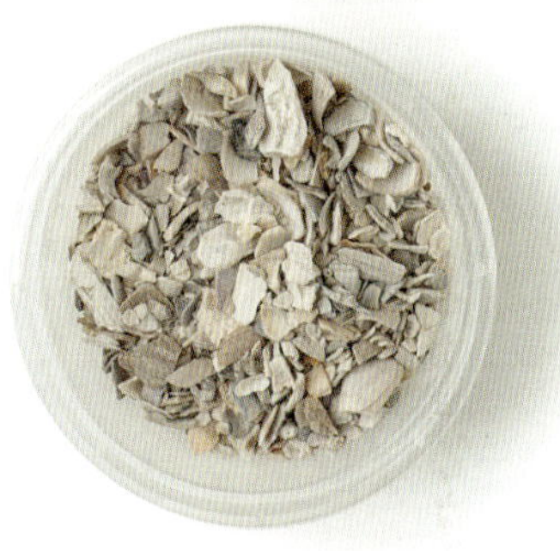

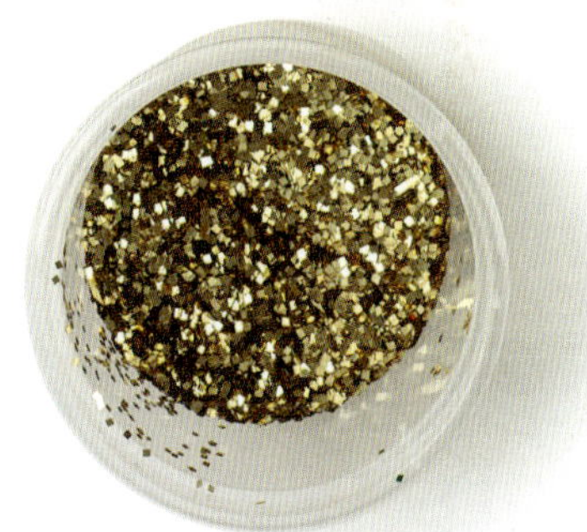

Suitable materials to add to pastes and gels. From top to bottom: wood ash, eggshells aquarium gravel, beach sand, broken seashells, glitter.

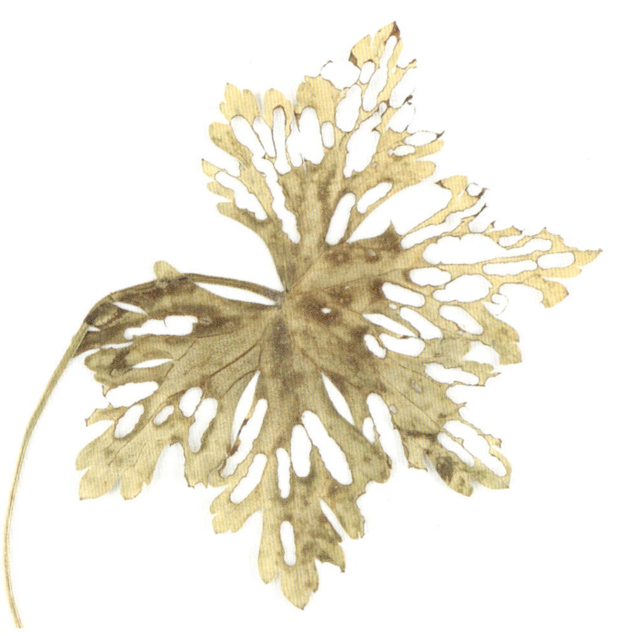

Stencils and texture paste

Craft suppliers stock a range of stencils that we can use to add pattern or texture to an artwork with the technique below. We can also gather subjects from nature or around the home for the same purpose – leaf or flower skeletons, feathers, cotton scrim, doilies or lace trim will all work. Stencilling can be done with either paint, acrylic gel or texture pastes.

After painting and once completely dry, texture paste can be lightly sanded and either left white or scumbled over with paint, pastel or coloured crayon (see page 43 for an example).

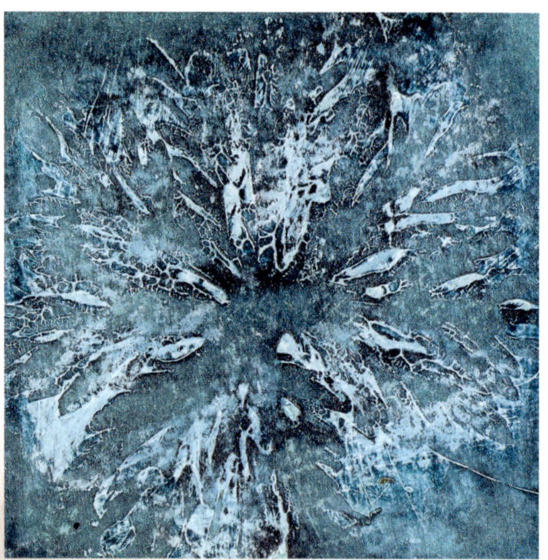

Geranium leaf print with texture paste

A partly-eaten away geranium leaf, almost skeletal, made a great stencil.

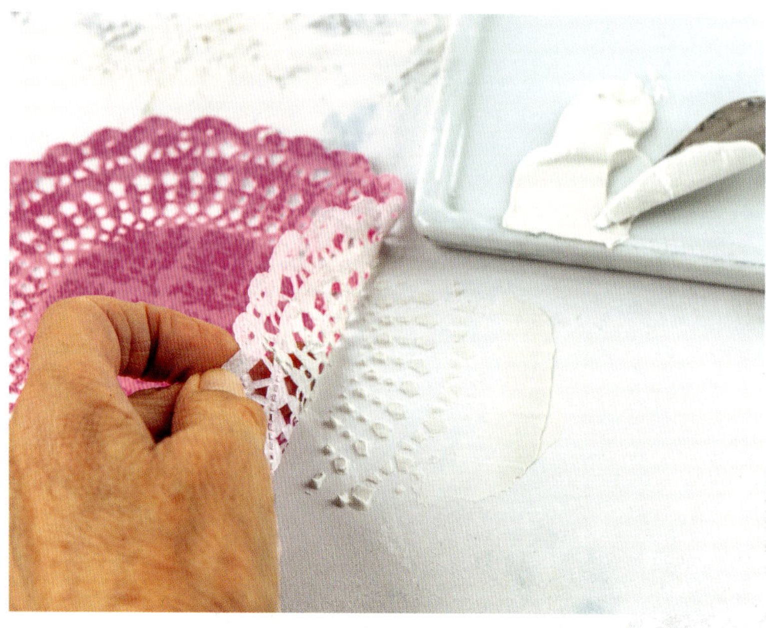

Creating stencilled texture

Use a palette knife, squeegee or piece of plastic card to apply the medium over the stencil. It will ooze through open areas. When the stencil is peeled away, it will leave a textured, patterned surface that reflects the design of the stencil. Here I've used a paper doily and fine-textured DIY filler.

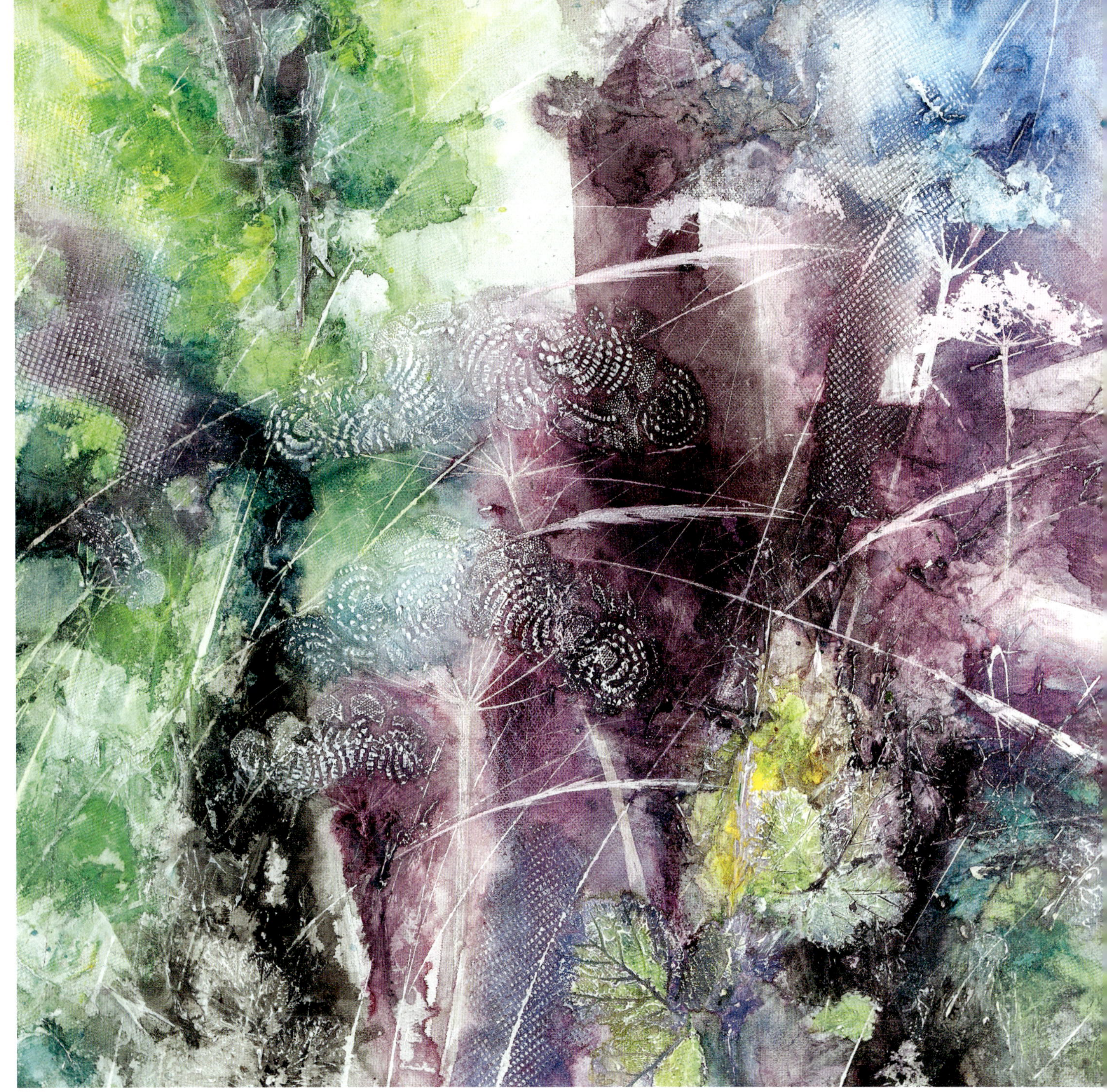

Queen Anne's Lace

50 × 50cm (19¾ × 19¾in)

A few years ago, I was given an unused roll of lace trim. It may never be used for its intended purpose, but different parts of it have been used many times in my artworks.

This painting uses the main lace motif as the umbellifer's seed head. It also has some tissue paper collage, and uses mark making and leaf prints in texture paste to enliven some areas, while others have been left clear.

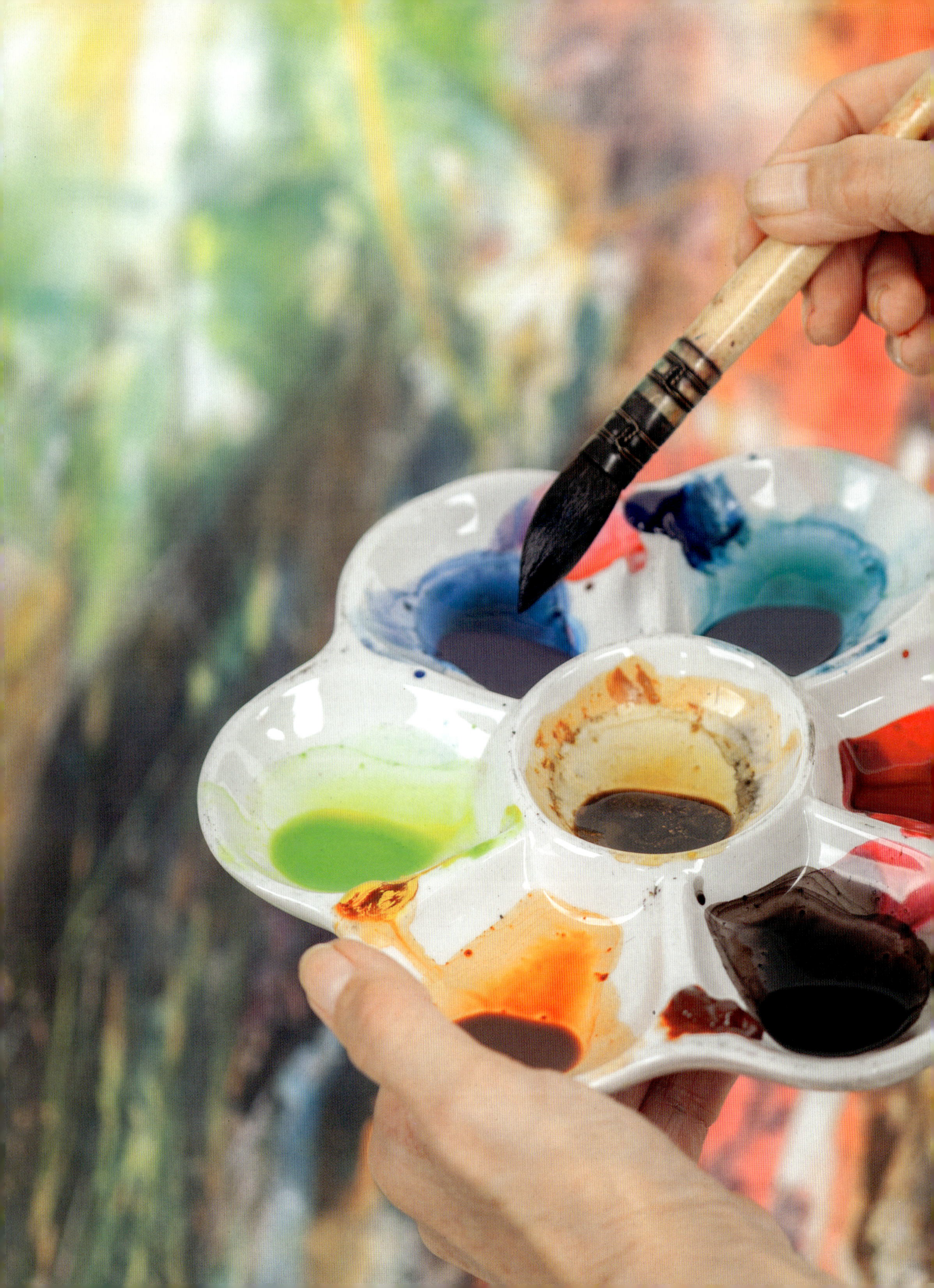

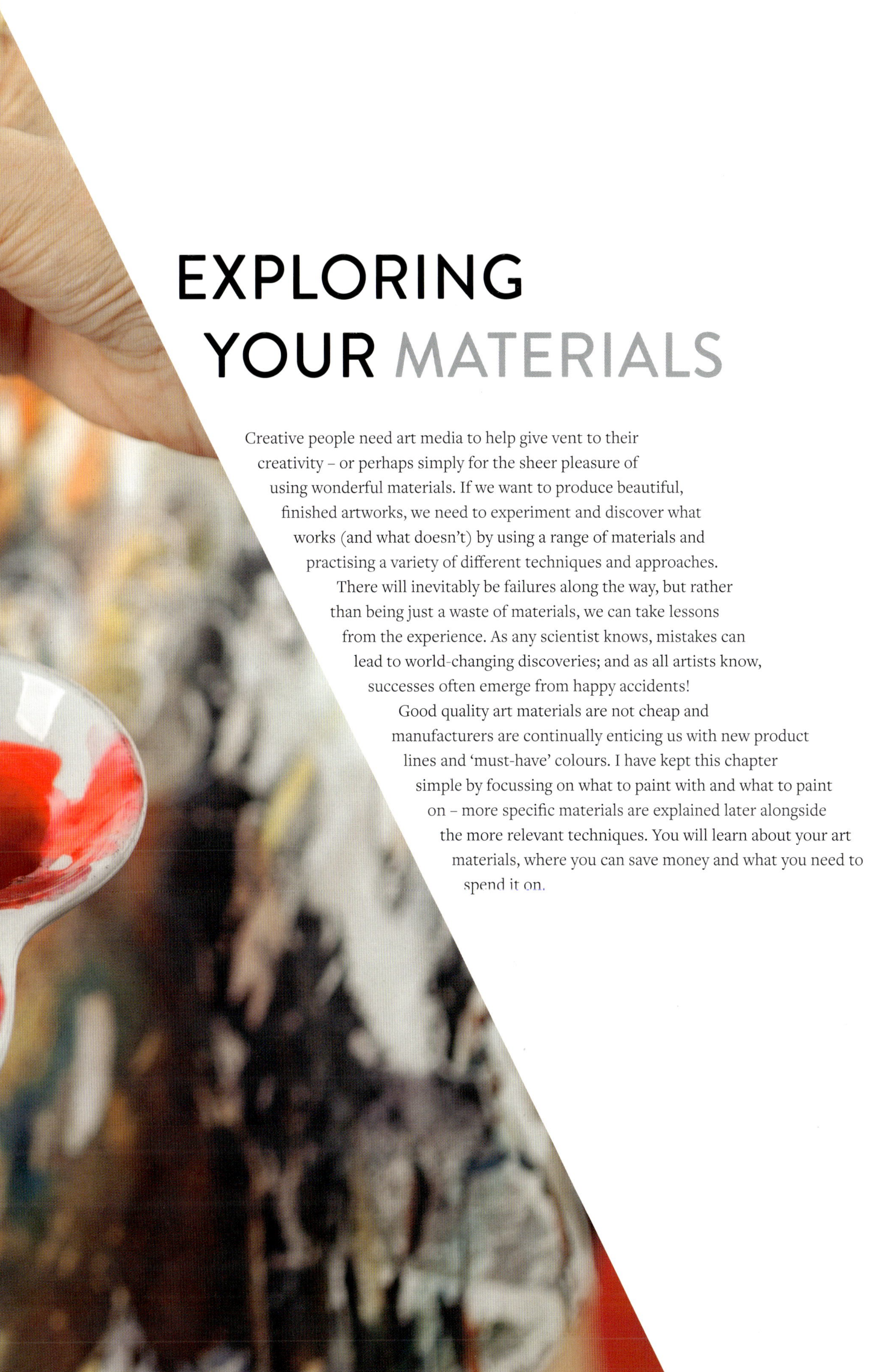

EXPLORING
YOUR MATERIALS

Creative people need art media to help give vent to their
creativity – or perhaps simply for the sheer pleasure of
using wonderful materials. If we want to produce beautiful,
finished artworks, we need to experiment and discover what
works (and what doesn't) by using a range of materials and
practising a variety of different techniques and approaches.
There will inevitably be failures along the way, but rather
than being just a waste of materials, we can take lessons
from the experience. As any scientist knows, mistakes can
lead to world-changing discoveries; and as all artists know,
successes often emerge from happy accidents!
Good quality art materials are not cheap and
manufacturers are continually enticing us with new product
lines and 'must-have' colours. I have kept this chapter
simple by focussing on what to paint with and what to paint
on – more specific materials are explained later alongside
the more relevant techniques. You will learn about your art
materials, where you can save money and what you need to
spend it on.

Pigment

Pigment is the ingredient that provides the colour in our media – whether they are paints, inks, pastels or anything else. The characteristics that we look for in our paints – such as how opaque or transparent they are; or whether they are staining or granulating colours – are inherent in the pigments themselves.

Individual pigments come from widely varying sources. The earliest pigments used by man were natural: carbon, coming from charred wood or bone, and the evocatively named ochres and siennas which occur naturally in clay. The semi-precious stone, lapis lazuli, gave Renaissance artists their only true blue. More expensive than gold, this blue mineral was mined only in Afghanistan – a fact reflected in the name of the paint made from it: ultramarine, meaning 'over the sea'.

Today, many natural pigments have been replaced by synthetic ones, for reasons of cost, health or their impact on the environment. The word 'hue' properly describes a specific quality of colour (e.g. 'duck egg blue' or 'royal blue'), but is also used by manufacturers when a potentially harmful pigment is replaced by one that is safer, as in cadmium red hue. This paint does not now contain harmful cadmium, but uses a synthetic pigment to produce a paint of the same hue.

Synthetic pigments, such as quinacridone or phthalocyanine (usually shortened to phthalo), have increased our range of colour choices exponentially. In many cases, synthetic pigments provide stronger, more transparent and more vibrant colours than natural pigments. The quinacridone pigments range between purple and orange, while the spectrum of phthalo blue is from a warm blue to cool green.

The contribution that chemistry makes to the art world can't be understated. As far as watercolour is concerned, it has changed its reputation forever from being regarded as a wishy-washy medium!

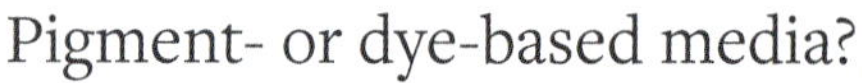

Pigment- or dye-based media?

I'm sure we've all experienced curtains or clothes that have faded over time, while other fabrics retain their colour. Likewise, there are some ranges of paints, alcohol inks and crayons that may be promoted for their powerful and vibrant colour. Rather than from pigment, their colour may come from dye, and therefore they are not archival. This means that they are not lightfast and, like your favourite jeans, may fade with time.

The sad story of quinacridone gold

Formulated for the car industry when gold cars were all the rage, the pigment no. PO49 was used for a paint called 'quinacridone gold'. It became an instant success in the art market. Loved by artists for its clarity and purity, it gave a satisfying glow to their paintings.

Sadly for artists, when the public lost interest in gold cars, pigment PO49 began to run out. Disgruntled artists continued to demand this beautiful gold paint and manufacturers scrambled to try and reproduce it by mixing existing pigments, but the truth is that the mixtures of pigments available in today's quinacridone gold paint can never replicate the magic of the old single pigment paint!

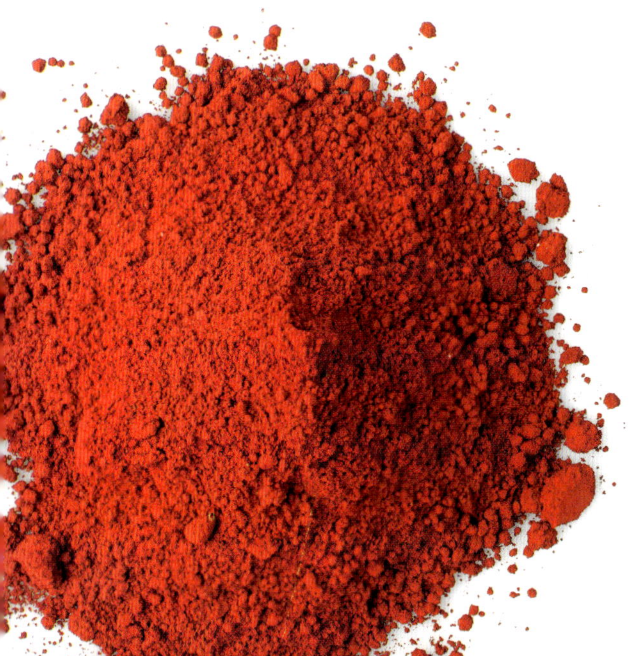

Wet media: paints and inks

The wet media that I describe in this book are mostly water-soluble, including watercolour, gouache and acrylic paint, as well as a variety of inks. The paint mixes are typically diluted to a similar consistency to the inks, so that they are sufficiently runny to flow over the support. They should not be watery, but pigment-rich and with a milk-like consistency.

Working with paint or ink of a fluid consistency is fun and can be very expressive. It is a loose way of working, with the liquid paint allowed to flow over and around any texture or collage that has been applied, streaming and pooling as it wends its way with a minimum of guidance from the artist.

Using ink-like consistencies of wet media has other advantages. They can be applied with a dip pen, quill, ruling pen, stick or any number of homemade tools. With these fluid mixes you can drip, flick or create interesting runs by moving or tipping the support.

Tubes or pans? Watercolours are available in both tubes or small blocks of colour, known as pans. In general, I recommend buying tubes, as the paint inside is already soft and moist, making it quicker and easier to mix. Pans, on the other hand, contain solid paint that does not rewet as easily. You need to work harder to mix sufficient colour from pans; the resulting mixes may be more dilute and may dry lighter.

Storage and transport A paint box with pans of watercolour paint is really useful to have when out sketching. I use a folding palette with empty wells, which I fill from my tubes of paints. I carry a few bottles of inks in a separate container.

Artists' or students' quality? The difference between these ranges is the quality of the pigment; how finely it is ground, and its proportion to other ingredients like fillers and binders. Artists' quality paints produce stronger, more vibrant results so, although they are more expensive, you need to squeeze less paint from the tube than when using cheaper students' paint. They are also easier to rewet, as the fillers in students' quality paints mean that they have a tendency to dry harder. Some of the larger manufacturers sell their own budget brands of artists' quality paints, which are a halfway house between artists' and students' quality. If you are just starting out as a painter, these may suit the pocket better.

Single pigments Our painting media contains either single pigments or combinations of pigments. You can usually find this useful information on the paint label or other packaging (see below left). Paints and inks that use just a single pigment will give purer, cleaner results.

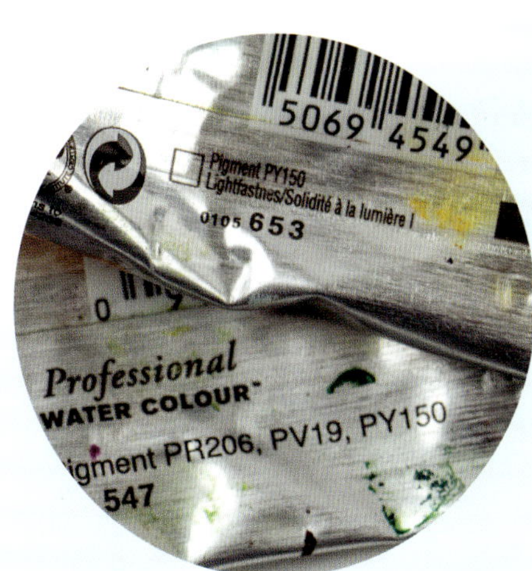

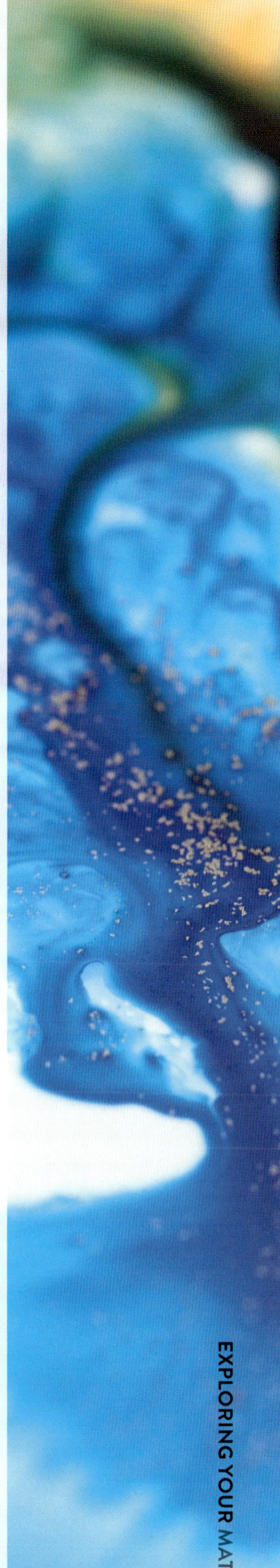

Single pigment paint at the top – as indicated by the lone 'PY150' pigment. Compare this with the paint at the bottom, which is made up of three pigments.

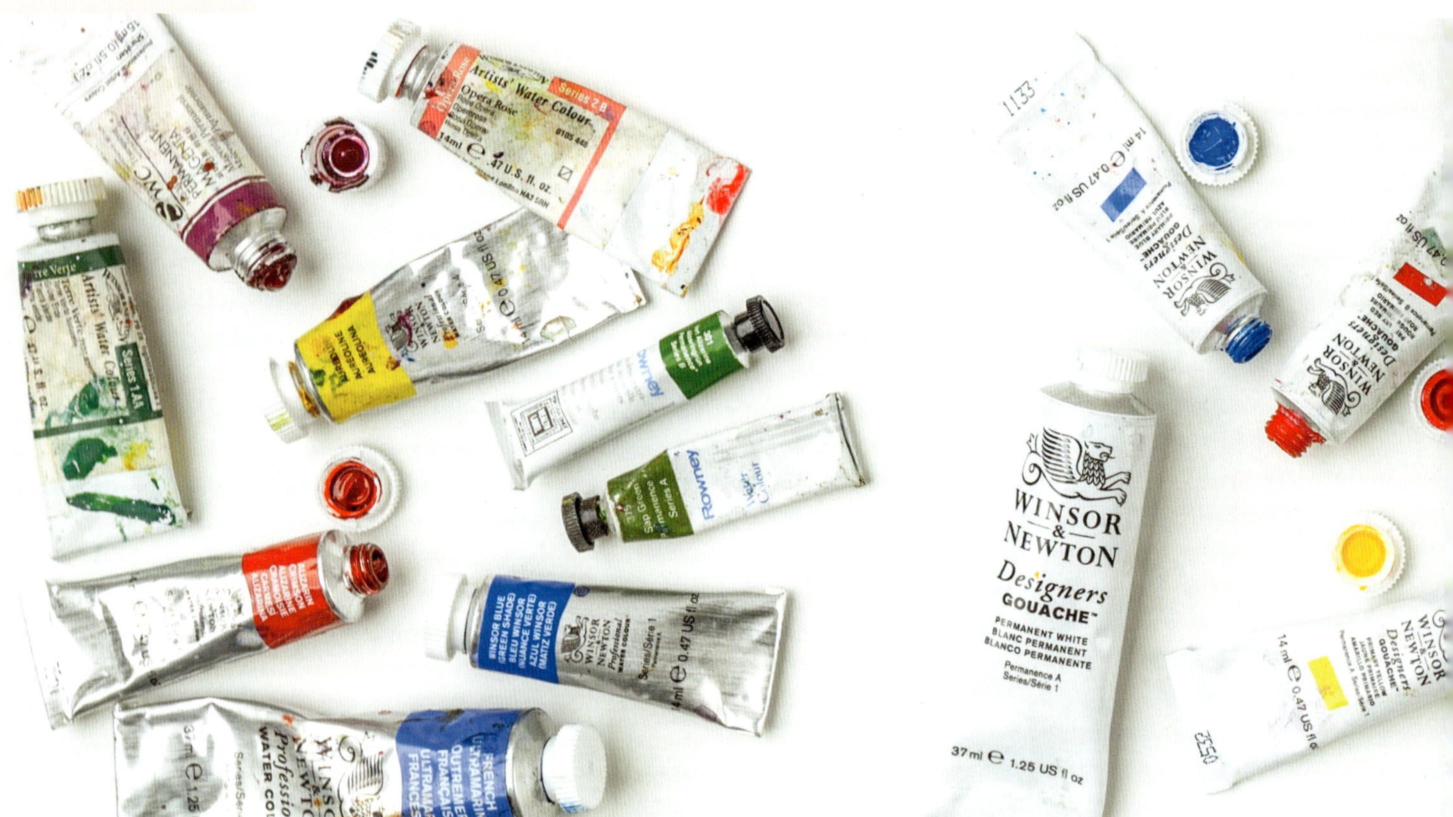

Watercolour paints

Choosing which colours to buy can be overwhelming, as the range of paints on offer is so huge. Many of us use the sweet shop method: eyeing up the mouthwatering selection and simply choosing the most visually appealing. I've been there myself and still have rarely used tubes of paint to prove it.

Experience has taught me to choose science over serendipity in making my colour choices. By choosing mainly single pigment paints (see page 55) and those that are transparent, we have the best chance of achieving both purer, less muddy colour mixes.

My regular palette includes the following pure pigment colours: quinacridone magenta, alizarin crimson, permanent rose, aureolin yellow, Winsor lemon, Winsor blue, French ultramarine and burnt sienna. I also have a few other favourites that are multi-pigment paint, including quinacridone gold, Aussie red gold, green-gold, perylene maroon and phthalo turquoise.

Gouache

Gouache is an opaque form of watercolour with a chalky consistency, traditionally used for illustration. In recent years, it has gained popularity as a painting medium in its own right. It can also be used in a watercolour painting to add highlights or to contrast with watercolour's relative transparency.

I like to use gouache paints, but as they dry out relatively quickly and are not my main painting medium, I restrict the number of colours that I buy. By using fewer, I allow myself to buy the better quality brands, which have richer colour. I buy primary red, yellow and blue, in order to have the widest mixing choices, together with titanium white.

There are two whites available in gouache, with quite different properties. Zinc white is the warmer and more translucent of the two and is best used in mixtures to make tints, while titanium white is more opaque and cooler in temperature.

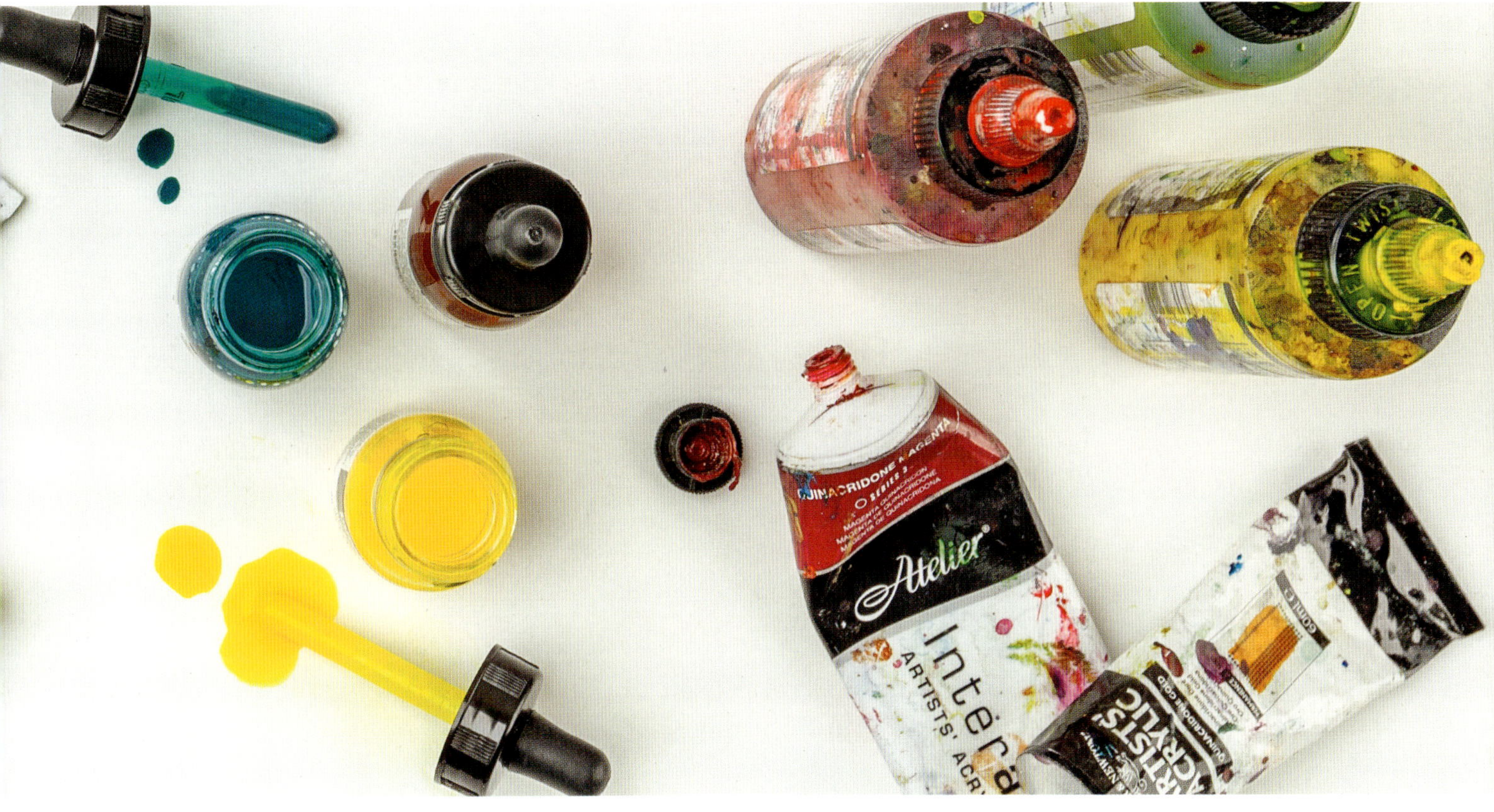

Inks

Acrylic inks Acrylic inks contain pigment that is suspended in an acrylic emulsion. The difference between acrylic paints or inks and traditional watercolours is that acrylics can't be rewetted once dry. Acrylic inks are pre-mixed to the perfect fluid consistency and are conveniently packaged in a bottle, often with a handy dropper. I often mix small amounts of acrylic inks in with my watercolours, to take advantage of the resist effects, which I describe in the chapter 'Irresistible Resists' on pages 70–79.

Indian Ink A velvety black ink made from carbon that has been used in China for thousands of years. It was only when it was imported from India in the mid seventeenth century that it became known as Indian ink.

Acrylic paints

As with acrylic inks, acrylic paints contain pigments suspended in a polymer acrylic emulsion that makes them waterproof when dry. This means that they can be applied in layers with no danger of disturbing what is underneath.

Acrylic paints are available in a variety of consistencies from fluid to heavy bodied, allowing a wide range of applications. Unlike oil paints, they can be applied either thinly over thick layers or thickly over thin, with no fear of the paint cracking. In addition to this, acrylic products are very adhesive, which allows them to be used on a wide range of supports.

Another advantage of acrylics is that, unlike other water media, they do not need to be framed behind glass – although varnishing is advisable, both to enhance and protect the surface.

Brushes

It's useful to have a variety of brushes and other tools for mixed media work. A palette knife is probably my most-used applicator after brushes, but plastic cards, various sticks, pens and much-loved quills are all indispensable to me.

When buying new brushes, the size you need will very much depend on the scale of your work. I suggest erring towards larger brushes. My round watercolour brushes are size 12 or larger, and my flat brushes range in size from 25–75mm (1–3in).

Brushes should be good quality, and make sure that round brushes come to a point. Once they have seen better days, they can still be very useful for mixing, making characterful marks and also for processes that may damage a more expensive brush. Some household painting brushes will also be needed if you plan to prepare your own supports.

These days it is possible to buy very good quality sable-synthetic as well as synthetic only brushes, which can be used to work in both watercolour and acrylics. Always make sure that you wash brushes well, especially after working with acrylic paints or inks. Clean them by working a little washing-up liquid into the base of the hairs just above the ferrule, then rinse out until the water is clear.

Dry media

Pencils

Standard graphite pencils are useful for sketching and other purposes. I recommend a softer 2B or 4B pencil. A harder pencil, such as a 2H or 4H, is also useful to transfer a traced-out design.

Charcoal

Charcoal can be bought in pencil or stick form, as shown. Its velvety pigment creates beautiful, tonal sketches that can easily be blended with fingers and worked up very quickly. Use a fixative to protect them from smudging, especially if you plan to add another media.

Pastels

There are two main types of pastels: soft pastels (also known as chalk pastels) and oil pastels. Soft pastels are made up of pigment, filler and a binder that holds these dry ingredients together. They can be bought as round or square sticks; the round type being softer and containing a greater proportion of pigment. As with any art materials, you get what you pay for, so it is advisable not to buy too cheaply. Some very cheap chalk pastels will crumble completely and not adhere to the support. On the other hand, the best quality soft pastels are a joy to use; they have a creamy consistency and are like drawing or painting with almost pure pigment.

Oil pastels are composed of pigment mixed with a non-drying oil and wax binder. This binder allows the pastels to be blended if desired, by either rubbing or using a brush or piece of rag dipped into a little low odour white spirit. Oil pastels can also be used as a resist with water media – see the chapter on resists, which starts on page 70.

Both chalk and oil pastels can be used to enhance a painting: whether on top of watercolour or acrylic media to strengthen colours, to add drawing, contrasting or complementary colour accents or to highlight texture by using the side of the stick. You can see an example of their use on page 43.

Top to bottom: graphite pencils, pastel pencils, charcoal sticks, oil pastels and soft pastels.

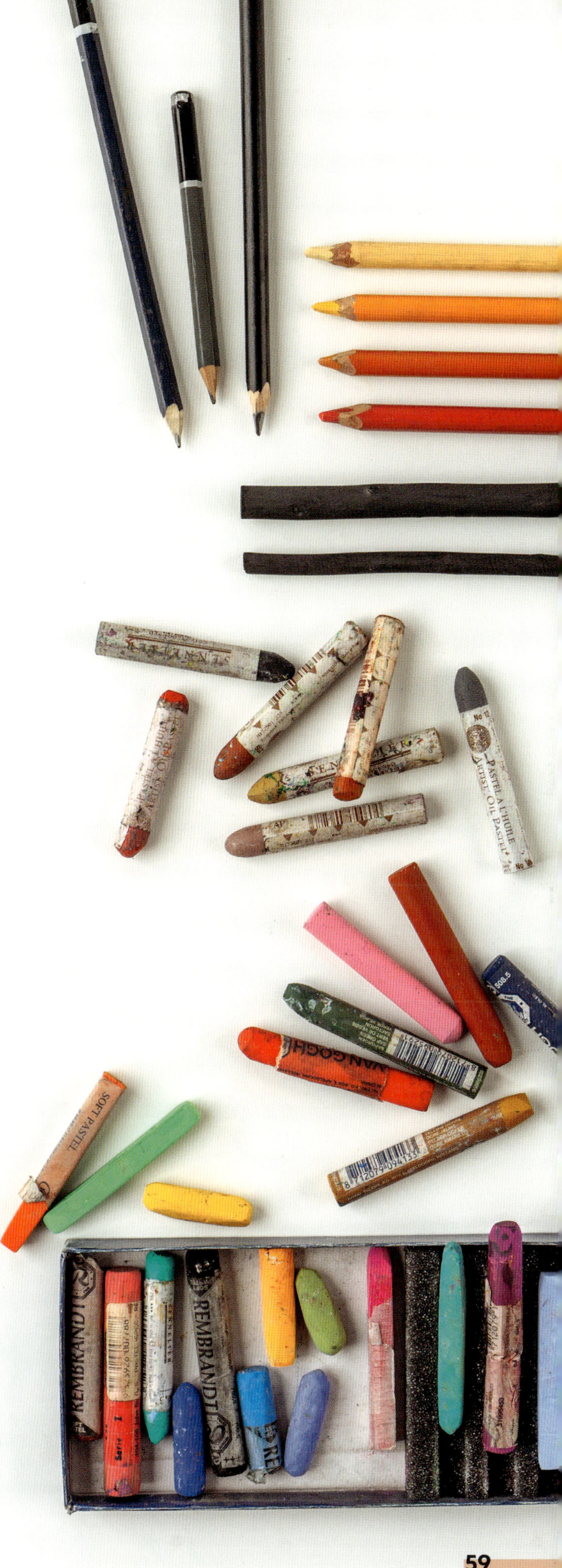

Supports

There are a wide range of supports that are suitable for painting in acrylics and mixed media. The important considerations are that the support is acid-free, robust enough, and also sealed and prepared appropriately. If you are working in watercolour, even as a beginner, a good quality watercolour paper (see opposite) is essential.

Stretching paper Watercolour paper that is larger than A3 (30 × 42cm/11¾ × 16½in) and either 300gsm (140lb) or lighter in weight needs to be stretched with gummed paper parcel tape in order to avoid it buckling. To do this, soak the paper in water for about eight minutes (too long can affect the sizing – see 'Paper storage', right), then lay it onto a board while wet. Use a dry cloth or piece of kitchen towel to wipe about a 1cm (½in) wide strip all the way round the edge (this ensures the tape adheres well) and apply the tape all round. The paper expands when wet and shrinks back as it dries to create a tight, stretched surface. Leave the tape on until the painting is finished and completely dry. To remove the painting from the board, insert the point of a scalpel or craft knife under the edge of the paper and cut around with the flat of the blade before lifting off.

Paper storage

Watercolour paper contains 'size' – a glue that holds the fibres together and maintains its stability. Without size, watercolour paper would soak up water like a sponge. It is important to store watercolour paper flat, in a dry place and away from direct sunlight in order to avoid deterioration. If watercolour paper is stored in a damp place, the size can be affected, making it unusable.

Mount board

Acid-free mount board makes a suitable and inexpensive support to use with a variety of media. If it has a smooth surface, any texture needs to be added – but happily it is robust enough to take a variety of collage materials.

Mount board can be used either just as it is or it can be sealed with a coat of gesso. You may also need to pin or staple it to a board for stability.

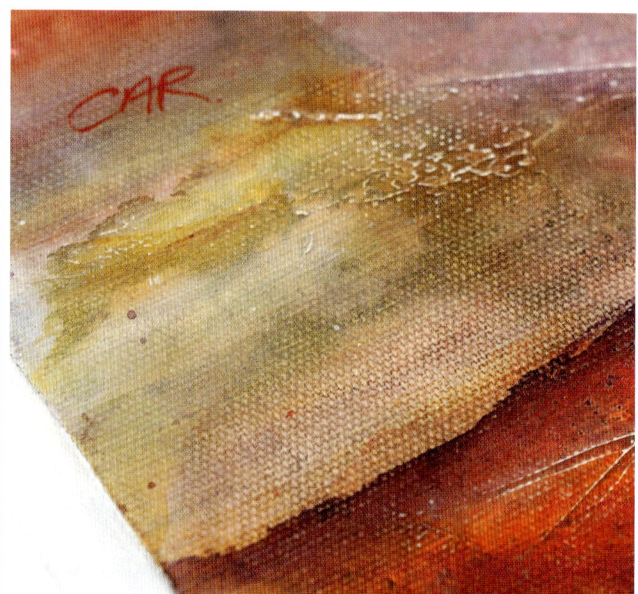

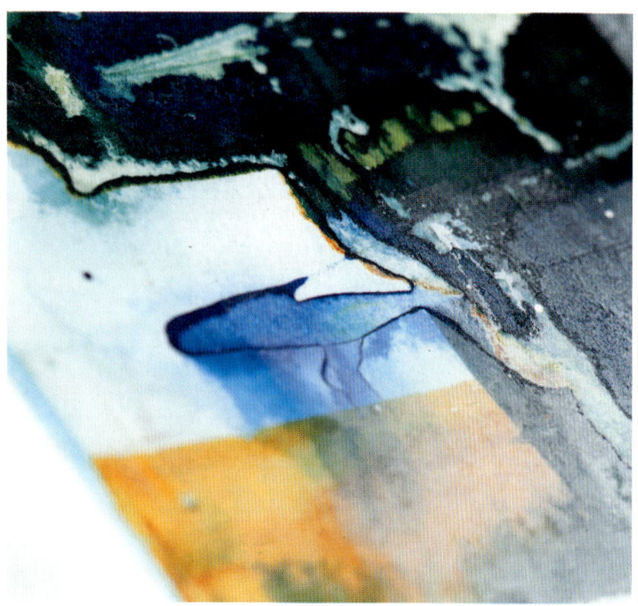

Canvas and canvas board

Both canvas and canvas boards can be bought ready primed to use with acrylic media. The choice that you make depends on whether you prefer the resistance of a solid surface or the bounciness of a stretched canvas.

Watercolour paper

Typically made from either cotton or cellulose fibres, this surface is designed to have just the right amount of absorbency to hold a liquid wash. Watercolour papers vary, so the only way to discover which suits your way of painting is to try different brands.

The most economical way to buy paper is in large, loose sheets, cutting them to size as required. While pads are convenient for sketching, they are the most expensive way to buy paper.

Surface There are different surfaces, ranging from smooth HP paper (standing for hot pressed), to Rough and Extra Rough. For most purposes, a Not surface (short for 'not hot-pressed', and also known as CP or cold-pressed), which has a medium texture, is a good choice. HP is a smooth surface and usually more suitable for detailed work. Rough surfaces help evoke texture and so suit seascapes or rocky subjects.

Weight Watercolour paper comes in a range of weights, with 300gsm (140lb) being the most widely used, although heavier weights are a good choice if you can afford them, especially for mixed media work.

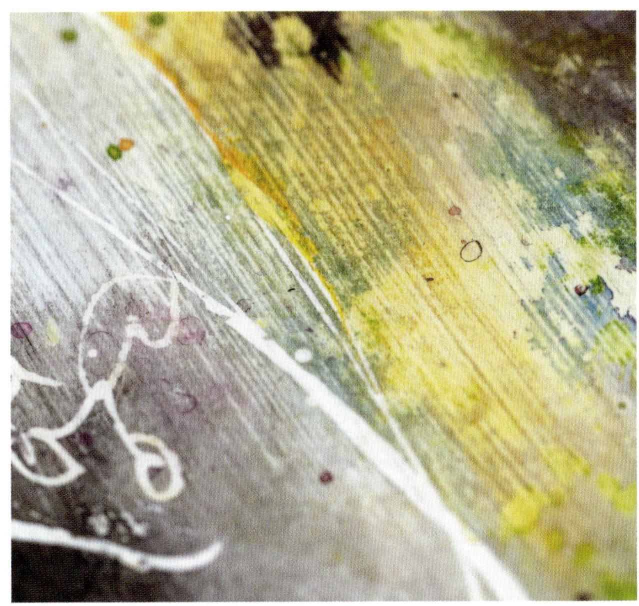

Wooden supports

Wood panels can either be bought from an art supplier, ready prepared or you can source your own. Prepared wooden panels have the advantage that the gesso primer is sprayed on, giving a very smooth surface.

Supports that you source, such as MDF, plywood, recycled or even driftwood, need to be both sealed and primed, which are terms that are often confused.

Sealing Sealing creates a waterproof barrier and protects the surface. A bare wood surface must be clean and dust free before sealing. To seal, apply two coats of acrylic gloss medium, allowing each coat to dry completely. A light sand in between coats is recommended.

Priming Once the surface is sealed, priming will make it ready to receive paint – without priming, the colour will bead or simply slide off the surface. To prime, apply at least two coats of gesso to the sealed wood surface. Gesso is absorbent, and does not seal the wood when used on its own. Gesso's role is to prepare the surface in order to accept other painting media.

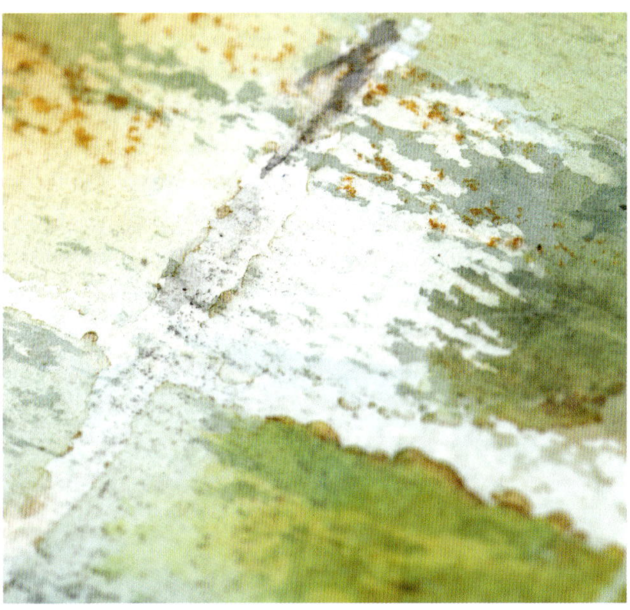

'It is only by deduction, by elimination, by emphasis, that we get at the real meaning of things.' **Georgia O'Keeffe**

TOWARDS THE ABSTRACT

Art that is abstract or towards the abstract presents more of a puzzle to the artist than representational art, which lays out its cards openly on the table. It places more emphasis on the formal elements that we looked at in the early chapters of the book. While the subject remains recognizable to a greater or lesser degree, the forms may be simplified, stylized, partially erased or even added to and made more complex. Adding and subtracting elements are actions that may be repeated back and forth during a painting's progress in order to edit and develop the image. In this section, I suggest ideas and experiments that use a variety of techniques, tools and surfaces. Some of these could be small-scale exercises, which are good for working through a quantity of ideas while larger pieces help to loosen up and allow the paint to flow.

If you are new to abstraction, remember that there are no fixed rules to follow: whatever you do is right because you are doing it in your own way. The biggest barrier to succeeding is not to try. If you are lacking in confidence, begin with a very simple subject, either what I have suggested or one of your own. Trust your own intuition; practice is your best teacher and in time you will get a sense of what works and what does not.

Georgia O'Keeffe

The American artist Georgia O'Keeffe (1887–1986) is well known for her beautiful paintings of over-sized flowers and abstract landscapes, especially of the desert in New Mexico, where she spent a great deal of her life. Many of her floral images are greatly enlarged, which in itself abstracts them, but they are also cropped close in, emphasizing a particular aspect such as the overlapping shapes of leaves and petals or the central reproductive areas – you can see one of my paintings in this style on page 79. O'Keeffe also smoothed surfaces, simplified colour and kept realistic detail to a minimum, in order to focus on the abstract elements of her subject.

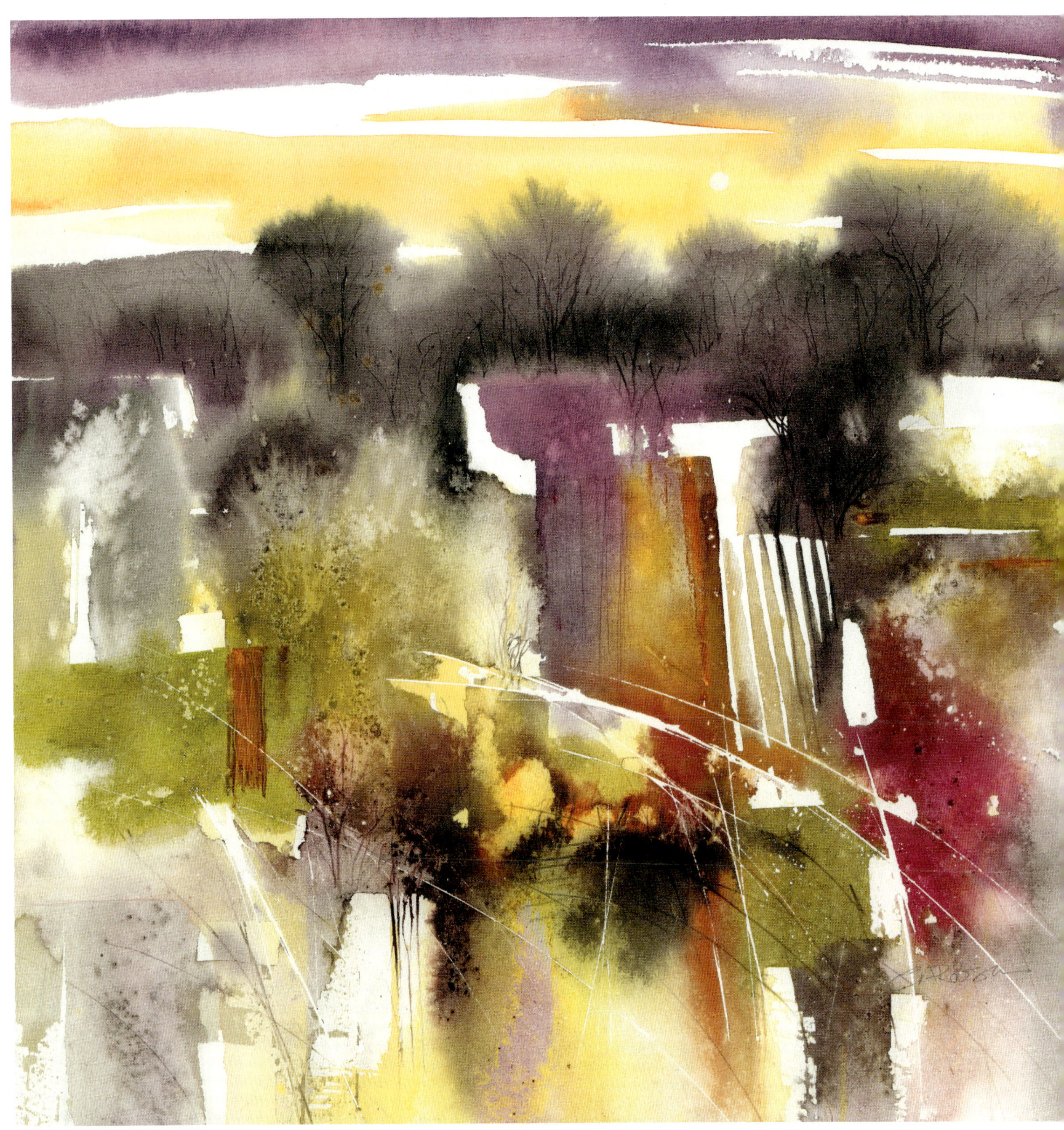

Winter Gold
35 × 35cm (13¾ × 13¾in)

'The paint follows the water!'

This profound little statement was announced by my ten-year-old neighbour when I was showing him and his sister some watercolour techniques. His words may sound obvious, but they struck me as being keenly observed. I was demonstrating the 'wet in wet' technique that will be very familiar to those watercolourists among you.

To my mind, my young neighbour's lightbulb moment hits at the heart of watercolour science and allows us to paint the kind of flowing, watercolour wash that is illustrated throughout this book.

The wet in wet technique relies on mixing a sufficiently loose consistency of paint (similar to milk in fluidity) and then applying enough water to the paper, so that when a loaded brush is merely touched to the water, the paint flows easily down.

EXERCISE Wet in wet

I used mount board for my support, but either hot-pressed or Not surface watercolour paper will do just as well – make sure it is taped all the way round onto a board to avoid the paper cockling.

It's worth practising these kinds of washes over and over, varying the colour scheme and media that you use. You can draw directly with the dropper from ink bottles, for example.

1 Apply the water using a large round watercolour brush with a good point. Vary the marks to leave open areas.

2 Begin adding your wet media, touching it into the wet areas and tipping the support to allow it to flow. The paint should move and spread over the wet paper. If it doesn't do this, you need to add more water.

3 Continue to apply your paint. You might also try giving some areas a light spray of water to allow the colour to run further. Colour will continue to flow where the paper is still wet.

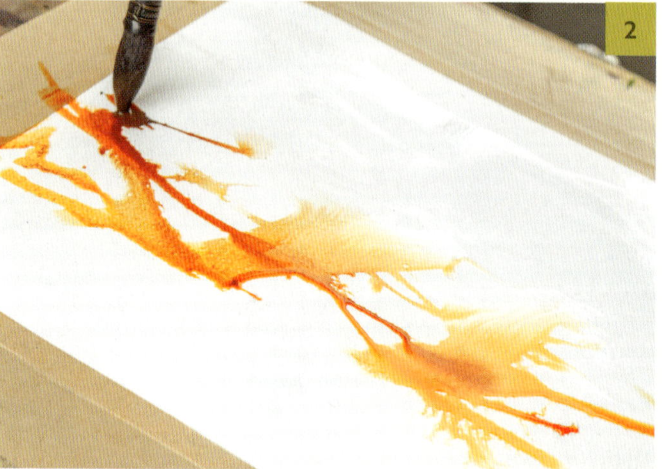

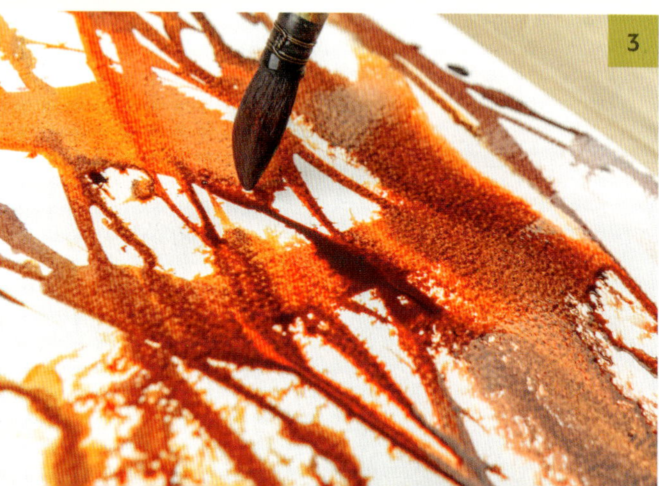

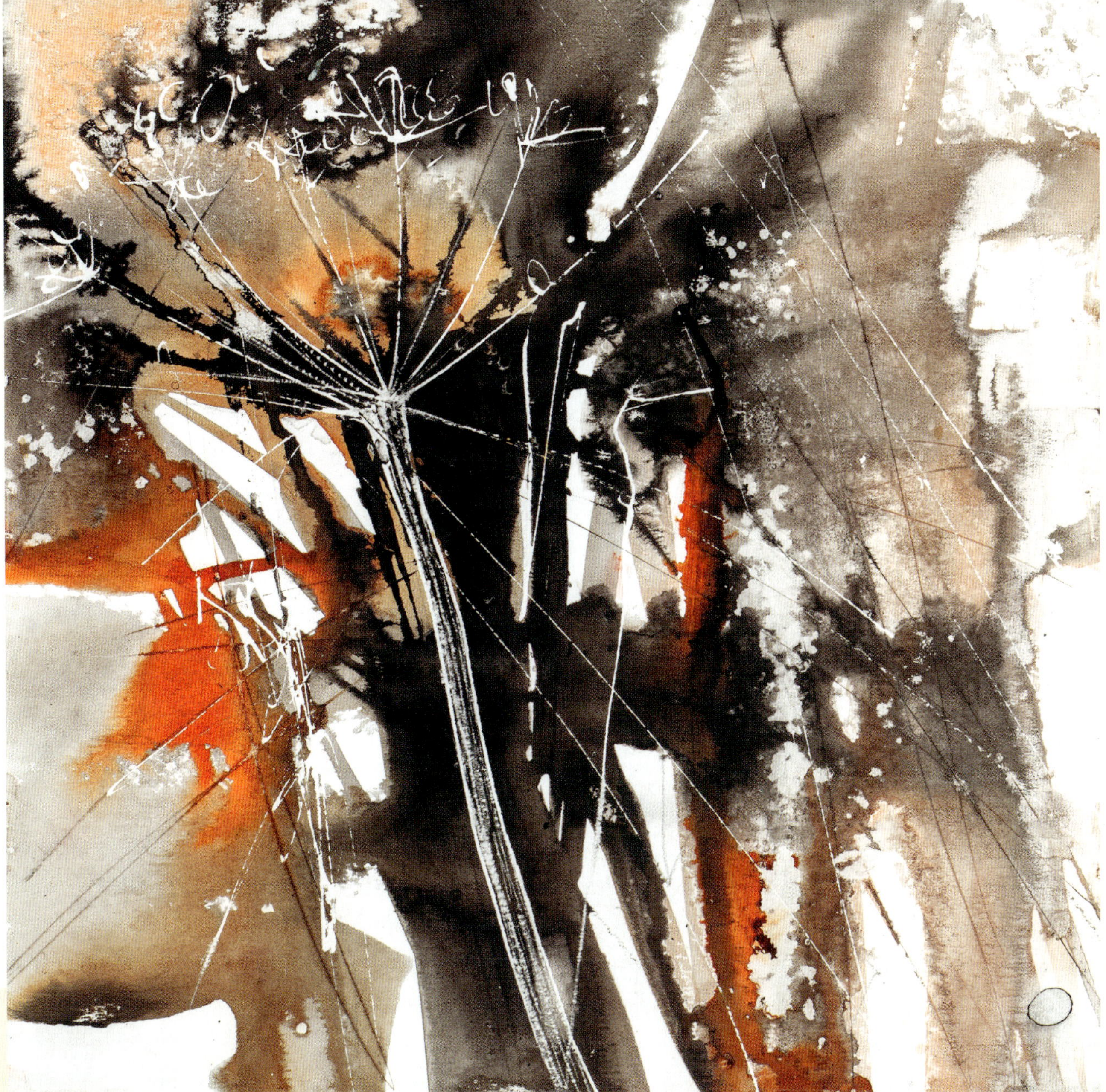

Painting *Autumn Seed Head*

Autumn Seed Head uses the simple motif of a seed head reduced to a skeletal state, but the idea could be adapted to suit any number of subjects. The seed head was sketched loosely in masking fluid (see page 74) and, once completely dry, clean water was applied using the technique described in the exercise opposite. I varied the marks with my brush, sometimes filling in areas with water and at other times drawing with the point of the brush to leave open shapes reminiscent of a background of grasses and foliage.

The colour scheme is very simple, made up from two wells of artists' quality burnt sienna watercolour mixed to a milky consistency. Add a few drops of burnt sienna acrylic ink to one of the wells, and a couple of drops of black acrylic ink to the other. The inks serve to strengthen the colours and also give some variety to the browns. When either of these were touched to the wet areas, the paint moved and spread over the wet paper.

Mixing organic and geometric shapes

It's often said that there are no straight lines in nature. A look around at the landscape will reveal that large features such as the hills, trees, rivers and lakes that surround us are almost universally organic, irregular shapes – as are the negative spaces between them.

On the surface, geometric shapes and straight lines seem solely to belong to manmade structures like buildings and fenceposts. And yet, if we look more closely at nature, we see the hexagonal cells in honeycombs, the woven complexity of a spider's webs or the intricate structures of snowflakes. Nature's geometry is everywhere.

By using geometric elements in our paintings, we provide an echo to nature's grand plan, lend a more abstract feel to our paintings and often improve their construction. Whether in paint, collage, drawn or printed, they also provide an interplay with more rounded, amorphous shapes.

The examples shown opposite suggest ways to use varying sizes of flat brushes to add geometric movements or bars of colour to your work. They can be added either at the beginning or end of the painting, or freely and intuitively as the painting progresses.

A The natural and most direct way to add geometric shapes into your painting is to use a combination of round and flat brushes, moving from one to the other as you paint, as in this example.

B In this sketch a damp, flat brush was dragged through the watercolour while it was still wet, blurring and softening the subject.

C This minimal image uses the same technique as in example B. The ink lines were drawn first before the damp flat brush was dragged through the still-wet ink.

D Overlaying an image with bars of paint is a way of either partly obscuring or breaking up the image, depending on how opaque the paint is. In this example I used a wide flat brush and white gouache paint.

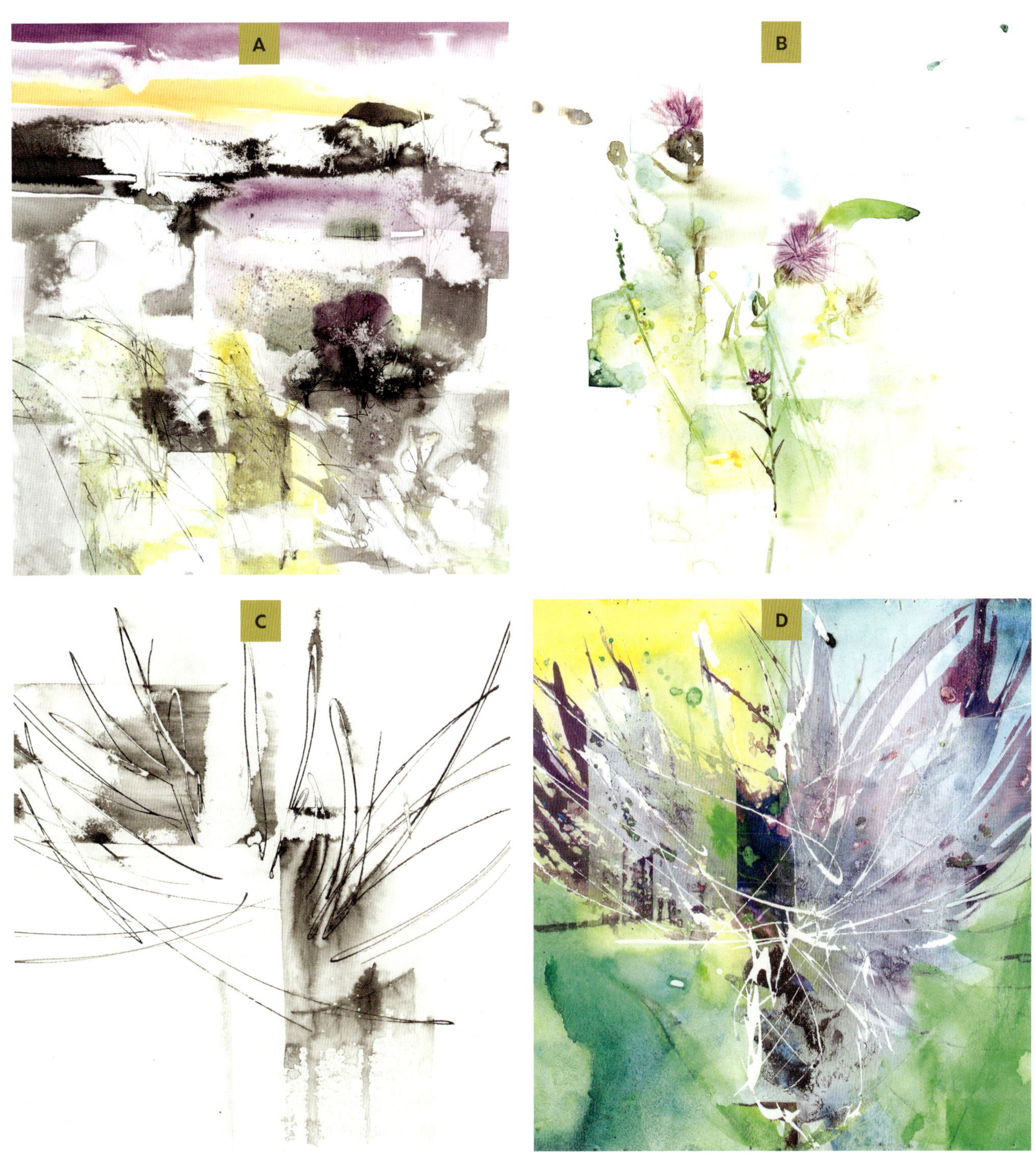

TOWARDS THE ABSTRACT

Painting *Season of Mists*

This is a painting with an environmental message that asks 'What price nature?'
A few collaged newspaper snippets torn from the stock market pages are used
to reflect nature's plight, our discarded litter mixing together with natural detritus.

This painting is only loosely tied to realism – the tree forms at the top provide
a visual anchor for the viewer, but the remainder is almost purely abstract.

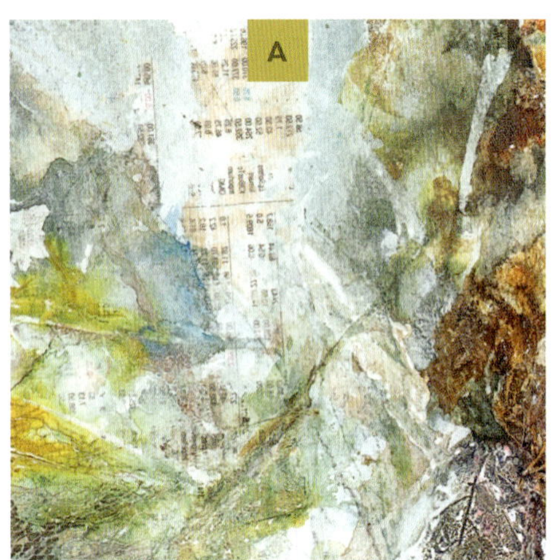
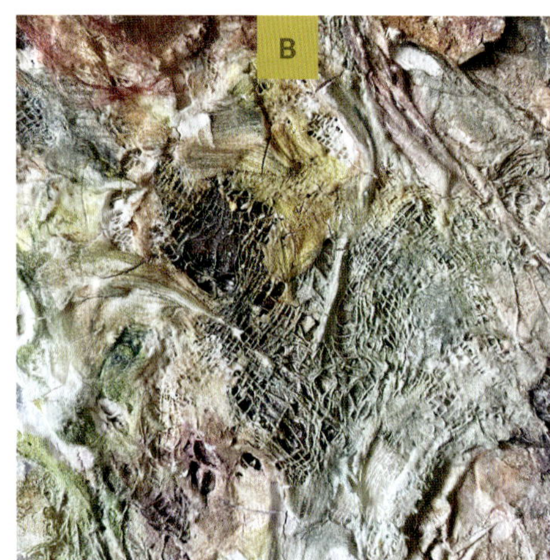
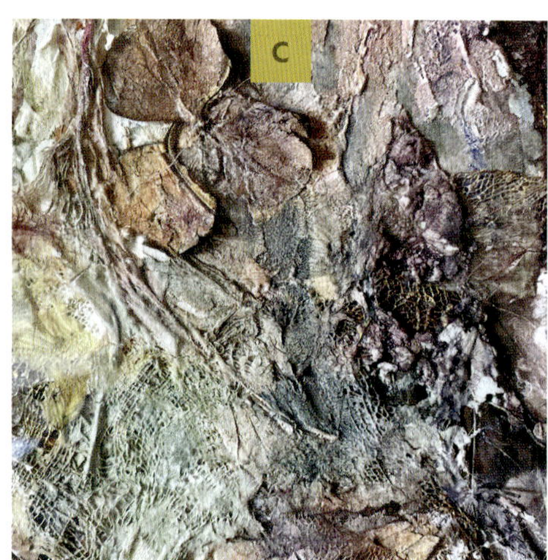

A Newspaper cuttings with lines of stock market figures, together with
texture paste and loose watercolour washes, form an initial layer to the
painting. They make a combination of organic and non-organic shapes.

B Scraps of coarse fabric, including both cotton scrim and tissue paper,
contrast with smooth textural effects.

C Dried hydrangea flowers and stems are held into the strongly adhesive,
acrylic texture paste.

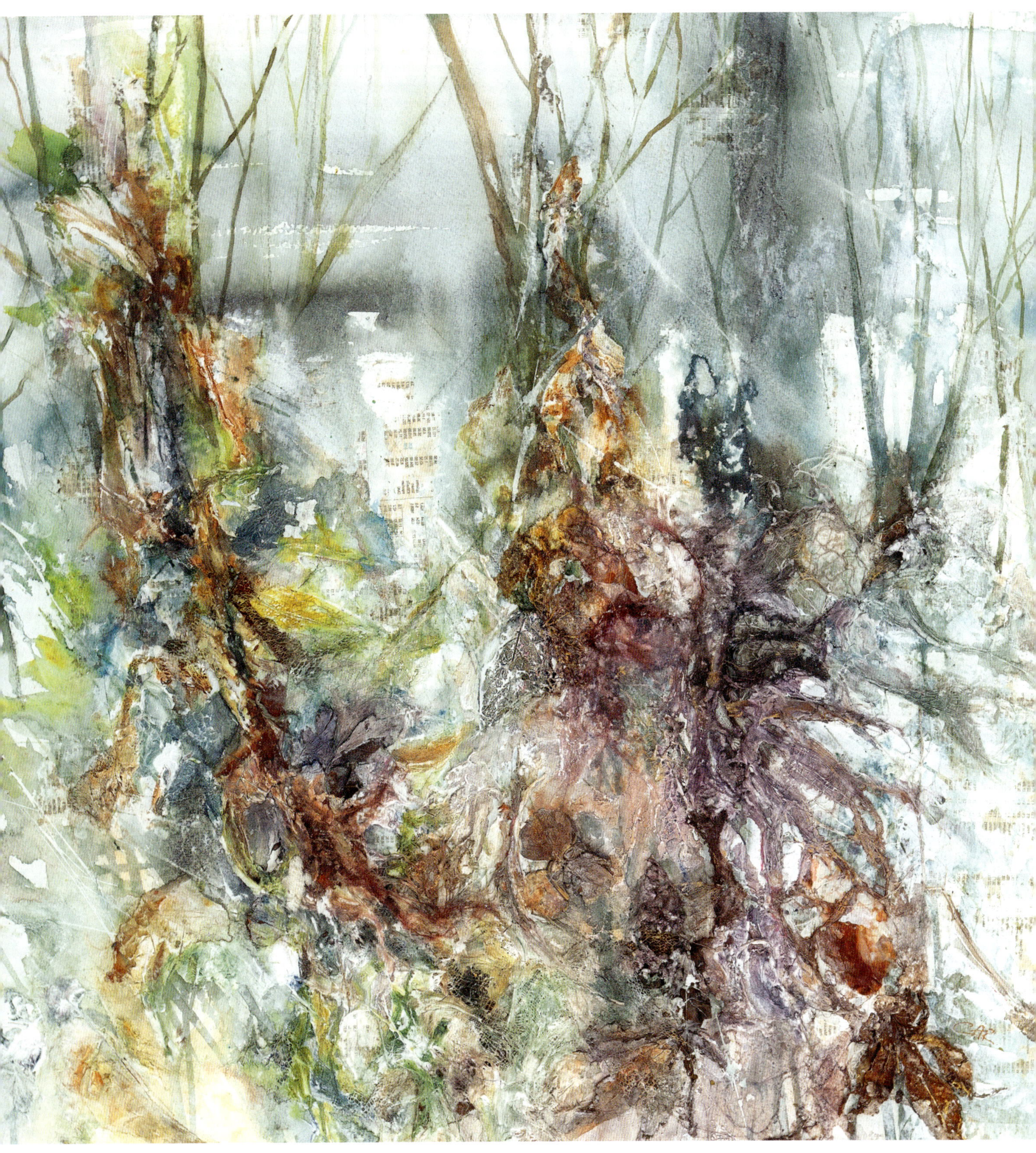

Season of Mists

53 × 53cm (21 × 21in)

IRRESISTIBLE RESISTS

Many of us use a wide variety of art materials from a range of manufacturers and you may have noticed that while some mix quite happily together, others resist each other to a greater or lesser degree. The most well-known resists are perhaps wax and masking fluid, both of which are often used in watercolour painting to reserve highlights or the white of the paper before applying a wash, as in the earlier exercise on page 46.

Other art materials resist each other in less obvious ways. By experimenting with materials that have some amount of incompatibility, we can exploit these properties in order to enhance our work. Art materials that resist each other set the stage for chance effects to happen – and serendipity to rule!

Barbara Rae

The Scottish painter and printmaker Barbara Rae (b. 1943), who is a great favourite of mine, freely combines materials and explores resists in her paintings and prints. When asked, in her book *Barbara Rae Prints*, about how she starts work in her sketchbook, she replied:

'Usually a wash of colour. Then I might use oil pastel or candle wax or acrylic medium to provide a waterproof barrier. It's all about activating the surface.'

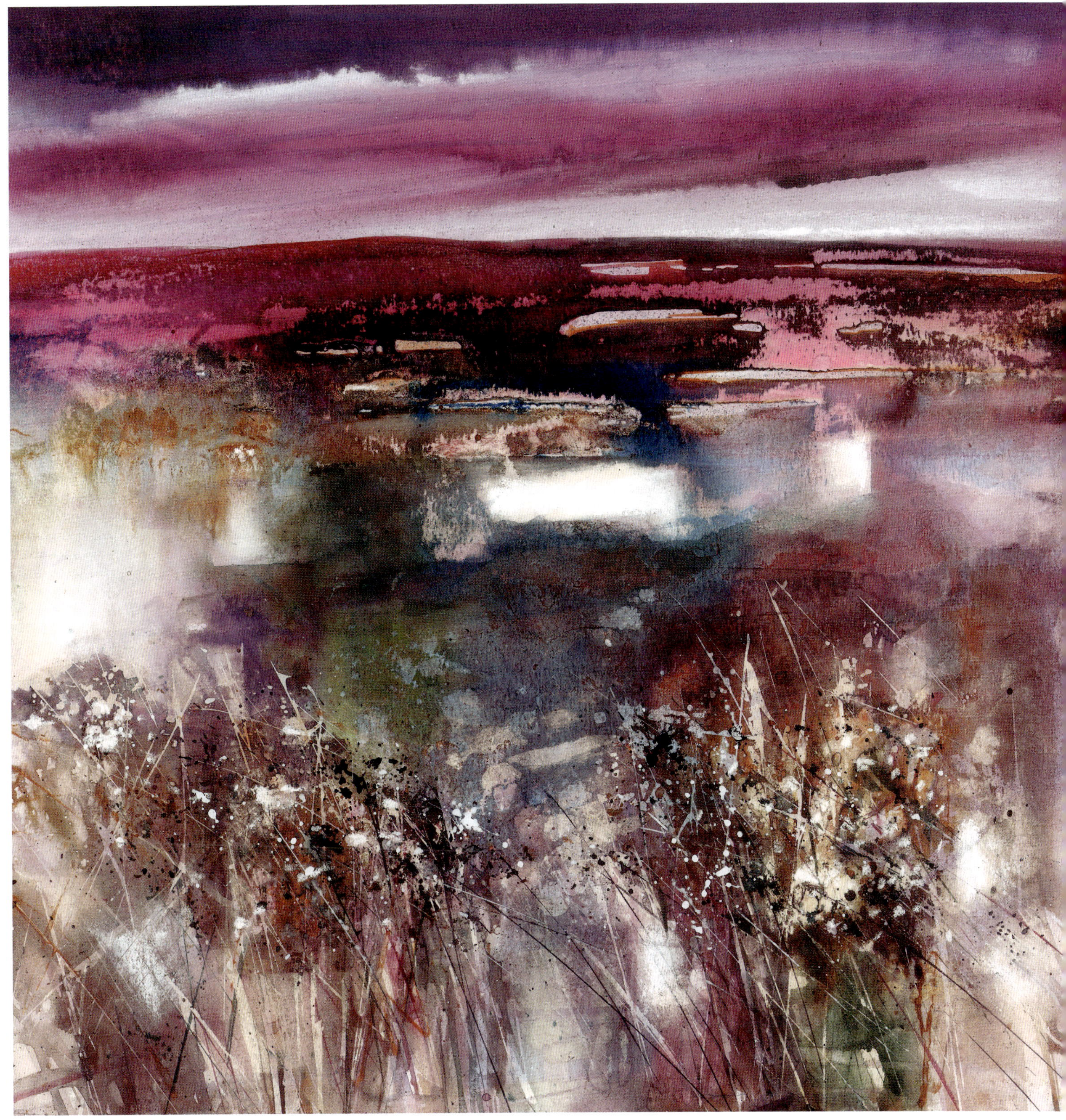

Magenta Landscape

35 × 35cm (13¾ × 13¾in)
*This artwork was painted in watercolour with a few
drops of acrylic inks added to the mixes. This allows
the acrylic ink to resist the watercolour when it is
washed off as described on page 77.*

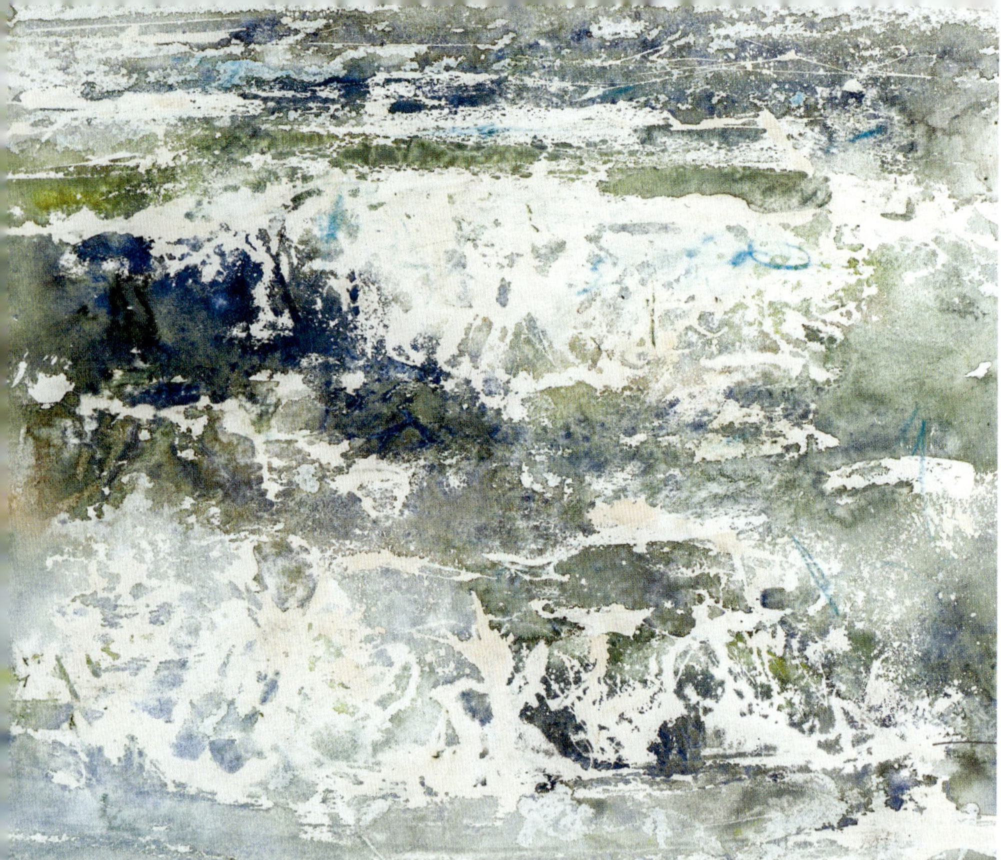

A sketchbook study of a rough sea with sea horses and foamy waves. To create texture on the smooth cartridge paper, a piece of wax candle, used on its side, was rubbed in places to create a resist. Rounded scribble marks were drawn with a wax crayon, too, before washing over the surface with watercolour.

Wax crayons, candle and oil pastels

Wax resist is an ancient technique that has been used for centuries to create pattern and surface decoration in textiles and ceramics. It can even be used in a simple way by children using wax crayons and watercolours, while experimental and creative artists use it widely in their work. Wax resist can be used in a variety of ways:

Working over Drawings, textures or marks made directly onto a support using wax crayon, candle or oil pastel can be washed over with thin layers of acrylic paints, acrylic inks or watercolours.

Rubbings Rubbings of various textured surfaces can be made through tissue or lightweight papers such as copying paper, and then used as collage. Textured Japanese papers, wood chip wallpaper and so on make good collage papers and can be enhanced with oil pastels, glued onto a support and then washed over with watercolours or acrylics.

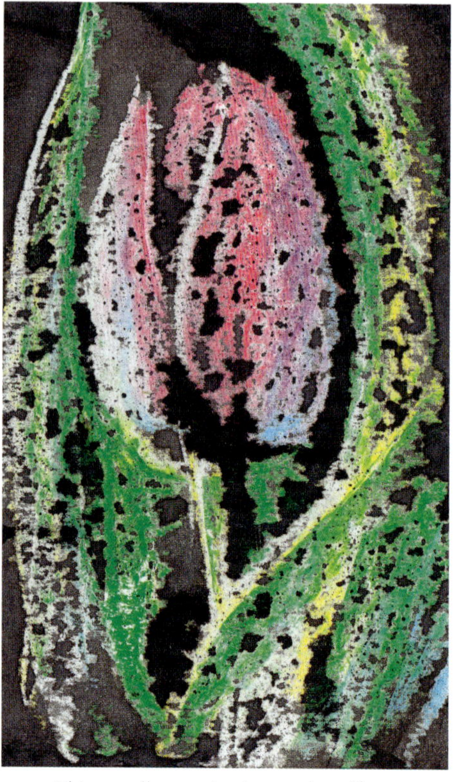

This small sample shows the effect of wax resist.

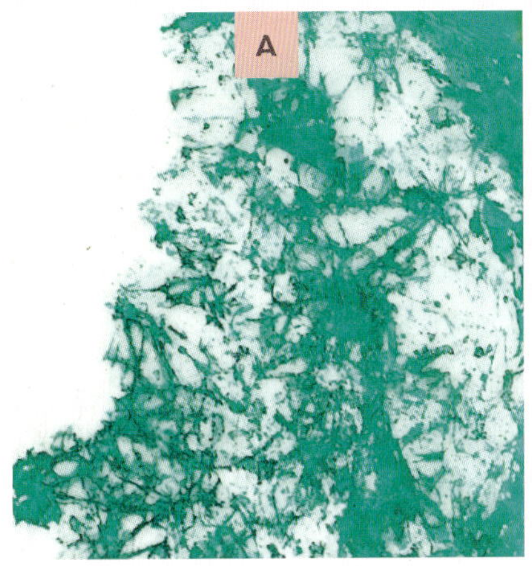

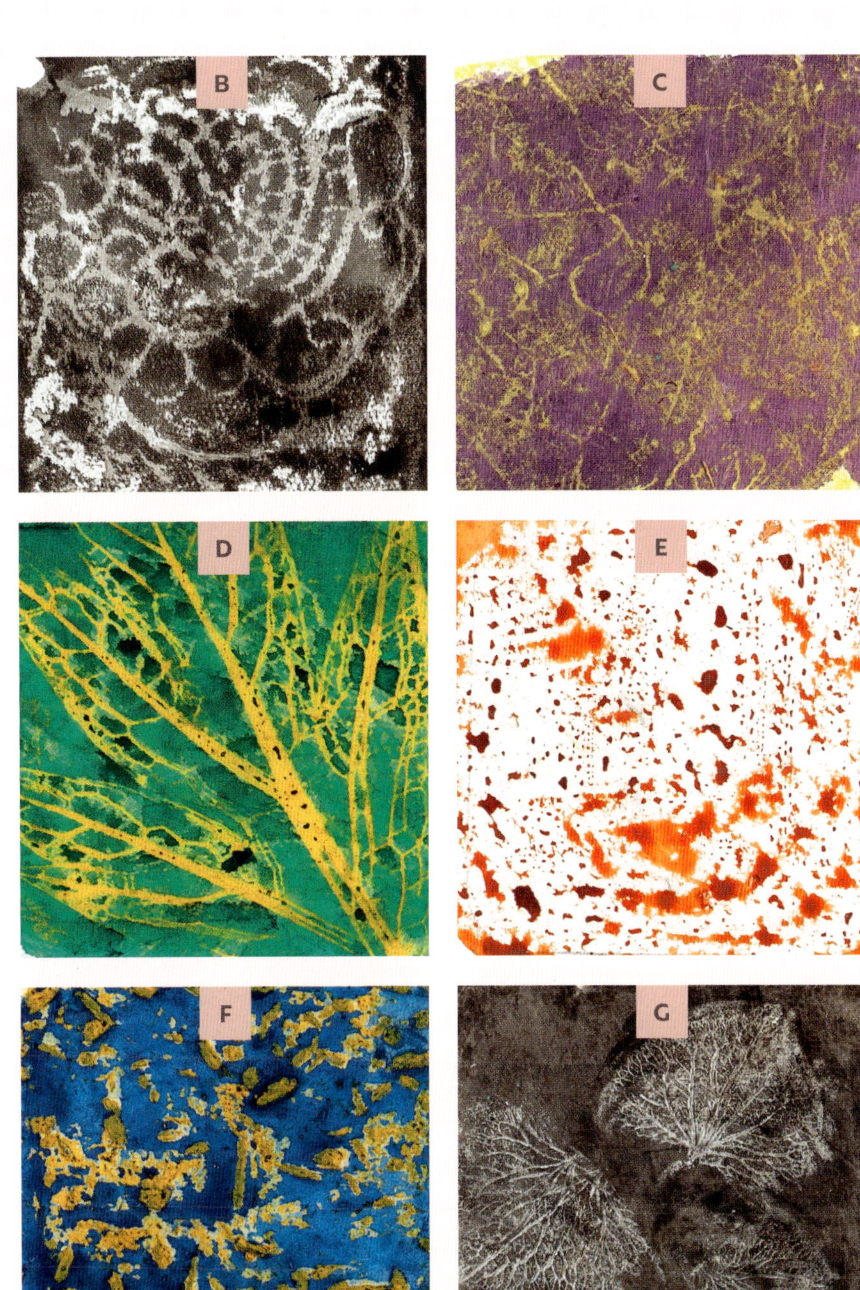

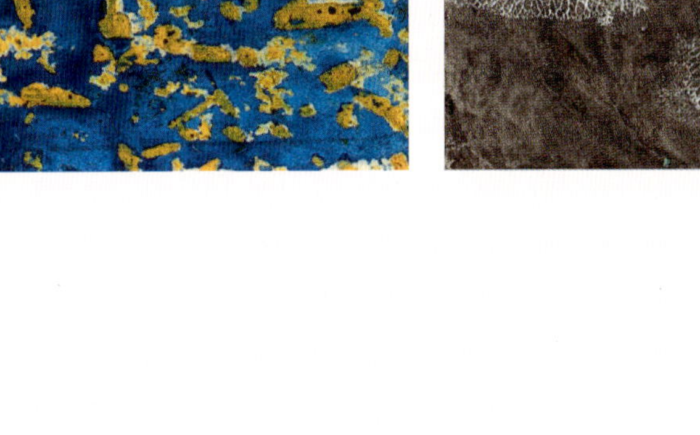

A A batik effect made by melting wax in a tea light and spreading it onto tissue paper with a strip of plastic card. I crumpled the tissue, opened it out again and then washed it over with paint, which seeped through the cracks to form the spidery, batik-like patterns.

B To prepare this surface, a sheet of tissue paper was laid over lace and worked over with candle wax.

C Here, yellow oil pastel was rubbed over Japanese paper with a raised texture. I then washed over it with a purple watercolour.

D I made a leaf rubbing through tissue paper using a yellow oil pastel, then washed over the result with green acrylic ink.

E I rubbed candle wax over thin copying paper, then washed over the surface with burnt sienna acrylic ink.

F Here, I took wood chip wallpaper, and rubbed over it with yellow oil pastel before washing over it with phthalo blue acrylic ink.

G Oil pastel can capture fine details, as this rubbing of skeletal hydrangea petals demonstrates.

Masking fluid

Masking fluid is a waterproof latex solution that is applied to a support as a resist to both watercolours and acrylic inks. Although it is frequently used to reserve just a few highlights, with practice it can be used to draw and create gestural marks, as shown opposite in *Greater Knapweed*. Here I used the long edge of a palette knife to apply the fluid.

You may find, as I do, that some brands of masking fluid are too thick a consistency to draw with. The answer is to decant a little into a small bottle and dilute it with a very small amount of water until the consistency is runny and similar to ink.

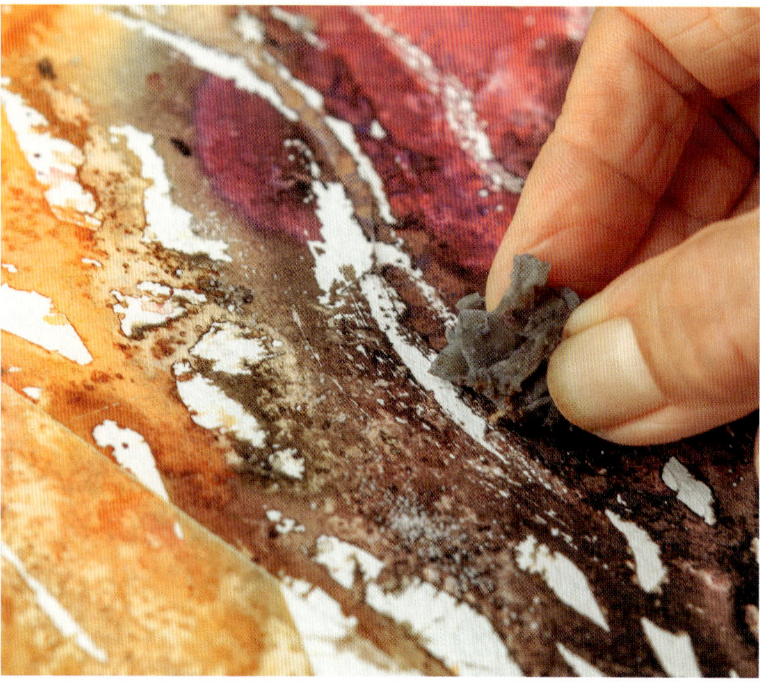

Removing masking fluid to reveal the clean underlying surface

To remove masking fluid, you can rub it gently with your fingertips (make sure they're clean!), use a shop-bought masking fluid eraser, or – as shown here – use a ball made from bits of masking fluid rubbed off your previous paintings.

Using masking fluid

Masking fluid can be applied like paint to temporarily protect the surface from paint. It is removed once the paint has dried simply by rubbing it gently.

Masking fluid can be applied with a range of tools, some of which you may already have, so try to be inventive rather that just using those that you can buy. Ideally, the tools that you use to apply masking fluid should allow you to draw fluently and expressively.

Applicators that are currently on the market, such as rubber shapers or nylon brushes, are very limited in the marks that can be made. Instead, choose metal or plastic tools that are smooth and allow the masking fluid to glide off, such as an old fashioned ruling pen, a palette knife or piece of plastic card. Homemade quills – or even twigs stripped of bark at their tips – also make good applicators. After use the dry masking fluid can either be easily rubbed off or the tool itself discarded.

Another tip when buying masking fluid is to avoid buying large expensive bottles where the contents will go off or solidify before you can use them up.

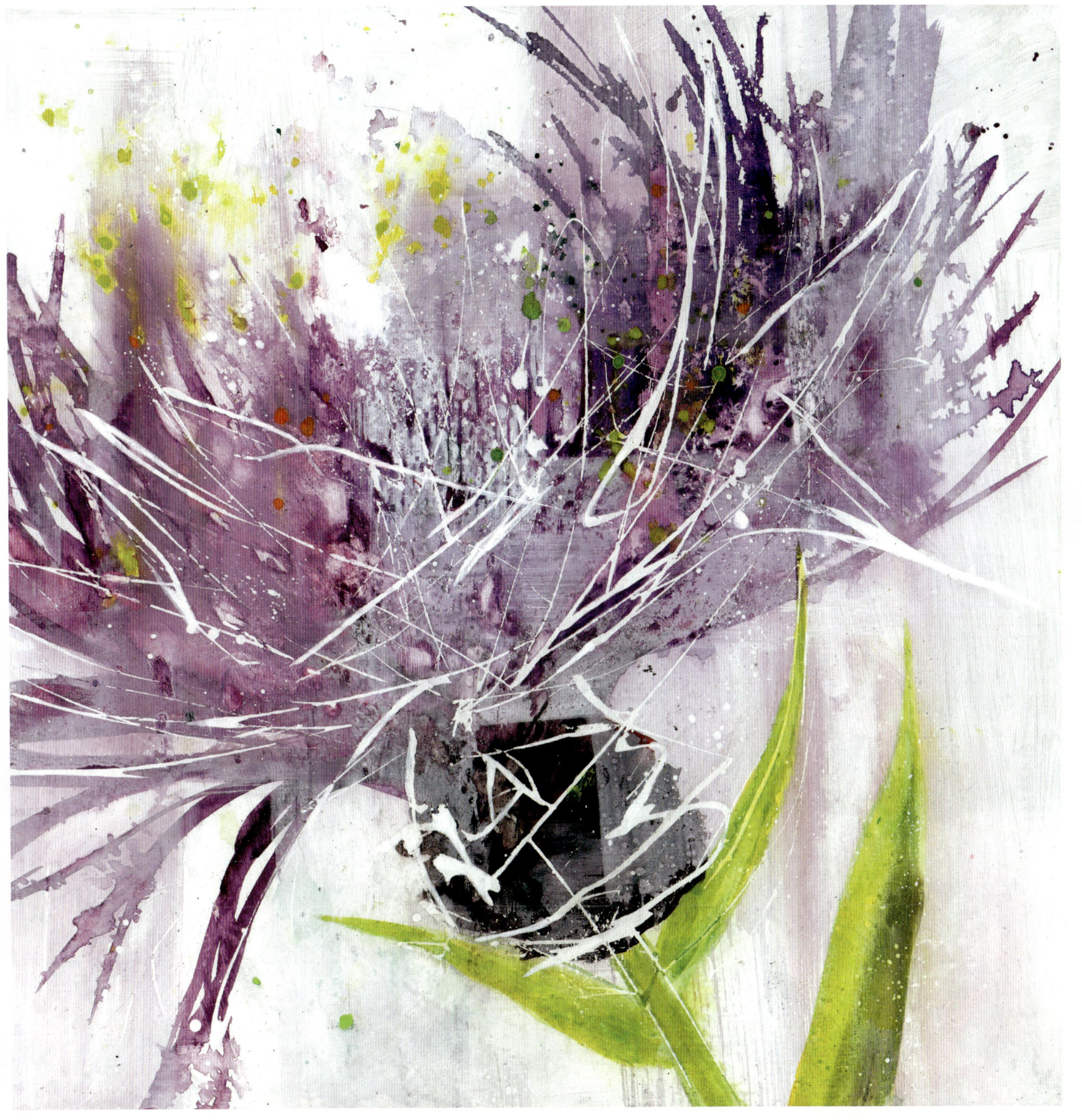

Greater Knapweed

30 × 30cm (11¾ × 11¾in)

Acrylic inks on board. These gestural lines and marks were made using the edge and the tip of a palette knife, both to draw with and to flick the masking fluid. Once dry, the masking fluid was washed over with acrylic inks – and once the ink had dried, the masking fluid was removed to reveal the white lines and marks.

Supports and media that resist

Some materials have inherently resistant qualities – just as water will soak into a newspaper but slide off a glossy magazine. Likewise, combining materials can have unexpected – but beautiful – results as the ingredients resist one another. Watercolours are normally bound with gum arabic, acrylic inks have a polymer or plastic base, and Indian ink contains shellac, a kind of varnish.

Surfaces that resist Supports with smooth surfaces, such as primed canvas, gessoed surfaces, smooth or shiny papers and mount card can be made to behave as natural resists to acrylics, when they are washed off. While these surfaces are designed to take acrylic media, if they are washed off at the right drying stage, some of the paint or ink will lift off, leaving unexpected shapes and interesting textures. *Spring Light*, opposite, shows an example of this.

Incompatible media Adding ink to watercolour will create interesting speckled textures as the different binders or carriers interact, as you can see below. Granulation medium is a product that is formulated to induce this effect but it is not necessary: the variance in their ingredients means that these materials yield up their magic with very little effort. The painting *Spring Greens the Winter Gloom* on page 125 is a good example of this type of resist in action.

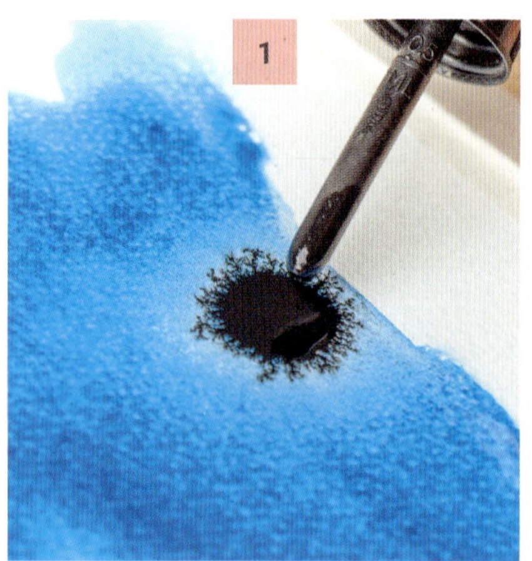

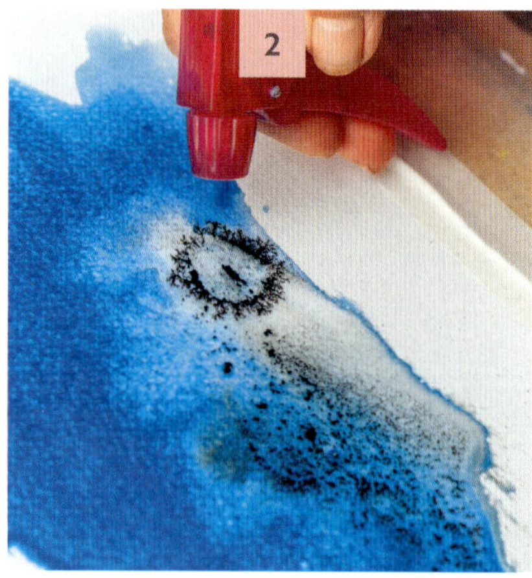

1 Try making a wash on watercolour paper and use the dropper from the acrylic ink to squeeze in a few drops and you will see the watercolour being pushed out of the way.

2 Tipping the paper, or adding water, will encourage the separation.

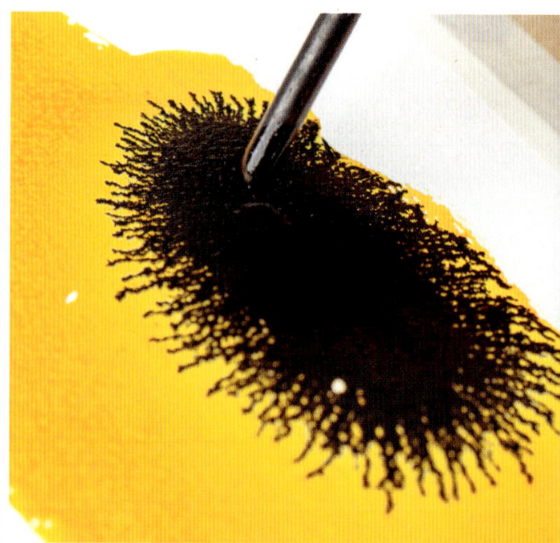

Using Indian ink will give a stronger effect, as you can see here. The 'halo' as the ink pushes the paint away is clear, and the separation occurs almost immediately.

Washing off

This technique results in interesting textures and abstract marks that can't be made any other way. It involves combining watercolour and inks at the colour mixing stage, allowing some areas of the painting to dry while others remain wet, then pouring clean water over it.

When washing off from paper, ensure it is fixed firmly to a board with tape, as described under 'Stretching paper' on page 60. See page 84 for more on this technique.

1 Start by adding a few drops of acrylic ink (less of Indian ink) to watercolours in the mixing wells, then begin to paint as normal.

2 As you work, aim to leave some areas wet and allow others to dry completely – water can be flicked into areas that you want to preserve and other areas can be given a quick blast from a hair dryer.

3 At the stage when some areas are dry and others remain wet, wash off the painting by pouring clean water from a jug or the tap – either over the whole painting, or selected areas. The flow of water will dislodge pigment from the wet areas in a semi-controlled way.

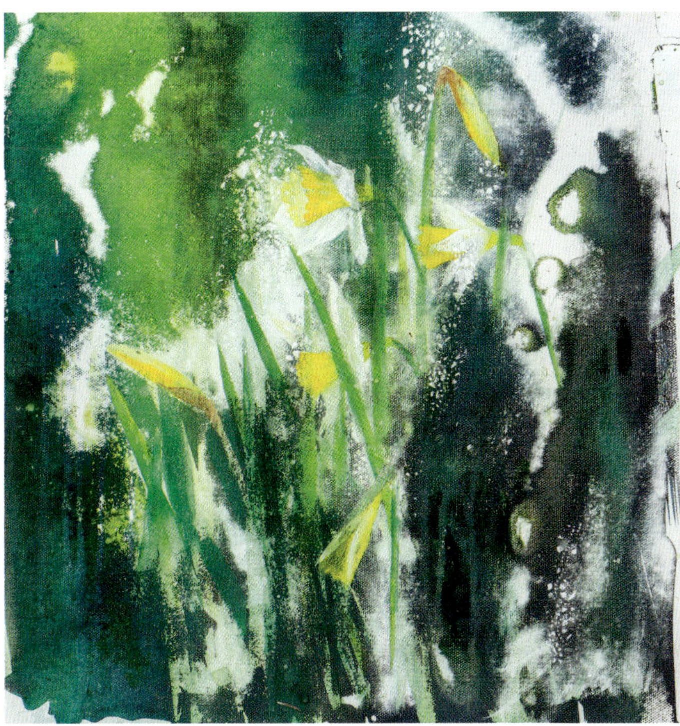

Spring Light
35 × 35cm (13¾ × 13¾in)
Painted with acrylic inks on canvas, the abstract shapes and textures in this painting are a result of choosing the right time to wash off: when some of the paint was still wet.

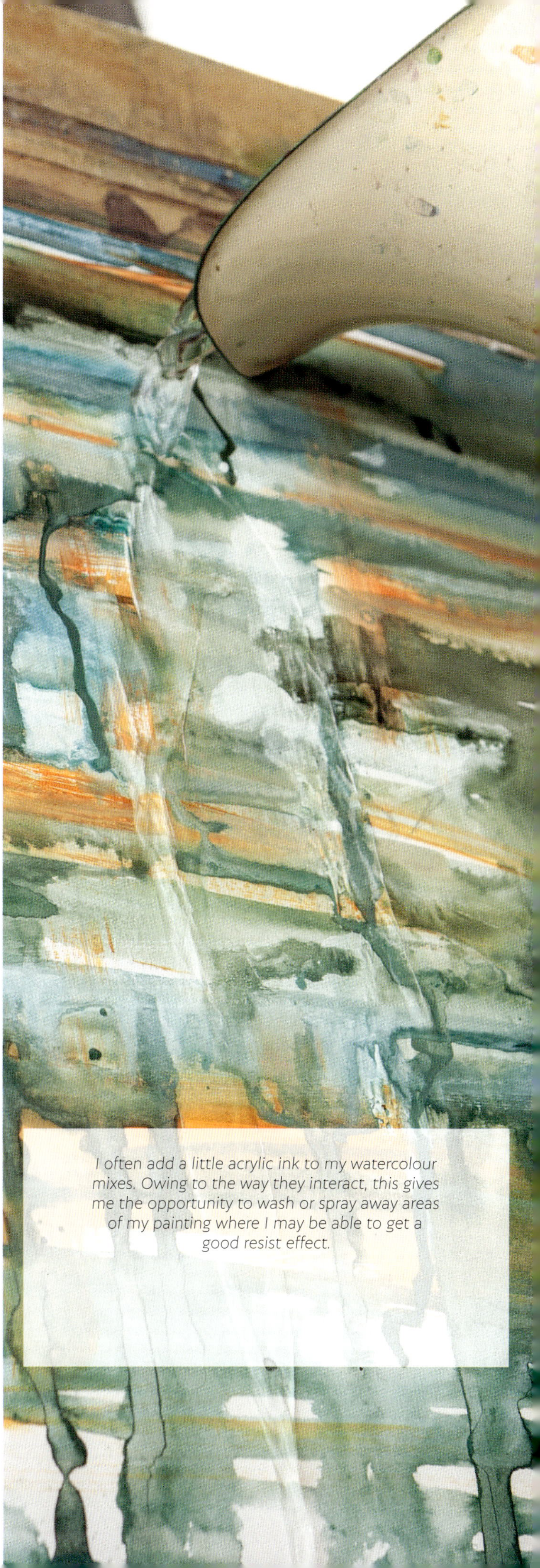

Gouache lift

Gouache lift involves painting the subject or motif first in gouache. The gouache is then painted over with ink before being washed off, as described on the previous page.

The gouache areas needs to dry, either partially or completely, because brushing the ink over disturbs and liquifies it. By giving the gouache a short blast with a hairdryer, parts of it will dry, while other areas stay relatively moist. As with the washing off technique described on page 77, the thicker (and therefore still slightly wet) parts are the ones that will wash away.

The amount the ink is allowed to dry before being washed off will also affect the results: this is where experiment and practice come in.

What materials?

Support For this technique I prefer to use a good quality white or off-white acid-free mount board as it is economical and sufficiently sturdy to cope with getting very wet. You can staple it to a board beforehand, or dry the finished piece by pressing it between two boards, protected with either tissue paper, clean newsprint or blotting paper.

Gouache For this process, the white gouache needs to be titanium white, sometimes called permanent white, as it is the most opaque (zinc white is better used in mixes and for tinting colours).

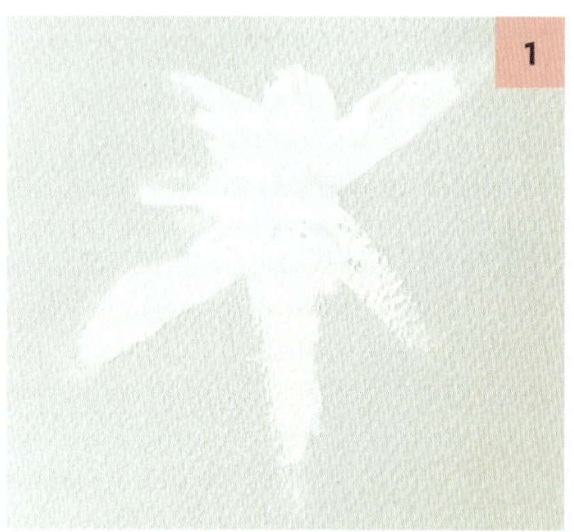
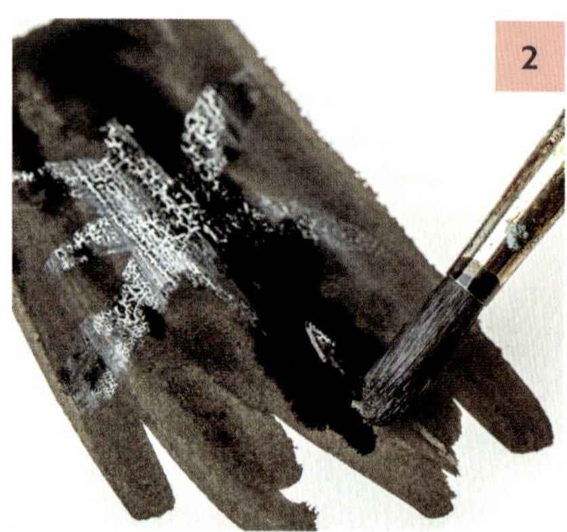
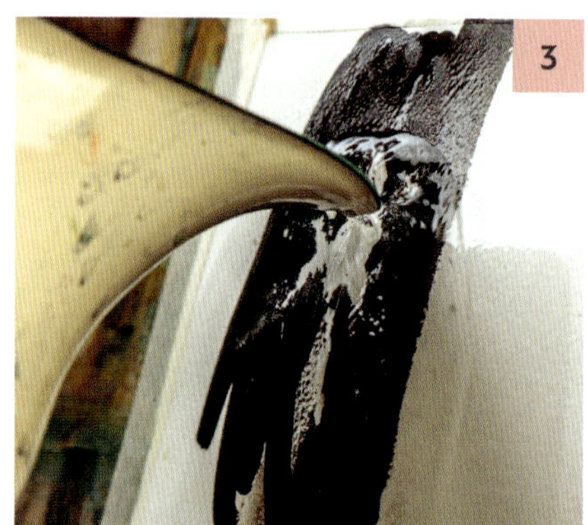

1 Paint the subject in gouache, applying it generously in order for it to resist the ink. Use a hairdryer to dry it.

2 It is important to change to a clean brush and palette to eliminate the resist effect of the gouache. Working quickly with a fairly light touch, paint ink over the whole image (see 'Indian ink or acrylic ink?', opposite). Some of the gouache will dissolve, but try to ignore this.

3 Allow the ink to dry. If you are using acrylic ink, you can use a hairdryer to speed up this stage. Very dry ink will give you a more contrasting black and white effect, while slightly damp ink will give a greyer and more textural finish. Once you are happy, wash it off under a gentle stream of water. You can use a soft brush or a finger to gently assist the gouache to lift.

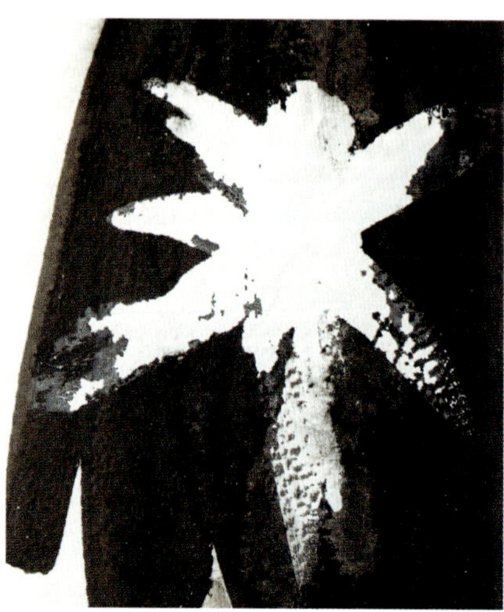

Gouache lift is fun to try and hopefully gives you an exciting reveal! As with any experimental technique, there is the potential for failure and so practice is needed to achieve good results.

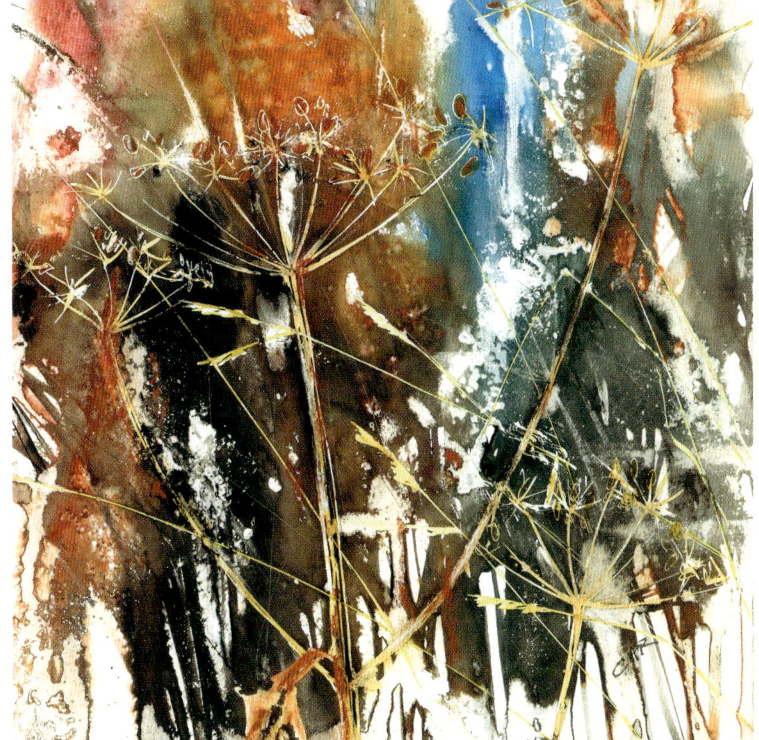

Seed Head Sparkle
35 × 35cm (13¾ × 13¾in)
Used with acrylic ink, here the gouache lift technique left interesting textures, edges and linear patterns from previous dribbles of paint.

Indian ink or acrylic ink?

The effects you get will depend on the type of ink you are using.

Acrylic ink Using acrylic ink rather than Indian ink results in a softer, more naturalistic and less dramatic effects. Gouache lift with acrylic inks is also more flexible and combines well with other techniques in a painting.

Indian ink If you are using Indian ink, it is inadvisable to use a hairdryer as it will make the gouache very difficult to remove.

A splash of colour

If you decide that you want to use coloured gouache with this technique, I recommend a good brand such as Winsor & Newton – with other brands I have tried, the colour tends to wash away. This combination will allow a wide range of mixes to be made: Winsor & Newton primary red, primary yellow and primary blue, plus titanium white.

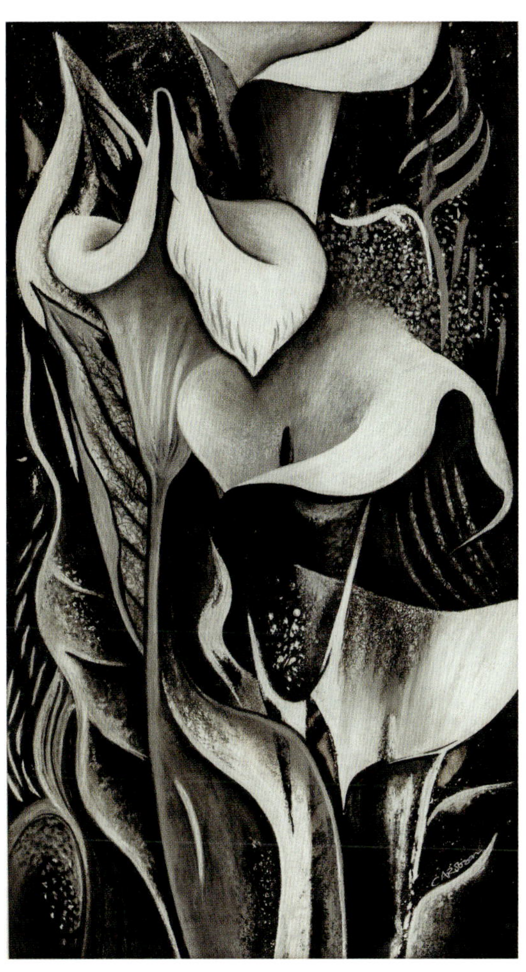

Calla Lilies
40 × 70cm (15¾ × 27½in)
A striking monochrome example of Indian ink used with gouache resists. Painted using a gouache lift technique, the subject was reserved with white gouache and overpainted with black Indian ink. The subject was then worked up using black and white chalk pastels.

This painting is similar to the type of cropped flower abstractions for which Georgia O'Keeffe (see page 62) was famed.

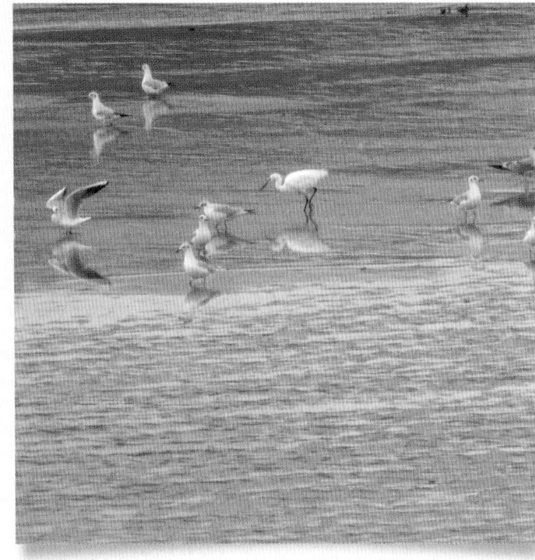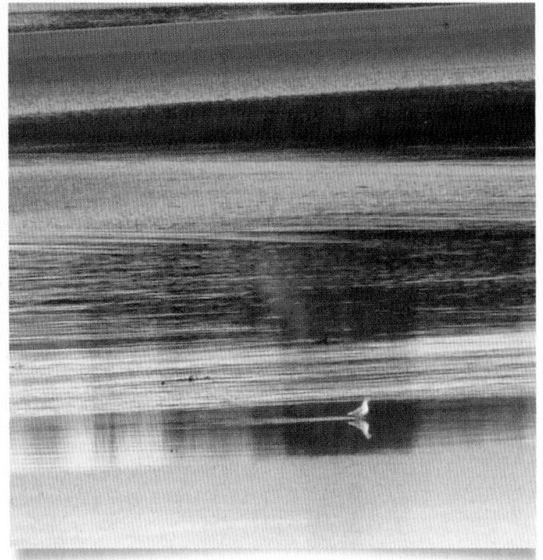

River Birds

In this project we take a landscape subject and give it an abstract feel. We are not looking for realism here, and instead focus on the shapes and tones in the source photographs, rather than the other basic elements such as colour and form. The source photographs for this painting are shown above. We will be drawing specific details from the shapes and reflections of the birds in the left-hand one, and combining them with the zigzag shapes, bars of tone and linear marks visible in the right-hand photograph.

You will need

- Mount card, 32 × 32cm (12¾ × 12¾in) secured to a painting board

- Soft pencil, such as a 2B or 4B

- Gouche paints: titanium white, burnt sienna

- Watercolour paints: Aussie red gold

- Acrylic inks: (Liquitex) phthalo blue, burnt sienna; (Golden) carbon black

- Brushes: size 6 round, size 12 round, size 16 round, 25mm (1in) flat, 50mm (2in) flat

- Palette with deep wells

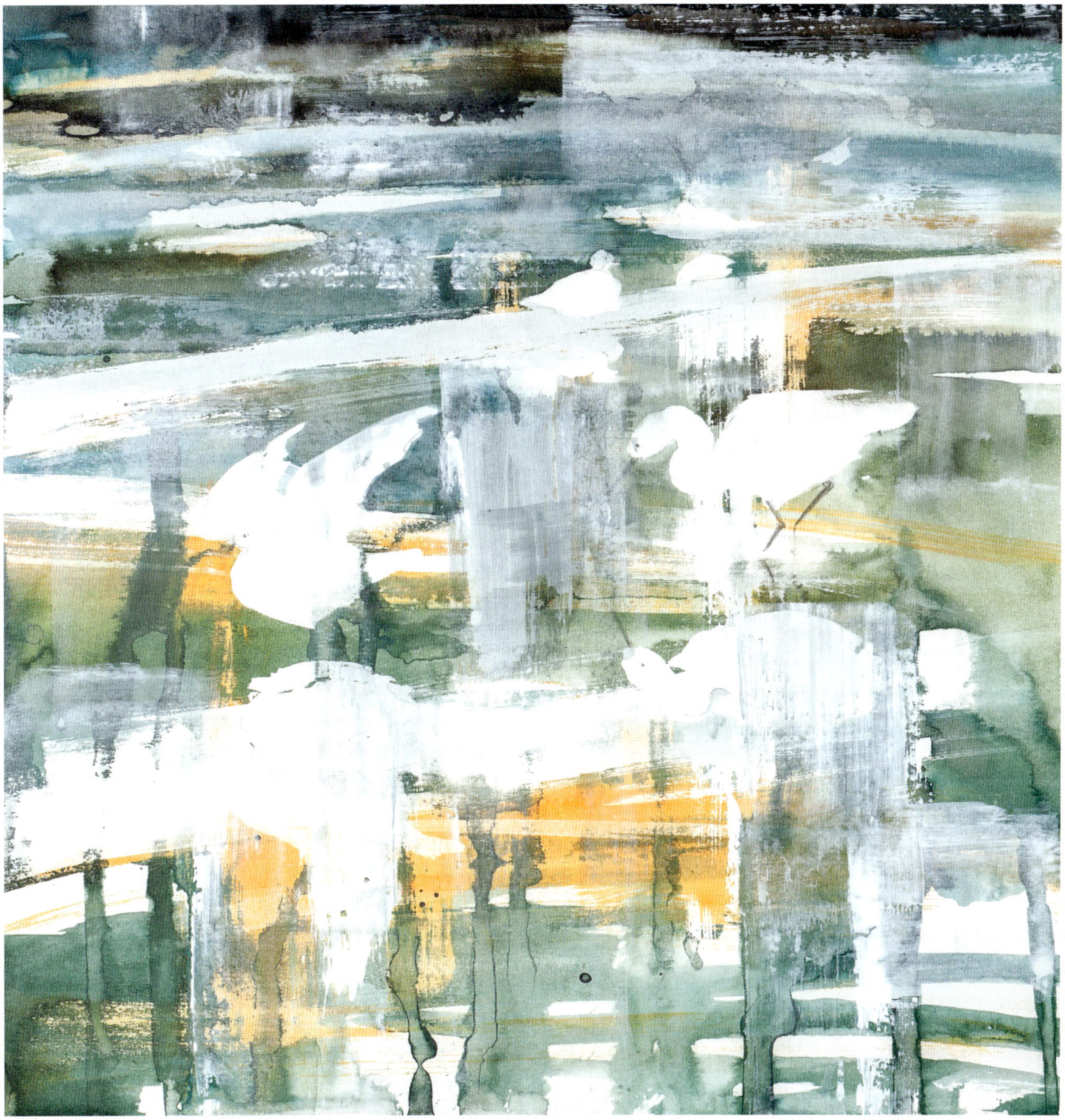

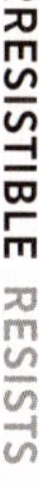

The finished painting
32 × 32cm (12¾ × 12¾in)

Establishing resists

There are two main shape elements in the photographs that interest us:
the shapes of the birds and the zigzag shapes of the light reflecting on the
sand and water. Rather than copying the photograph, use those forms to
inspire you; try to ignore what is literally in front of you and instead create
a very simple composition that incorporates simplified bird shapes and
those zigzags.

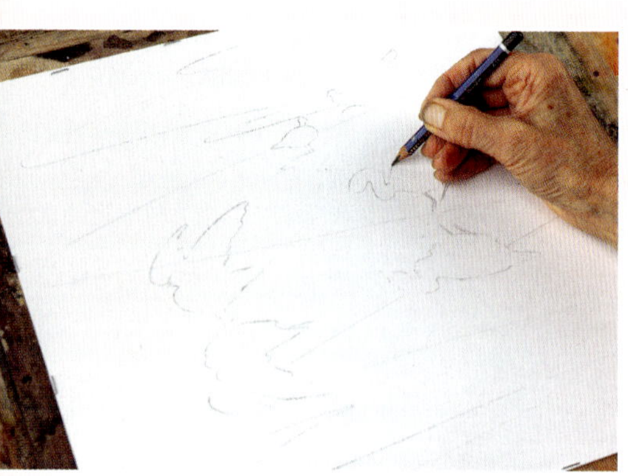

*Simplifying the shapes is the first
step towards abstraction. Try to
regard the birds as collections
of shapes rather than living,
breathing creatures.*

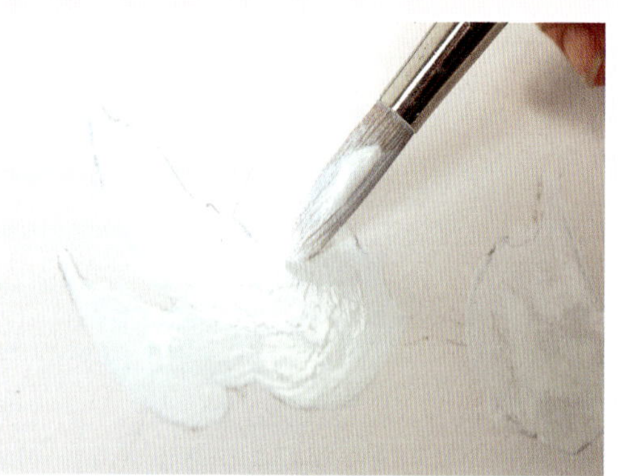

*This detail shows thicker paint being applied to
the shape suggested by the bird (on the left) than
that suggested by the reflection (on the right).*

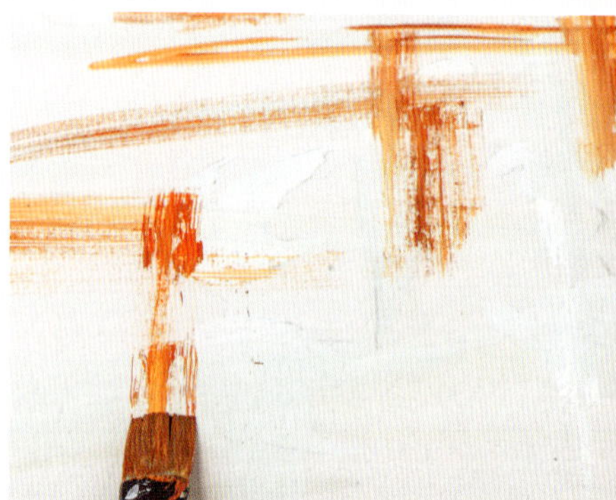

*Using loose strokes with an almost
dry 25mm (1in) flat brush will give
a broken effect.*

- Draw on the design using a soft pencil. Think about the
  rule of thirds (see page 24) when drawing on the design.

- Swapping between the size 6 and size 12 round
  brushes, paint the shapes with white gouache– both
  those suggested by the birds and those suggested by
  the water.

- Apply the paint more thickly on the shapes suggested
  by the birds, and more thinly on those suggested by the
  reflections. This will ensure the two groups of shapes will
  behave differently when working as a resist against the
  inks applied in the next stage.

- Still using white gouache, use larger gestural shapes
  of the size 12 round for larger linear marks. Take these
  right across the other shapes already established so that
  the two groups are integrated. Swap to the 25mm (1in)
  brush for those nearer the bottom of the painting and
  contrasting vertical strokes.

- Add a little colour by introducing the burnt sienna
  gouache into the painting, hinting at the sand colours
  of the inspiration. I mixed a little Aussie red gold into
  the burnt sienna gouache to warm up the colour. Once
  satisfied, allow to dry.

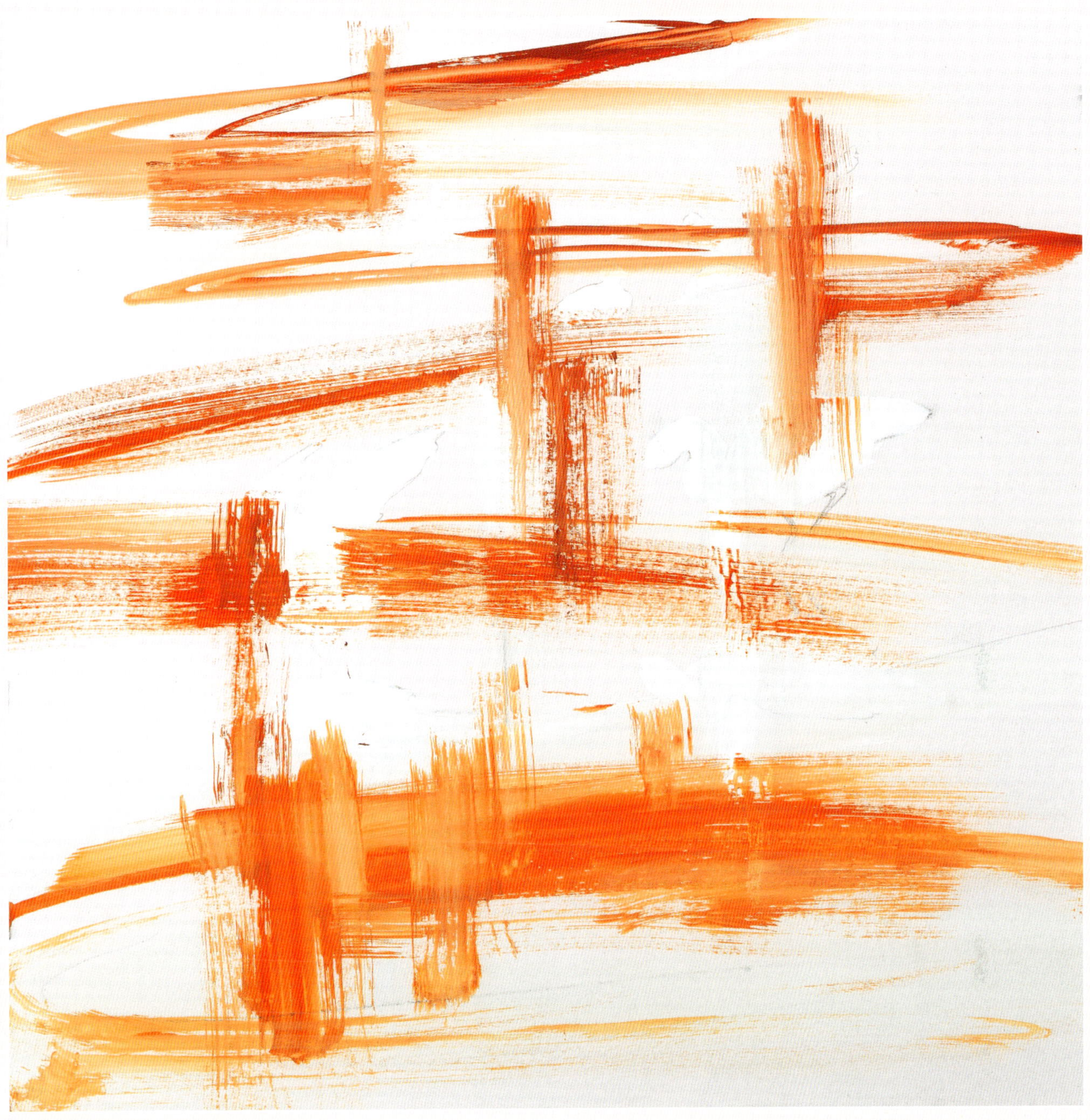

The painting at the end of this stage.

Fluid paint and washing off

With the gouache completely dry, we are now going to add variegated washes of acrylic inks over the top of the gouache paint. It is important to change to clean brushes and palette so that there is no residue of gouache that would further resist the acrylic inks.

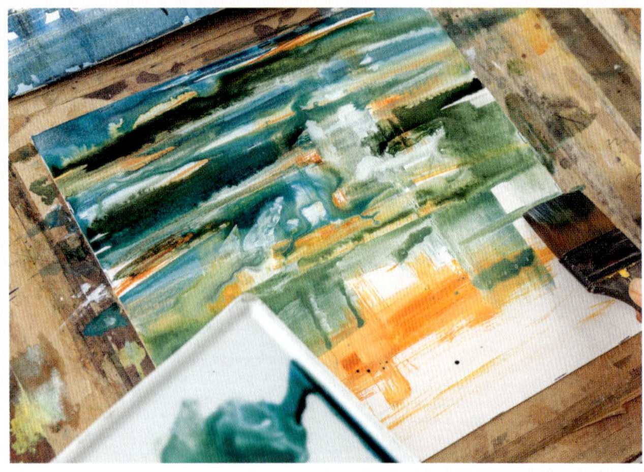

A large brush gives stronger, more dominant marks, which adds to the abstract effect.

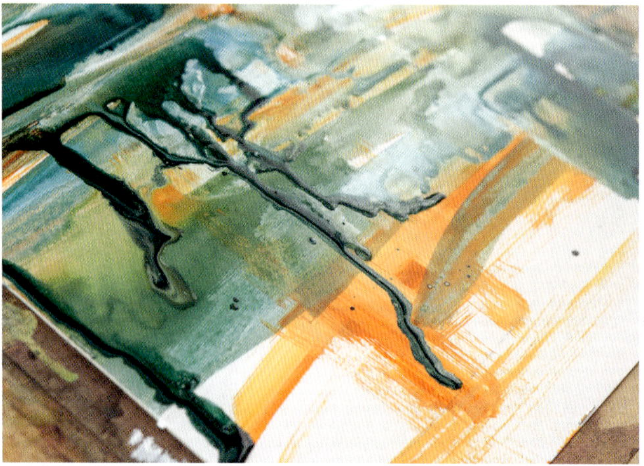

A variegated wash is varied both in colour and tone. Tipping and tilting the painting encourages the fluid paint to mix and flow in interesting ways.

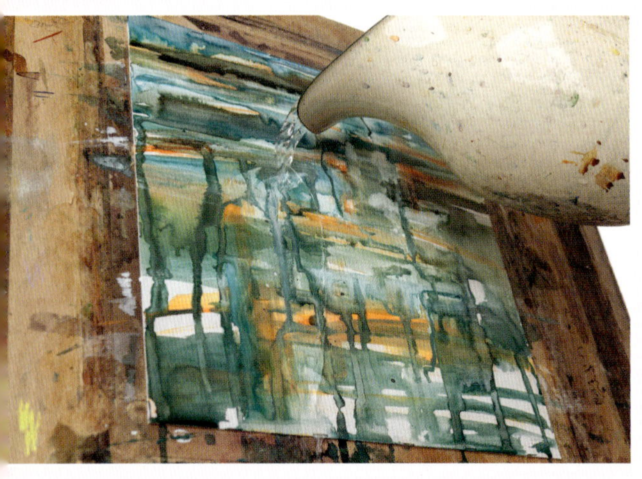

When washing off, paint that is completely dry will remain largely in place; while still-damp paint, or paint on top of resists like the gouache, will come off almost completely.

- Prepare two blue-green mixes in a deep-welled palette using phthalo blue and burnt sienna acrylic inks in different proportions. One should be more brown-tinged, the other more blue-tinged. Using a size 16 round brush, apply a variegated wash over the whole surface, straight over the gouache.

- The gouache will partially dissolve under the wet ink; try to ignore this as you work – keep a light touch to avoid over-agitating it.

- Paint using mainly horizontal strokes of the size 16 round brush, swapping between colours as you go and allowing them to mix wet in wet. Swap to the 50mm (2in) flat brush to add some bold verticals as you work.

- Throughout the wash, aim to create abstract geometric shapes with the way you apply the paint. Leave some gaps of clean mount board to show through.

- Allow the paint to dry, but not completely – then use a jug of water to wash off the whole painting. You can use a soft brush to agitate the gouache areas in order to bring them up.

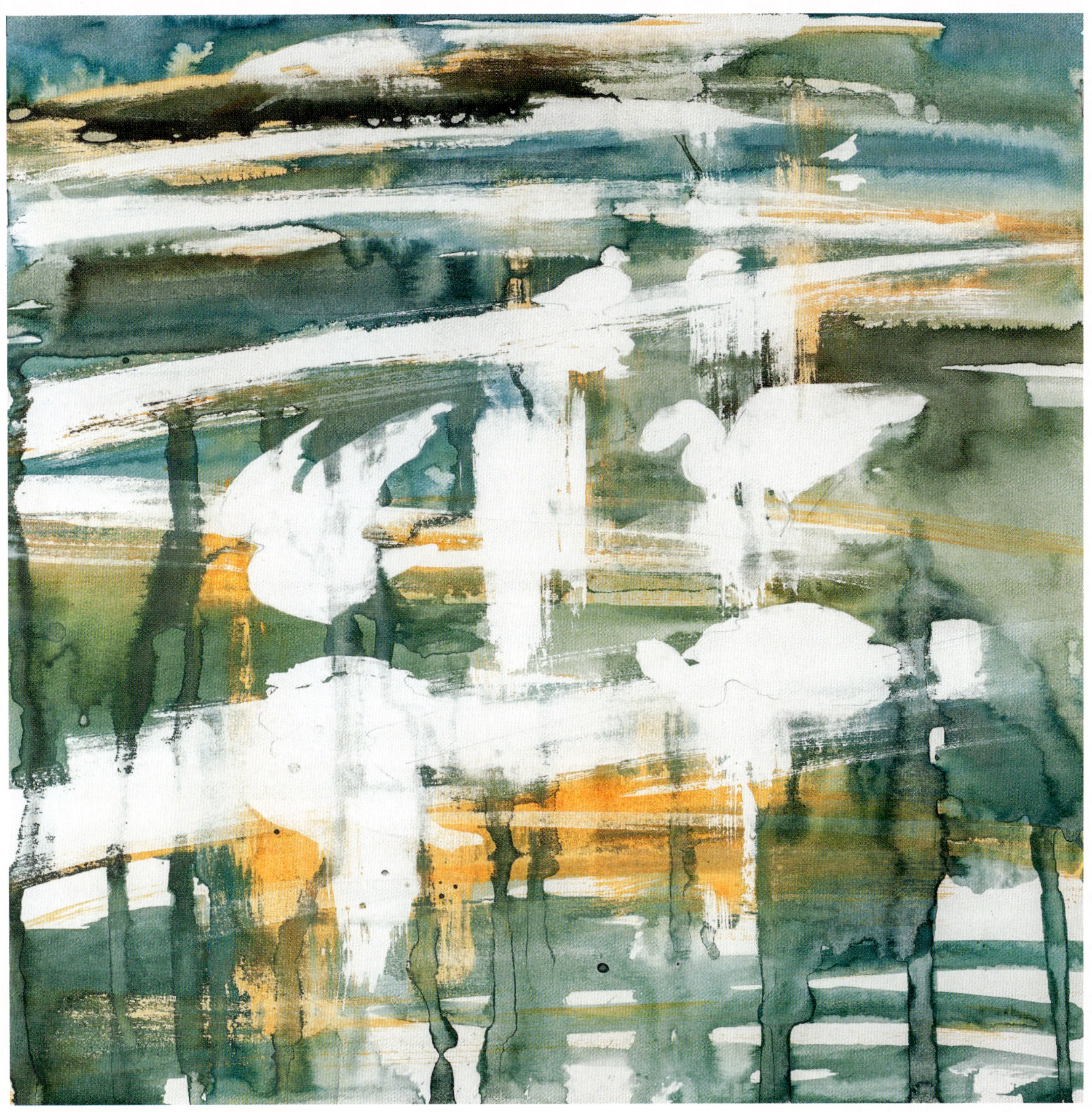

The painting at the end of this stage.

Finishing touches

Because of the nature of the technique, the results will vary, so how much you refine will require you to respond to your painting. It helps to have a clear idea of what you are aiming to achieve with your work.

- Start by using the tools and techniques from earlier stages to further develop the work once it is completely dry.

- You may wish to simplify the piece, rather than adding detail – in this case, you might use washes to unify or blend areas together.

- Subtle details made with a pen or pencil can add a bit of familiar realism which serves to heighten the abstraction elsewhere.

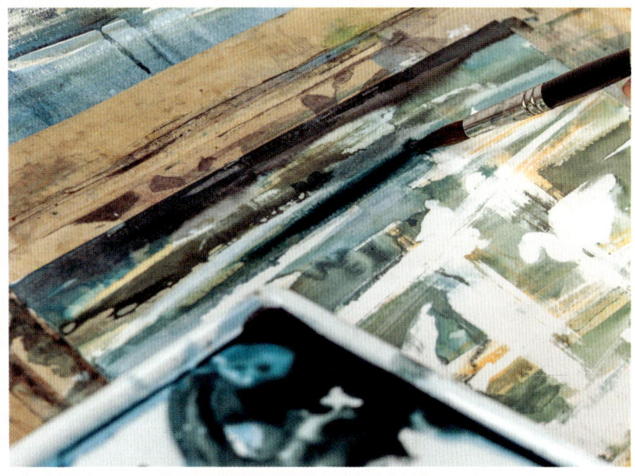

Strengthening and making the band at the top more continuous helps to frame and keep the eye within the composition.

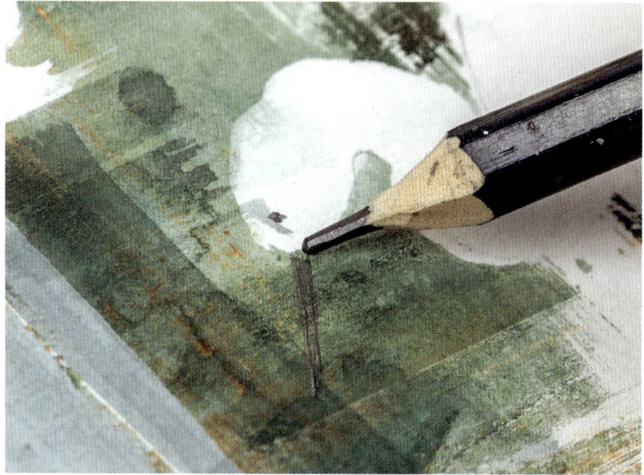

A few pencil marks help to add some context to the bird shapes – but don't over-detail the painting.

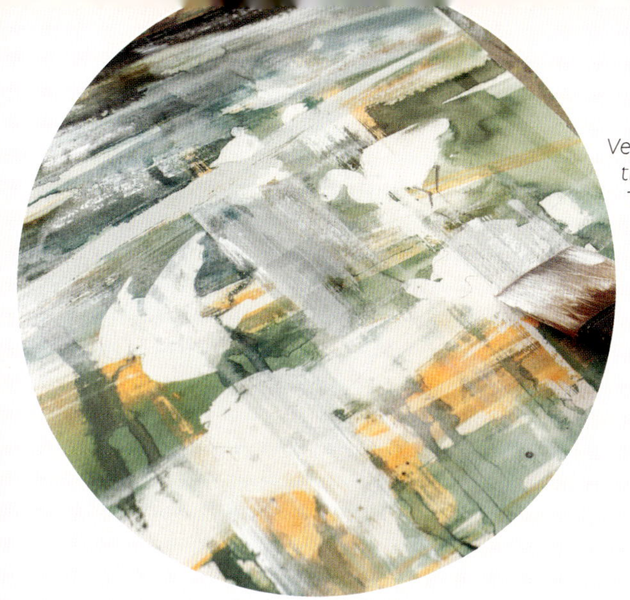

Vertical strokes that echo the bars of reflection in the source image help to unify the overall piece. They were made with dilute gouache and the 50mm (2in) flat. The finished painting can be seen on page 81.

This finished alternative below has greater impact and contrast than the version on page 81; a more continuous, strongly contrasting top and a looser lower area. Refining will help to introduce those strengths into the project.

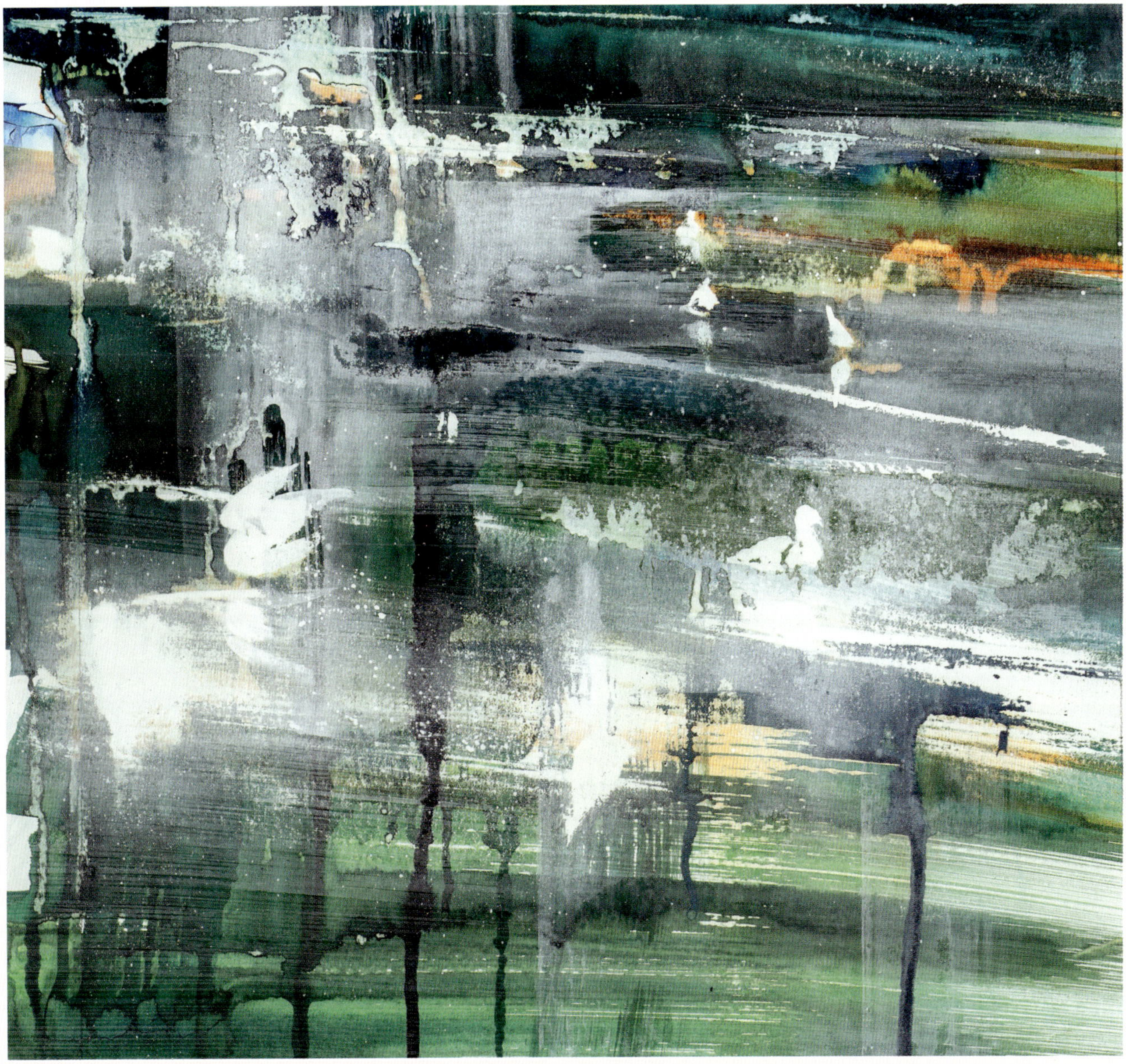

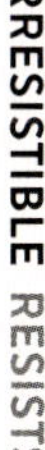

LAYERS

This chapter explores how we use layers to develop a mixed media painting using fluid acrylic paints or inks. Working in layers is a way of building a painting in definite stages, rather than the more direct approach of a wet in wet watercolour, for example, that is finished in one sitting.

The act of layering a painting takes time, as each layer needs to dry before the next one can be started – and working in this way means your painting can begin either with or without a firm plan of action. The slower pace enforced by the layering approach will give you more time to think and make creative decisions based on what has gone before. Each layer is like a question, begging a response. Building a painting in layers is needed for this interaction to happen; an idea to be explored, a decision to be assessed, perhaps altered or even obliterated.

Responding to your painting

Artists often talk of a painting needing to speak to them. Two British artists describe their experience slightly differently. Tracey Emin (b. 1963), well-known for her raw, candid art practice, has described this dialogue as being almost like a fight, as paint is thrown at the canvas. In stark contrast, Maggi Hambling (b.1945), a multi-disciplinary artist, describes her way of developing her work as a negotiation, and every painting a love affair.

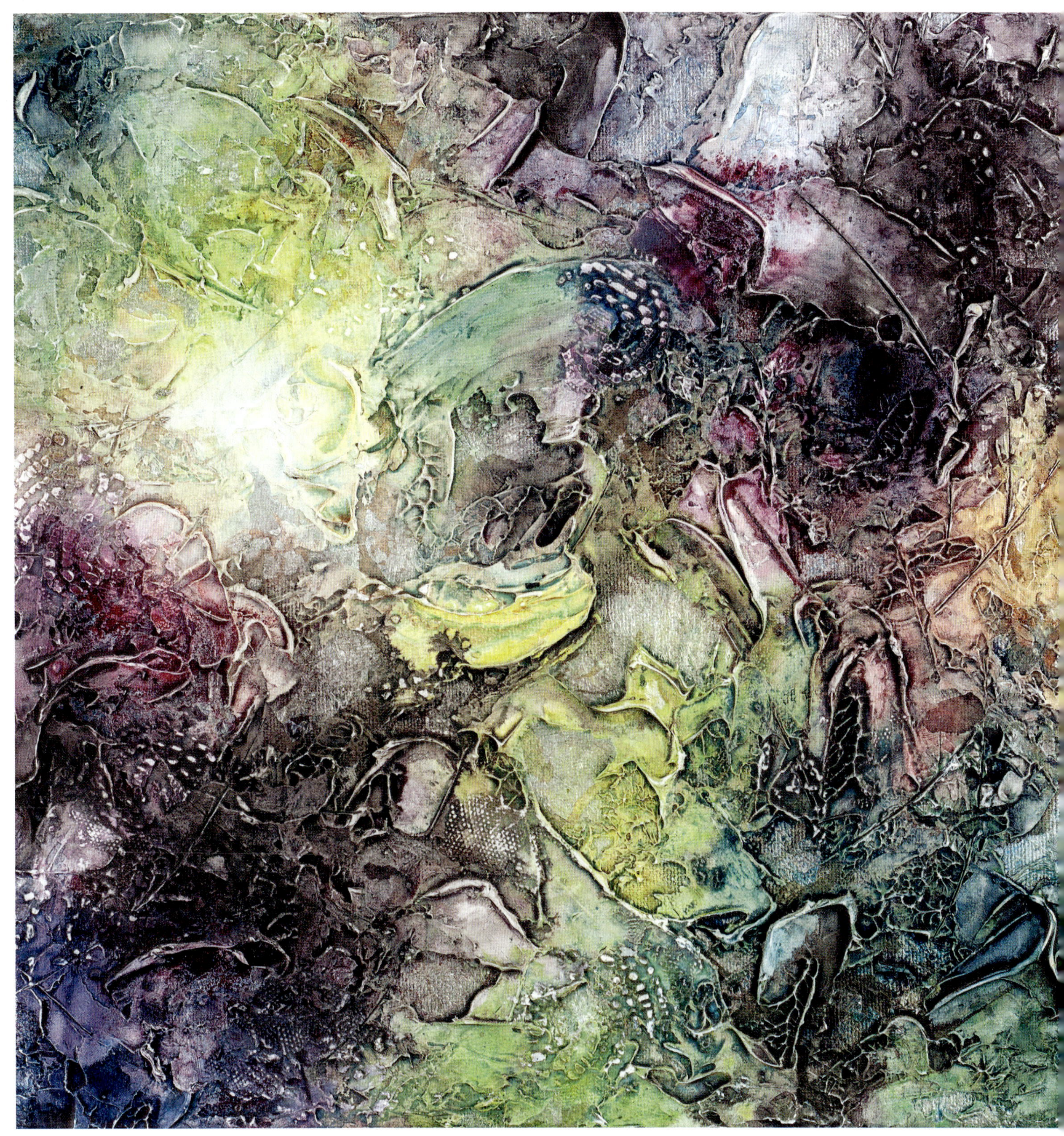

Nocturne
30 × 30cm (11¾ × 11¾in)

First layers

A clean, white piece of watercolour paper or canvas might be beautiful to look at, but – just like the author's dread of an empty page – that pristine surface can be daunting to an artist. The initial colours or textures added to your support while you find your way in these early stages are sometimes known as 'starts'.

One approach is to begin with a layer of texture or collage. This is particularly useful if you are working on a smooth support such as mount board or a wooden panel. It can be used just in places to vary the surface of the support, or over the whole surface.

Textured beginnings

Texturing your support, whether all over its surface or just in part, gives the opportunity to create an interesting and varied surface with all kinds of marks and impressions.

Shallow texture can be achieved through textured papers such as wood chip wallpaper, decorative Japanese papers, braille paper or a combination of several different types. You can also apply thin layers of texture pastes and gels.

For coarser texture or deeper relief, you can apply thick layers of texture paste. You can use the edge or the point of a palette knife, plastic card or pointed stick to incise lines, or a range of other marks. Try bouncing the palette knife in the paste and then lifting it to make raised peaks and ridges or use it flat to smooth out areas.

You could also try using materials such as sand, grit, beads and flakes, ground-up eggshells, shreds of fabric, threads or dried natural materials. These can be combined into texture paste beforehand or pressed in afterwards.

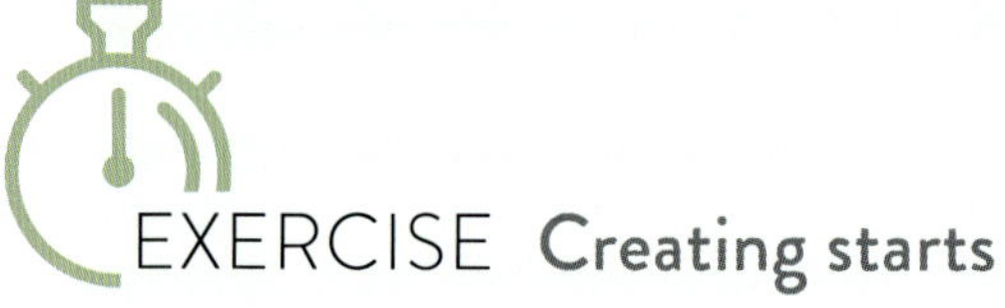

EXERCISE Creating starts

This exercise suggests some ideas for starts on mount board, together with ways that they might be developed.

Start 1

1 Apply a layer of gesso over the whole surface.

2 While wet, lay down a sheet of tissue paper that has been crumpled and opened out. Spray it with water, press creases into it and allow it to rip open in places.

3 Layer on smaller pieces of tissue paper in the same way.

4 Add another layer of gesso and crushed eggshells in places, leaving some areas clear in order to get varying depths.

5 Once dry, paint over the whole piece with titanium white acrylic paint. This softens the colours of the eggshells and further unifies the piece.

You could develop this start by building up the eggshell layers even more, perhaps adding larger pieces and leaving it as a monochrome piece. Alternatively, you could add washes of colour or bring up the high points with pastels.

Start 2

1 Build up gesso and a tissue layer as described in start 1.

2 Sprinkle on dried leaf detritus, stems and flower petals collected from nature.

3 To take the effect of the dark leaf detritus on the white background further, leave it to dry completely, then add wet in wet washes of burnt sienna, phthalo blue and quinacridone magenta acrylic inks.

4 Once dry, work a small area up with white pastel, mainly on its side, to give a frosty appearance.

Start 3

1 Use acrylic medium to glue down pieces of paper collage (see page 104), then leave to dry.

2 Paint over this layer with a descriptive wash, using yellow medium azo acrylic ink together with burnt sienna and phthalo blue.

3 Use a brush and palette knife to move the fluid colour about on the surface. Allow it to flow and make lots of linear marks with the brush.

4 Add a few sprinkles of salt.

5 When almost dry, wash some of the ink away, leaving textural marks in places.

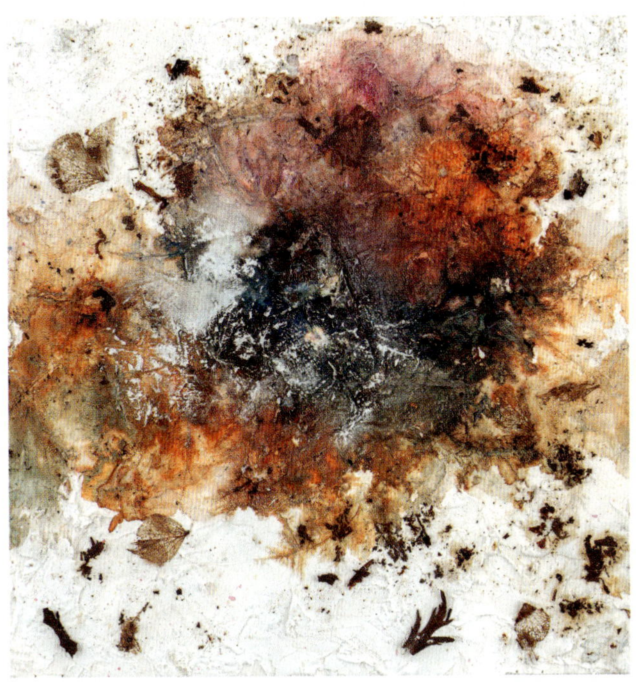

You could develop this piece further from step 2, by heating up the colour scheme with fiery reds, or lowering the temperature with freezing blues. The high points could be sanded back, brought up with pastels, or even have metal leaf added!

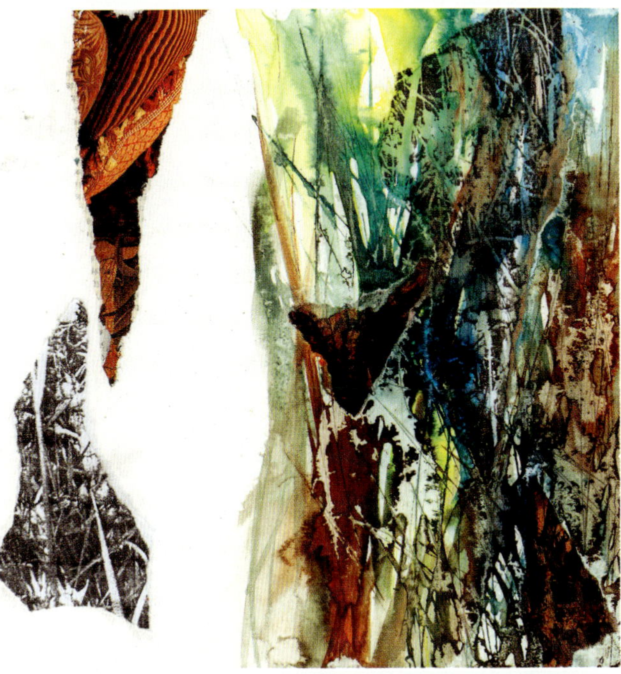

This piece could be given more interest with washes of hotter colour on the left-hand side. The small central piece of collage is accidentally shaped like a lone butterfly. If something like this happens in your start, try taking it further by adding more detail.

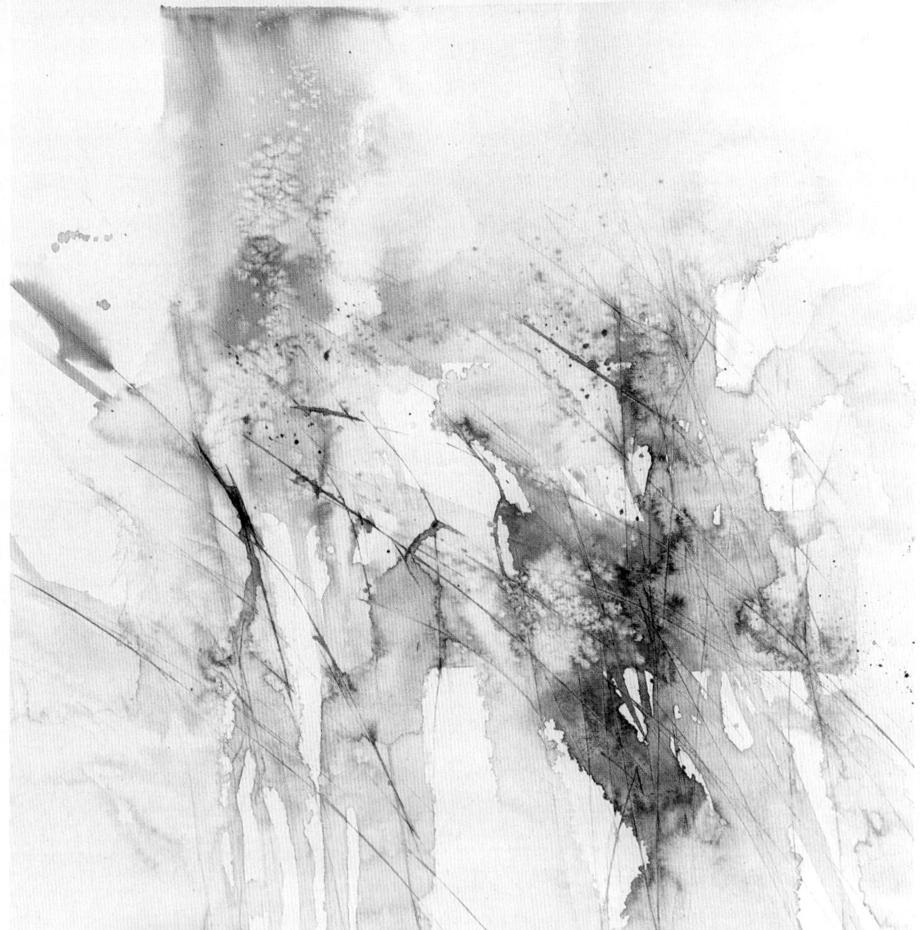

An example of a grisaille underpainting.

Underpaintings

An alternative way to make a start is to use an underpainting – that is, paint applied largely to get a feel for the composition and take away the white of the support. Underpaintings can be loose and spontaneous and not necessarily related to an idea or plan; it is a way of activating the surface in some way and making something happen.

Underpaintings were traditionally mid-toned, muted or greyed; known as 'grisaille' and often monochrome. They are usually understated so as not to be too dominant, early in the process. As well as its role as a start, an underpainting may be used to create a mood and have a unifying effect on the rest of the piece.

There are two approaches to choosing colours for an underpainting. The first is to balance and harmonize with the main colour scheme by using similar or muted versions. The second is to use complementary colours that will bring out the best in each other. In a colour scheme, cool colours such as blues, greens or cool purples might be used in an underpainting to their warm opponents of yellows, oranges or reds and vice versa.

More layers

Once you have a start in place, you can develop your piece by adding more layers. Here are just two approaches to get you started.

Washes of colour Additional washes of paint or ink can be applied at any stage of a painting as long as the layer underneath is completely dry. Use transparent colours to keep underlying layers visible or opaque colour to disguise or even blot out completely.

Angle or tilt the board or easel that you are working on in order to allow liquid colour to run and flow over your support. Have brushes and other tools to hand and use them to create evocative marks or shapes. The joy of liquid colour is watching it dribble and meander, finding its own way over and around texture or collage; pooling in places and causing runs of colour that fire the imagination.

Hide or reveal Layers allow for experiment and spontaneity. A painting can proceed forwards or even in reverse. Areas that are not working can be covered with paper, other sorts of collage or painted over with an opaque paint. If a painting has layers of collage, you might want to dig for buried treasure: peel back a layer, scrape, sand or even excavate!

If you have used texture paste, when the painting is finished and completely dry, any high points in the texture can be lightly sanded and either left white or scumbled over with paint, pastel or coloured crayon.

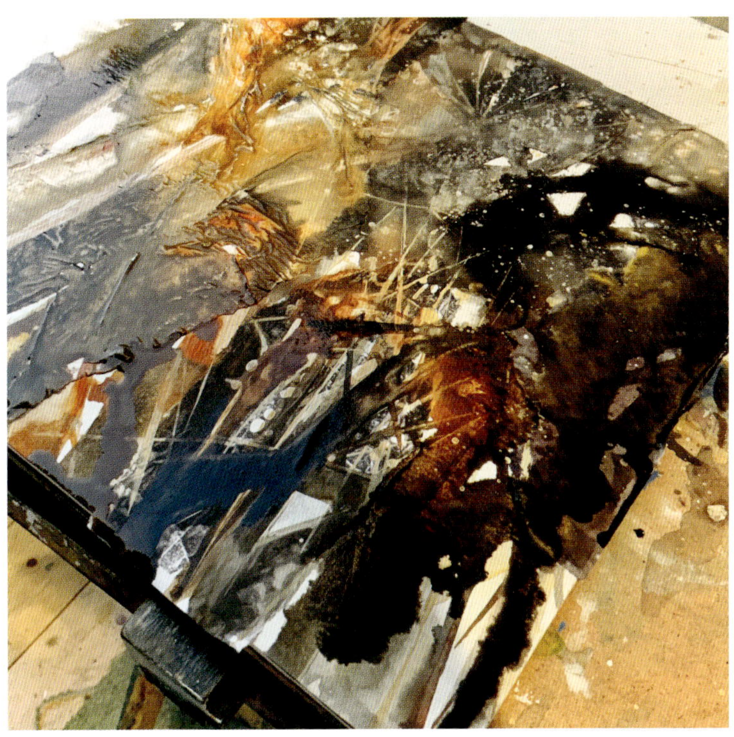

Watercolour wash being applied over a textural collaged start.

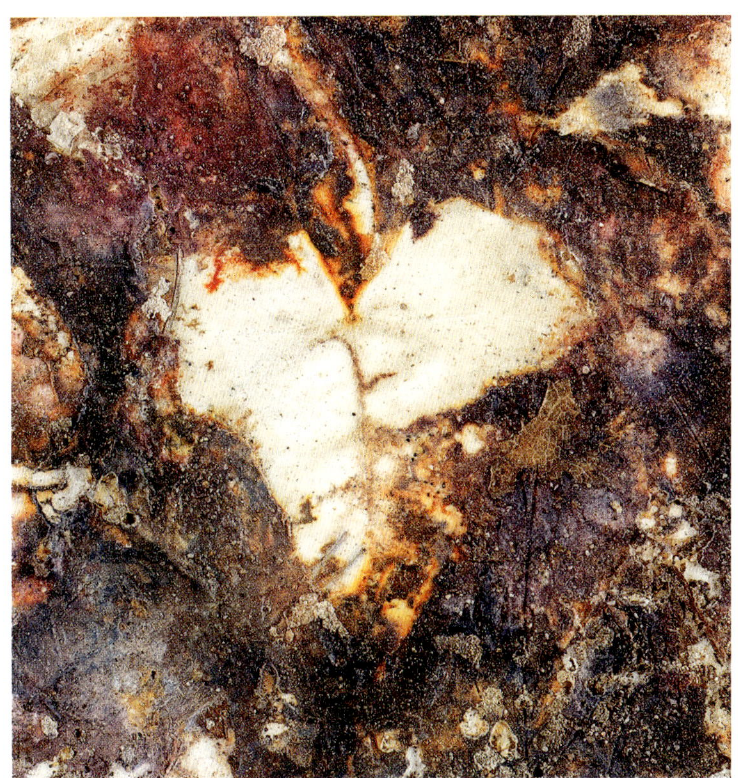

A rounded palette knife was used to scrape the shape of this leaf from a more textured overlayer.

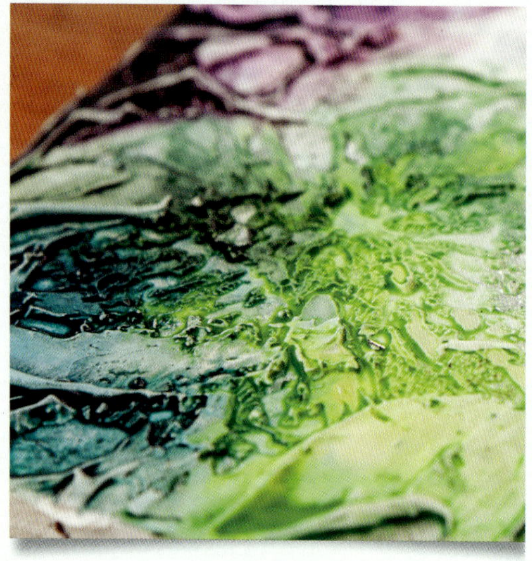

Nocturne

In this project, we will use layers of collage and deep texture to build abstract shapes. In terms of stencils, I'm using geranium leaves and lace fabric, but you can use almost anything you like. Similarly, you should feel free to adapt the texture and colours. The colour scheme I've chosen is intended to create mystery, a dark and dreamy mood. Likewise the forms are somewhat unclear; half-hidden shapes that seem familiar but can't be readily identified. The aim is to hint at the unknown to evoke the strangeness of the night.

You will need

- 30 × 30cm (11¾ × 11¾in) wooden panel primed with white gesso
- Metallic silver leaf
- Acrylic medium
- Tweezers
- Texture paste (Daler-Rowney texture paste and DIY fine surface Polyfilla)
- Stencils
- Acrylic inks: (Liquitex) yellow medium azo, burnt sienna, phthalo blue, quinacridone magenta, (Golden) carbon black
- Brushes: size 16 round brush

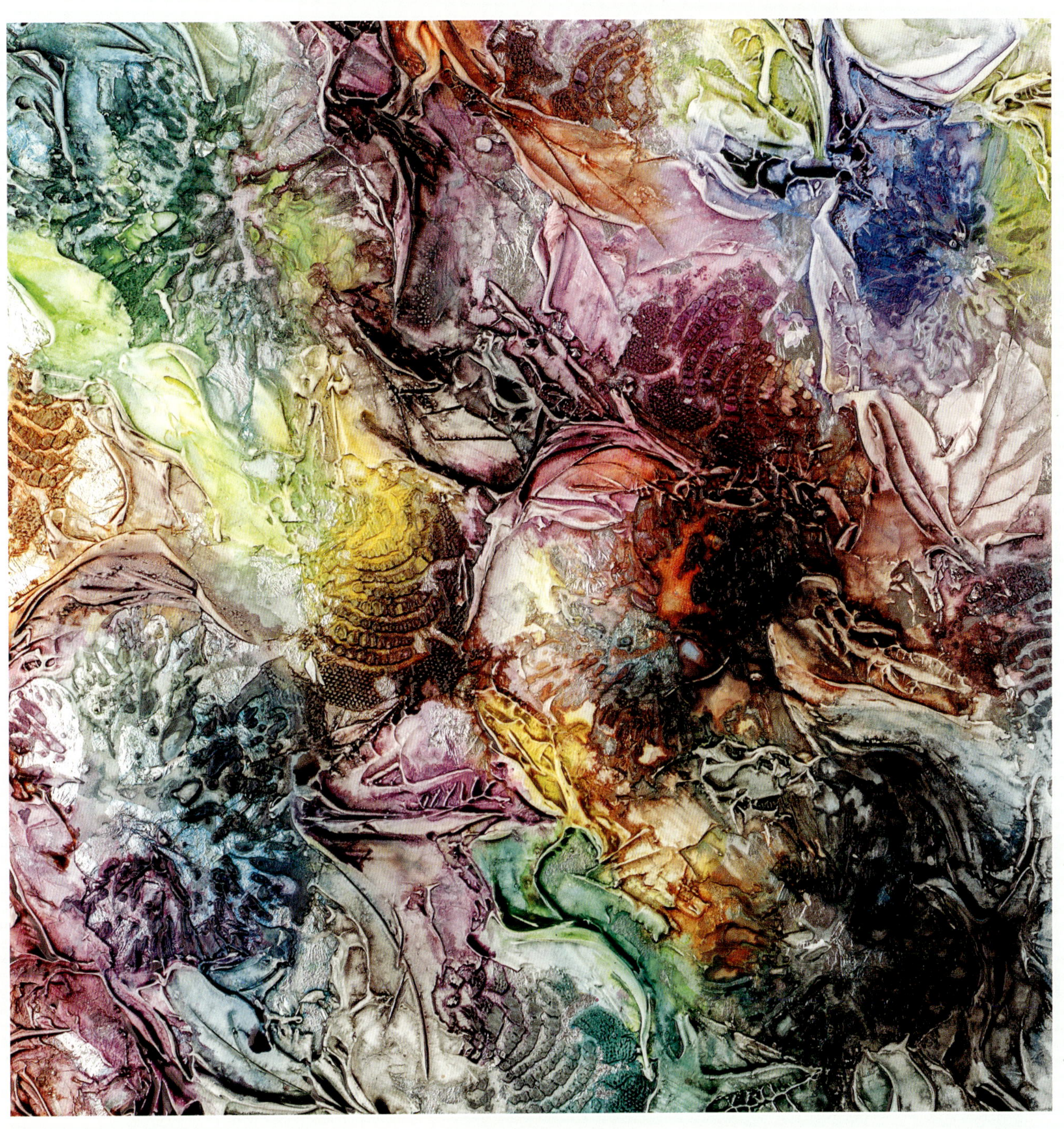

The finished painting
50 × 50cm (19¾ × 19¾in)

Creating the surface

This stage establishes the basic surface with silver leaf, texture paste and the use of stencils. Aim for a natural, uncontrived look – avoid even spacing and numbers of elements. Placing some of the stencils overlapping the edge of the painting will give a more natural and flowing appearance. By the end of the stage, some areas of silver leaf should still be showing.

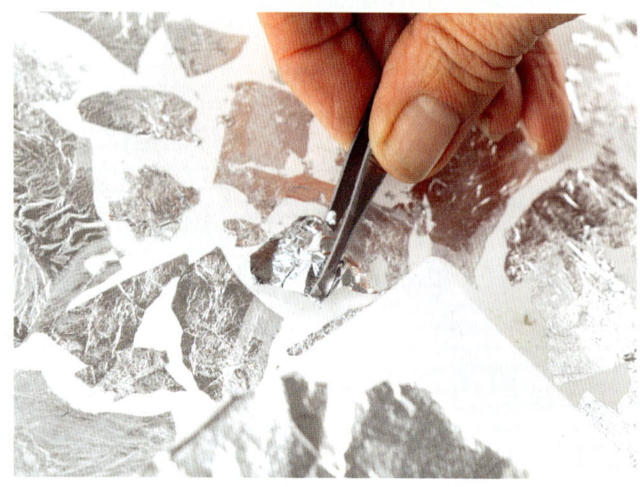

Applying silver leaf is a fiddly process, and metal leaf is very flyaway. Use tweezers – and ensure you have no windows open!

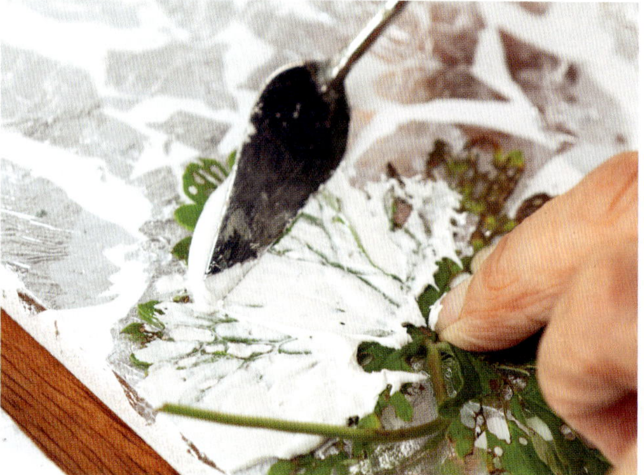

Smear the filler away from the centre of the stencil.

- Apply patches of silver leaf to the surface with acrylic medium. Work in small areas at a time, using tweezers to selectively apply small pieces of leaf.

- Place your geranium leaf (or other stencil) on the surface and use a palette knife to push fine surface filler over the top and through the gaps in the stencil. Gently lift it away to reveal a textural effect, then repeat, aiming to cover roughly a quarter to a third of the surface.

- Use your other stencil – lace fabric in this case – to add variation. Use the same technique, and avoid accidentally covering or spoiling the texture you have already created. Allow the piece to dry before continuing.

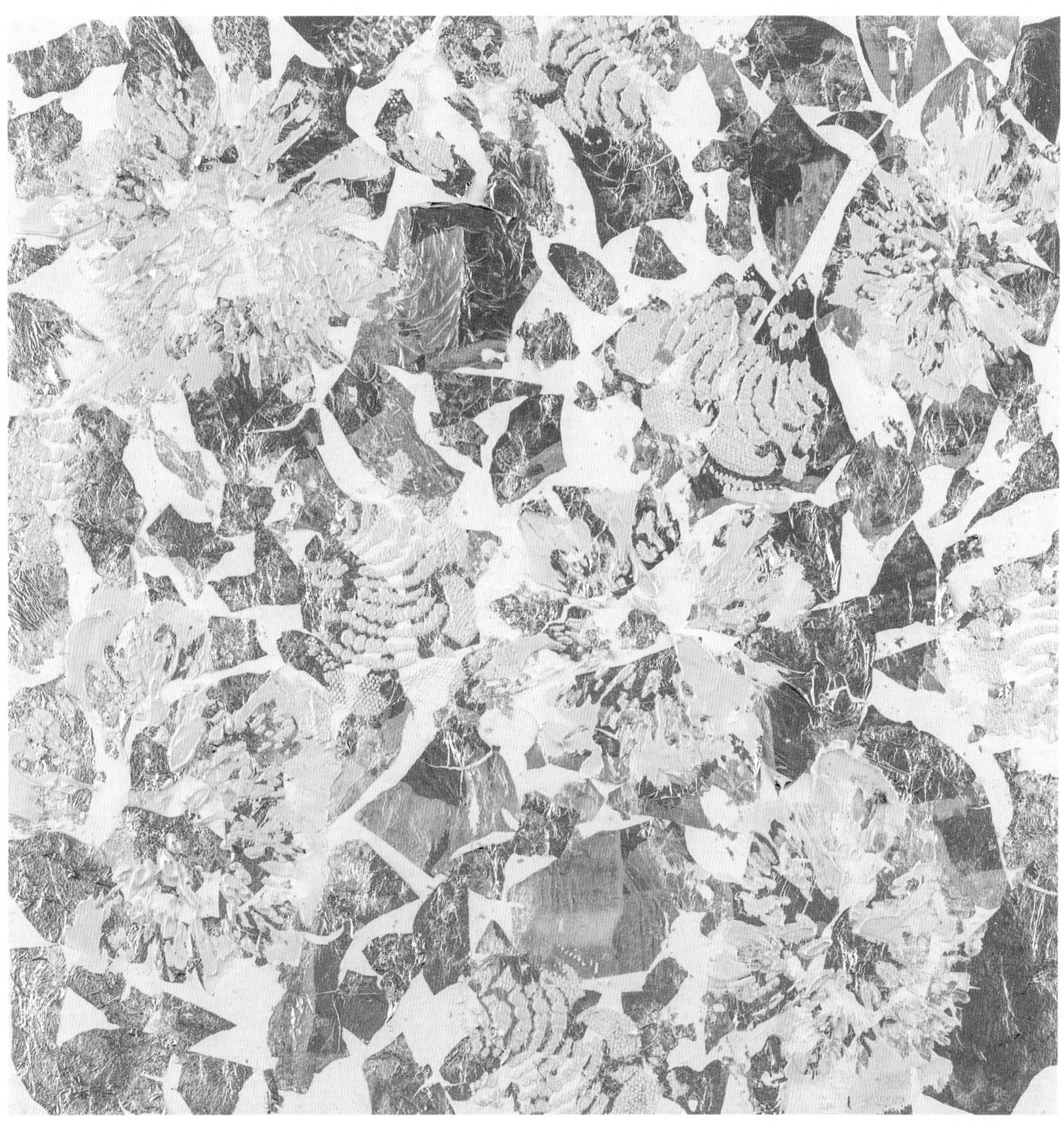

The painting at the end of this stage.

Developing the texture and relief

We'll now add the deeper relief to create more variation in texture, as well as suggest freeform leaf shapes and movement. This stage is about creating more controlled and considered visual interest and dynamism.

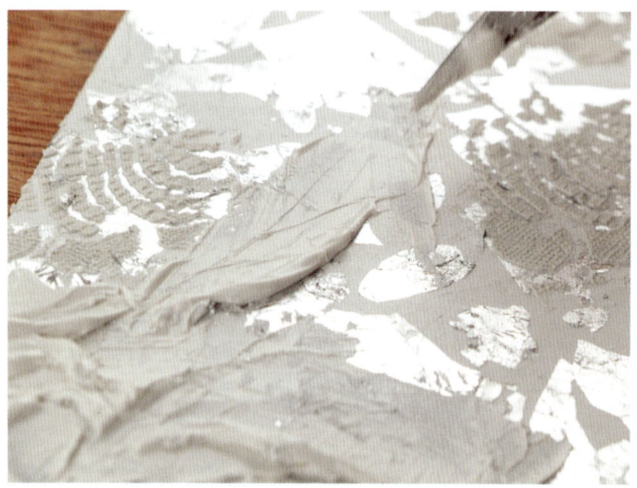

After adding a swooping mark in texture paste, you can use the edge of the palette knife to suggests leaf veins and markings.

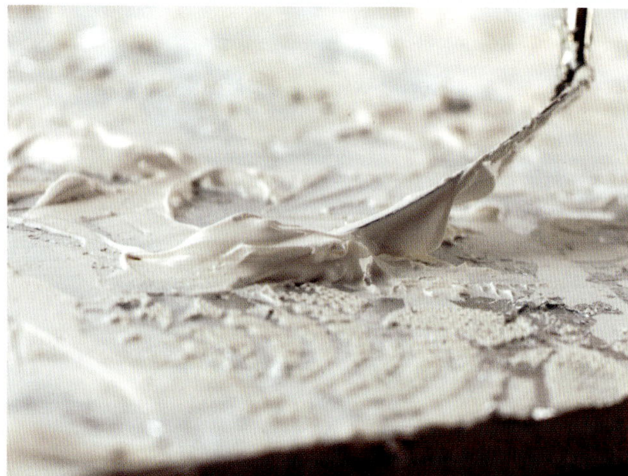

This shows the palette knife lifting and curling the edge of a leaf.

- Start to apply the texture paste using a palette knife, working in small areas with gestural movements and using all the parts of the knife – the flat, the tip and the edge. You might try pressing down and lifting away for a different texture.

- Avoid the areas built up in the previous stage, instead filling in some (but not all) of the spaces in between the stencilled areas. Leave some of the silver leaf showing, too.

- As you continue to work, always try to suggest motion by using sweeping, free movements of your arm and hand. Aim to create a surface that is so deeply textured that it appears almost sculptural, like bas relief.

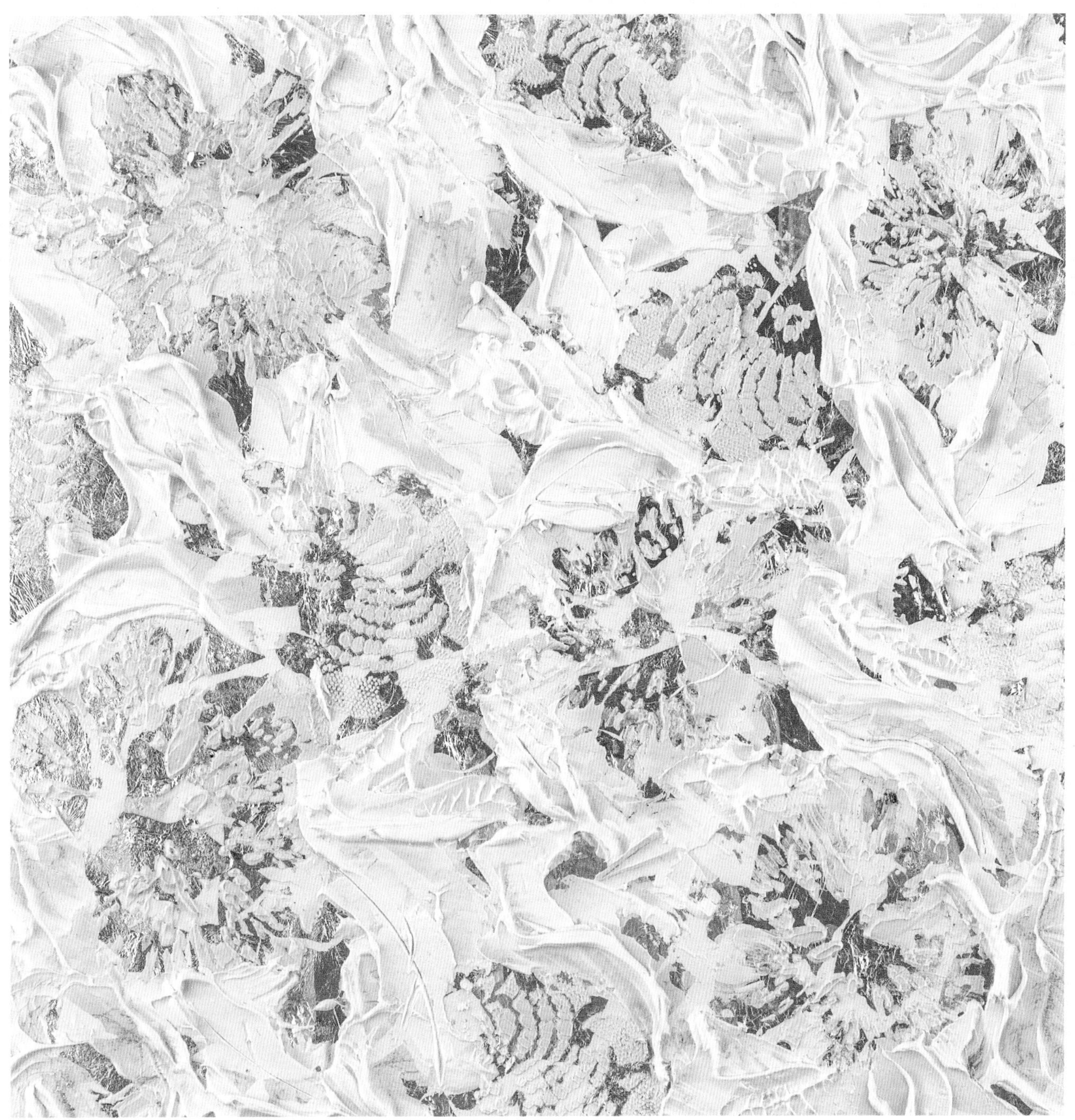

The painting at the end of this stage.

Adding colour

In a watercolour painting you would generally start with the lightest colours and values and gradually build towards the darks, but in this all-over design it is better to paint more directly, laying down strong tones next to light, repeating and balancing them across the picture plane. The aim is to enhance and draw the eye to main focal points and areas of textural interest.

Acrylic inks are a perfect consistency to use straight from the bottle so when working wet in wet, avoid diluting them too much with water. Combining them with an acrylic glazing medium will help to retain the integrity of the ink's binding medium and stop it from breaking down.

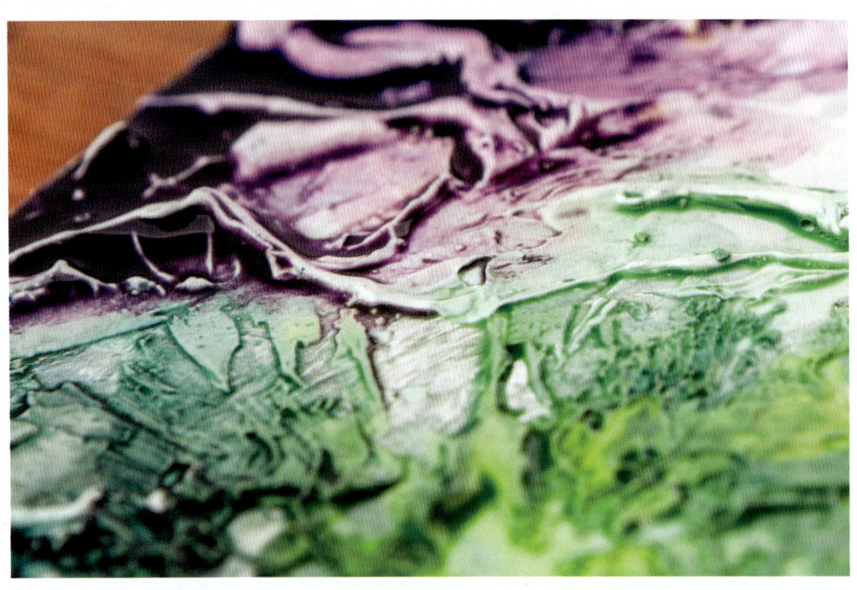

Using inks will keep the colour vibrant – you can see here how the wet medium settles into the recesses.

- Using a size 16 round brush and acrylic inks, wet the surface with clean water, then begin adding your colours. Much of the precise placement is intuitive, but the following tips will help guide you.

- Establish the areas you want to be light, and add the darkest tones next to them for maximum impact.

- Use areas of complementary colours – yellow next to purple and burnt sienna next to blue, for example. This will depend on your colour scheme.

- Build the work up gradually; there's no rush. Try to balance the colours across the whole piece as you work.

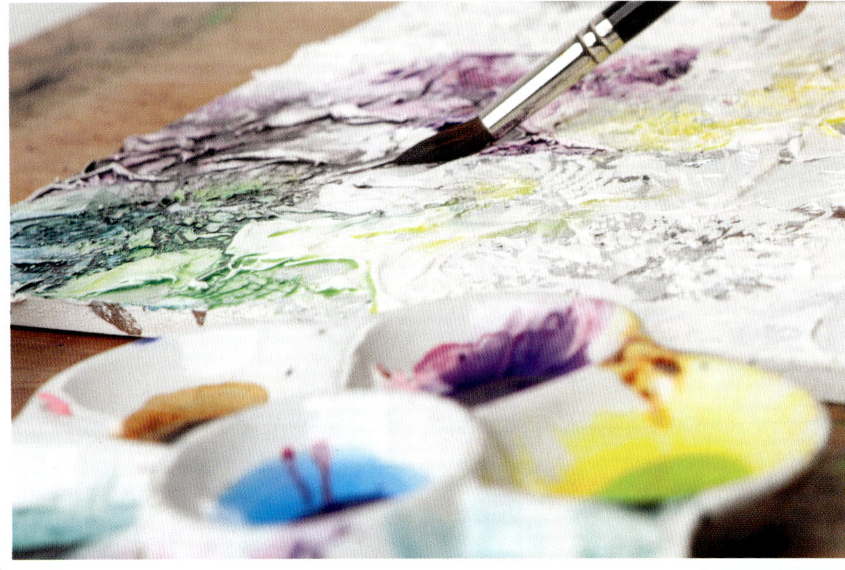

Keep your colours clean. Avoid mixing the colours in your palette too much – instead combine them wet in wet on the surface.

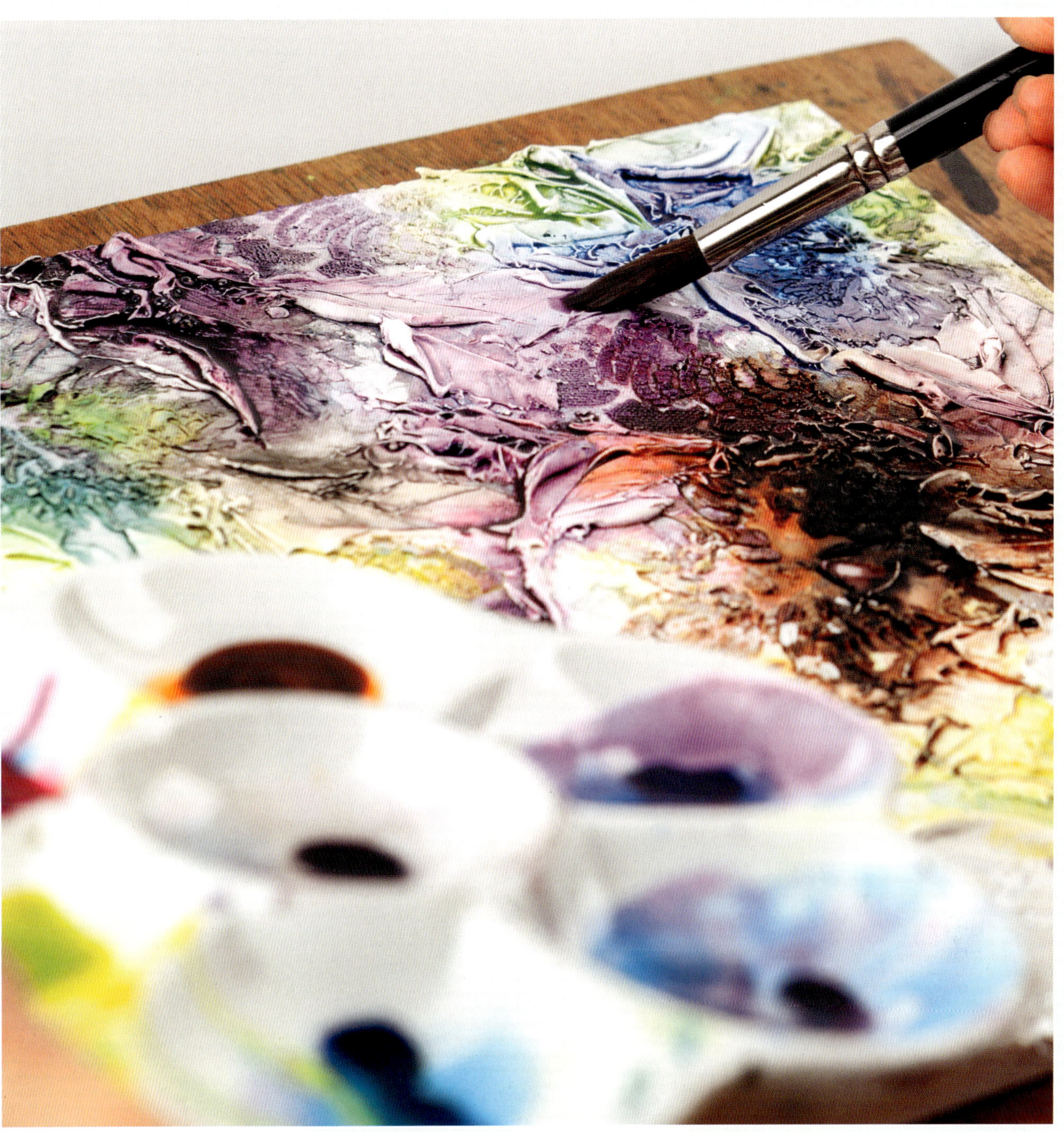

Keep an eye on the overall balance of the composition as you work – rather than fixating on isolated areas. As soon as you find yourself wondering 'when should I stop?', the painting is coming to a conclusion. The finished painting can be seen on page 95.

'Once an object has been incorporated in a picture
it accepts a new destiny.' ***Georges Braque***

COLLAGE AND PRINT

The word collage comes from the French word, *coller*, meaning 'to glue'.
It was first used as an artistic technique in the early twentieth century by
Cubist painters, George Braque (1882–1963) and Pablo Picasso (1881–1973). It
was a time of major changes in the world, following two World Wars that had
transformed and destroyed lives and communities. The art world had moved
away from conventional realism and sought a way to express the turmoil
that was around it. Collage allowed diverse and random images, surfaces and
textures to be taken out of their context and given a new meaning. It was a
new way of presenting ideas that reflected the state of the world.

Prints from both manmade and natural materials like leaves, leaf skeletons,
stems, flowers and feathers can be used as collage to enrich our artworks, or
be printed directly onto a painting, where they make beautiful standalone
elements in their own right.

Personally, I enjoy the fragmented and deconstructed appearance that
you can achieve through combining techniques like collage and printing,
and often use it to explore environmental and other themes. I'm interested
in edges and boundaries, in life as well as nature. Where one thing ends,
something new begins.

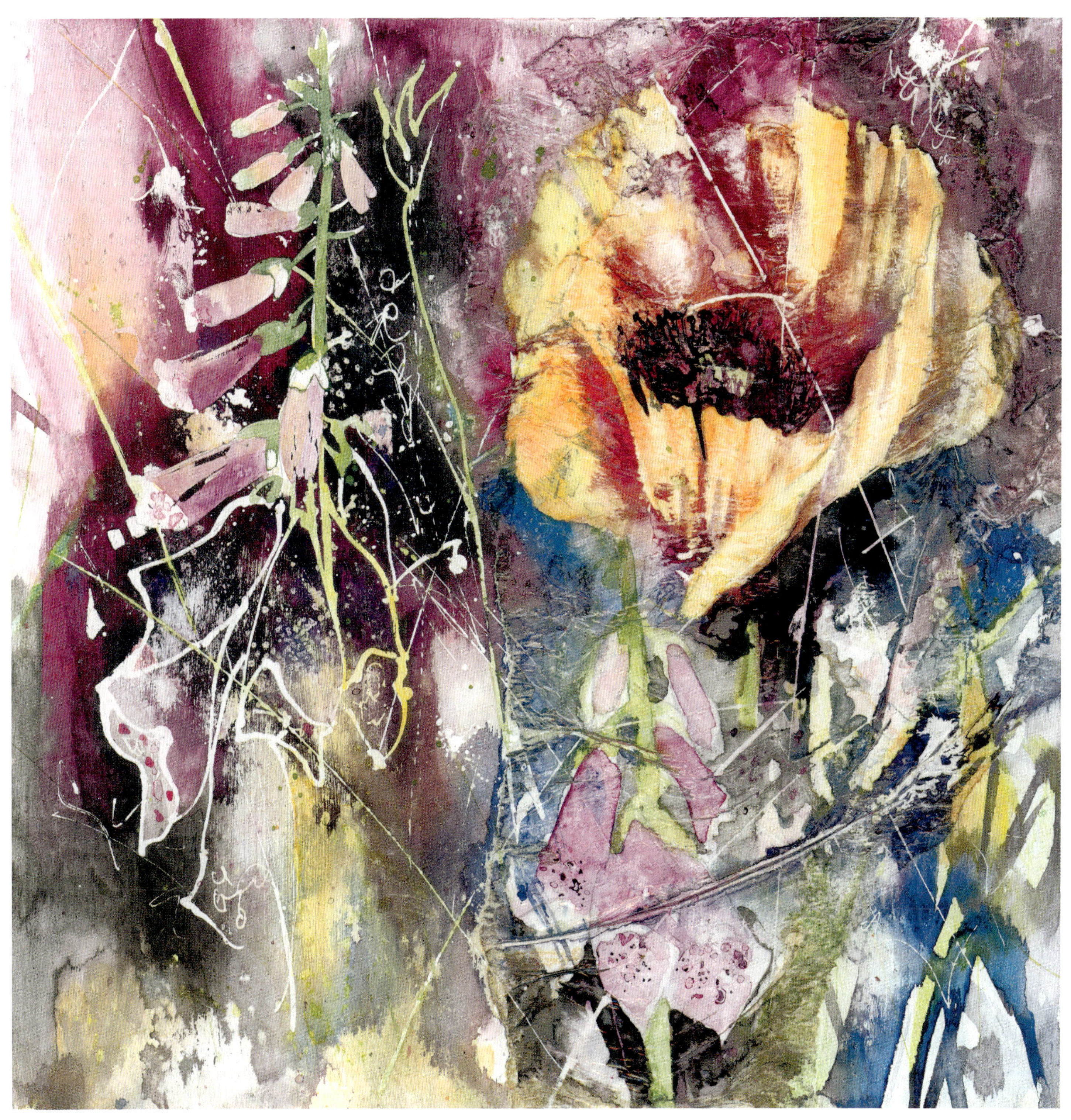

Bloom and Wild
35 × 35cm (13¾ × 13¾in)

Paper collage

Papers of any thickness can be collaged directly onto a support, as long as you use the correct adhesive. Magazines, newspapers, promotional material and wrapping paper are just some sources of collage that we can reuse and give another life. They can contribute random imagery and inject mystery with half-obscured images, printed texture, a pop of colour or hint of glitz.

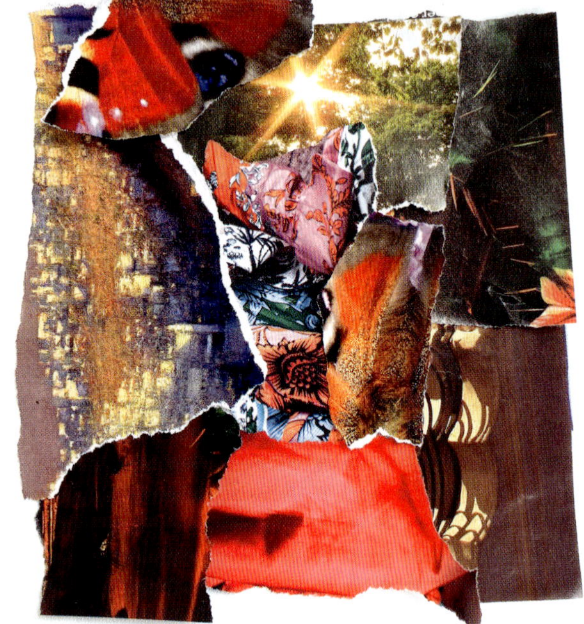

A simple collaged start (see 'Start 3' on page 91), using elements torn from magazines.

Securing collage Acrylic medium is suitable for lighter weight papers like tissue paper, magazine and newspaper cutouts; acrylic gel is more suitable for heavier weights of collage. The best adhesives to use are those that are artists' quality rather than those described for school or craft use. These are fine for experiments but they may yellow with age or be incompatible with other artists' products.

Layering Always check that collage is properly stuck down and lying flat before adding further layers (whether of collage, texture or paint), as it is difficult to rectify this in the later stages of a painting.

Sealing Any collage that is absorbent will take up the paint or ink that you are using, and its worth considering whether that is what you want. Sealing the surface of the collage before you start painting helps to keep the colours fresh and adds a little extra UV protection. In order to do this, brush over the area with an acrylic medium or apply a layer of self-levelling gel over the whole piece. These products can usually be diluted if you prefer a thin layer, but check the instructions first. Self levelling gel has the additional effect of adding a little separation to the layers, giving an appearance of depth.

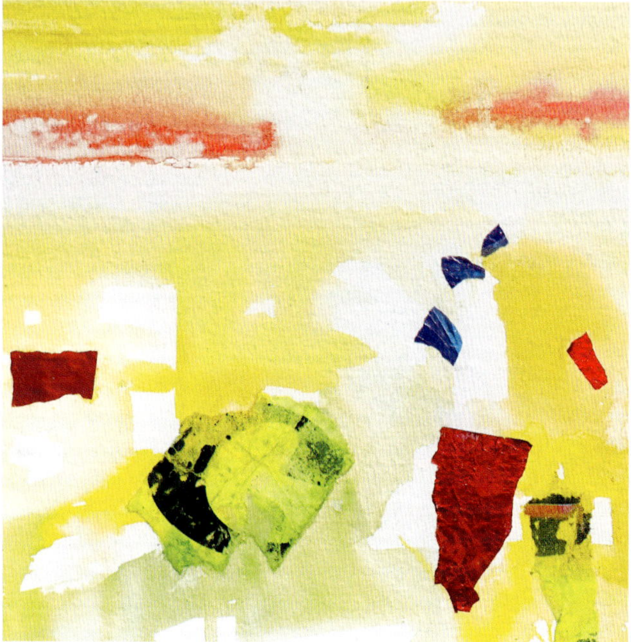

***Early stage of* Fragmented Landscape**

A collage layer may be kept to just one layer or built up with multiple layers to any kind of tangible depth. It may then be followed by either washes of colour, texture pastes, drawing or mark making with pastels, crayons or other dry media. There are no rules to follow; it is a question of learning to trust your intuition about what works and what doesn't.

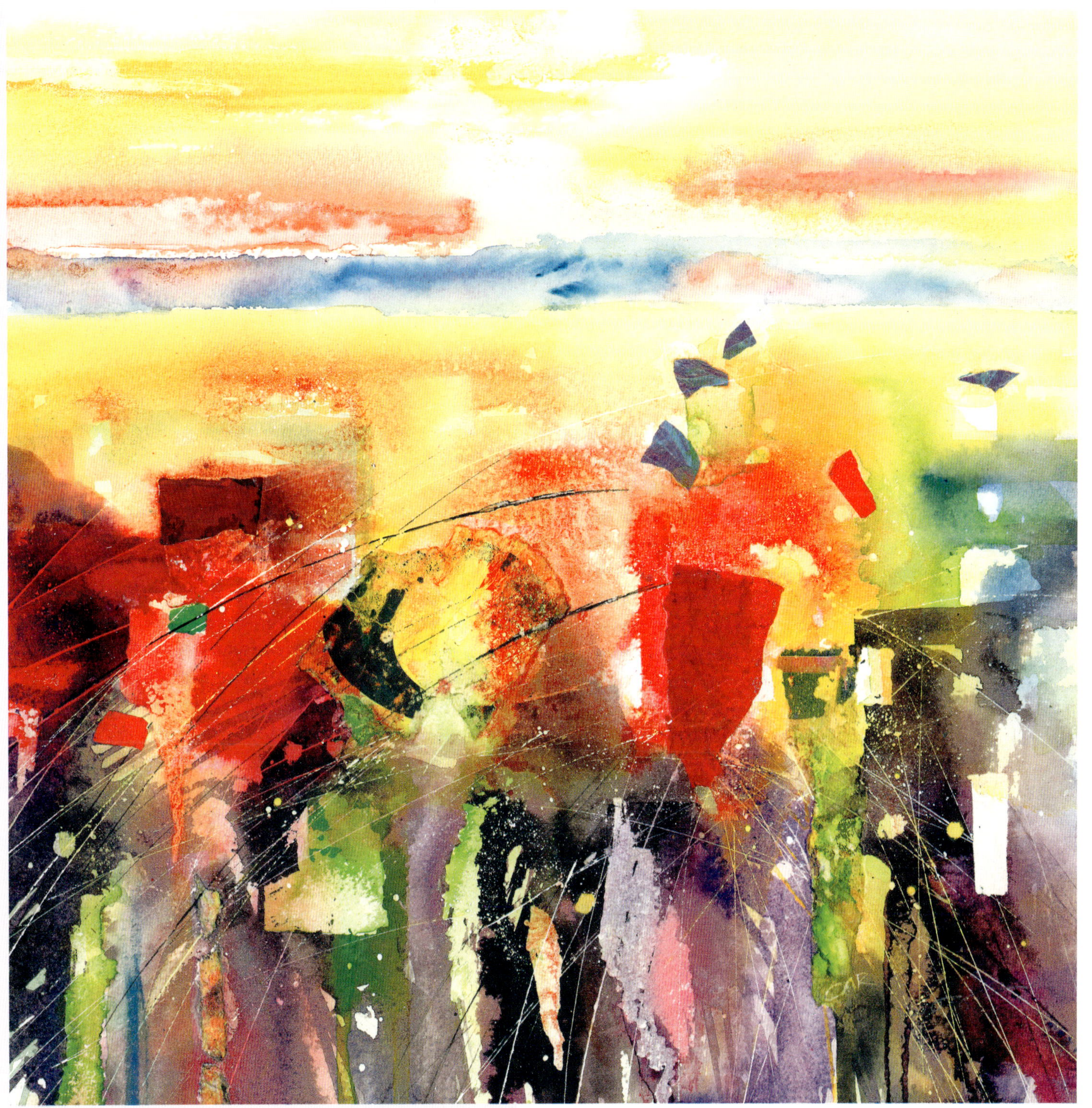

Fragmented Landscape

52 × 52cm (20½ × 20½in)

In the finished painting, the large brightly coloured collage pieces are emboldened further with the addition of painted shapes and strong contrast. Towards the horizon, colour and tones are softened, while the smaller receding shapes provide both perspective and variation of scale.

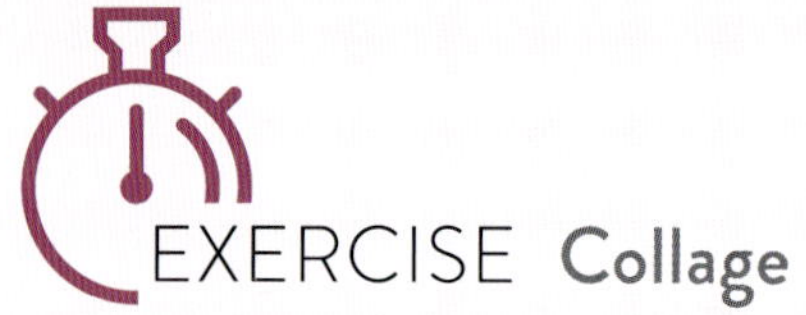

EXERCISE Collage

This meadow sample uses the wet in wet technique (see page 64), but it begins with a few pieces of collage. Choose your collage pieces with care as they could form a central story for the piece. They may, for example, contain a subject that suggests a theme. Here, a central daisy flower sets up the theme of a meadow. I decided to place the largest piece of collage horizontally as it suggested a distant landscape and its warm colours a sunset. I also

added an area of texture on the left-hand side of the piece, which involved using a strip of plastic card to pull texture paste through a piece of cotton scrim.

For this exercise, prepare a support and gather pieces of collage that vary in shape and size. They may harmonize in colour or be quite contrasting – it's your choice. Take your cues for the colour scheme from the collage papers and mix up wells of fluid colour.

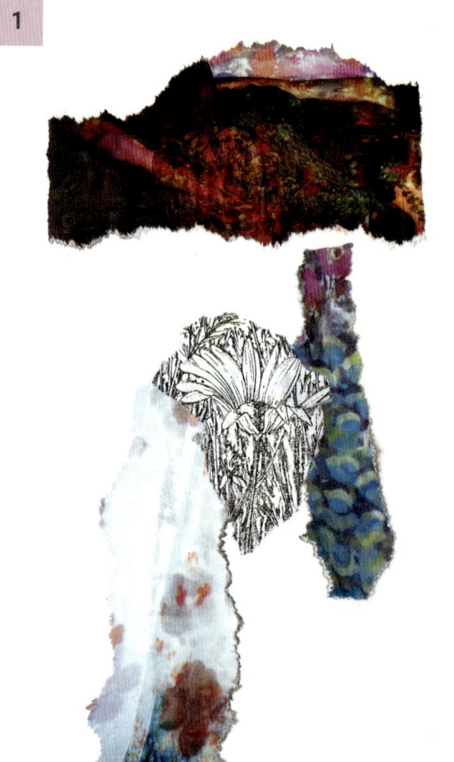

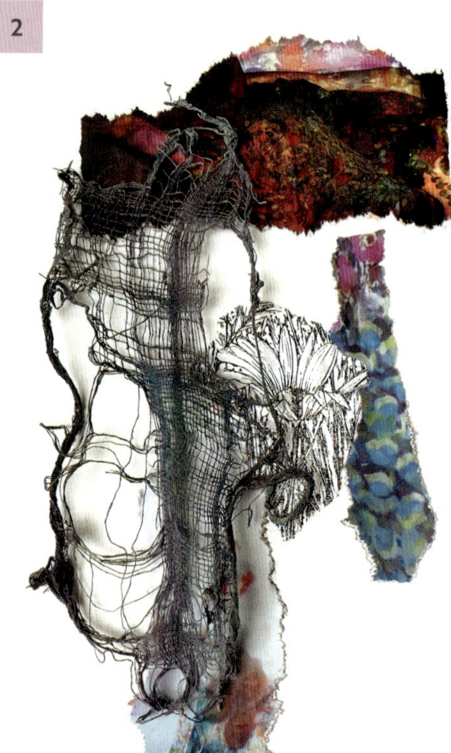

1 Play around with the pieces of paper collage until you are happy with the arrangement and then glue them down – I used acrylic medium.

2 Create the area of texture by holding down the piece of scrim and pulling texture paste through. Allow it to dry completely, before moving on.

3 Paint loose and flowing wet in wet washes over the collaged areas. Allow them to dry completely, then make any final additions. Having used a daisy flower, I brightened up some of the petals with white gouache and then used the edge of my palette knife to suggest some long grasses.

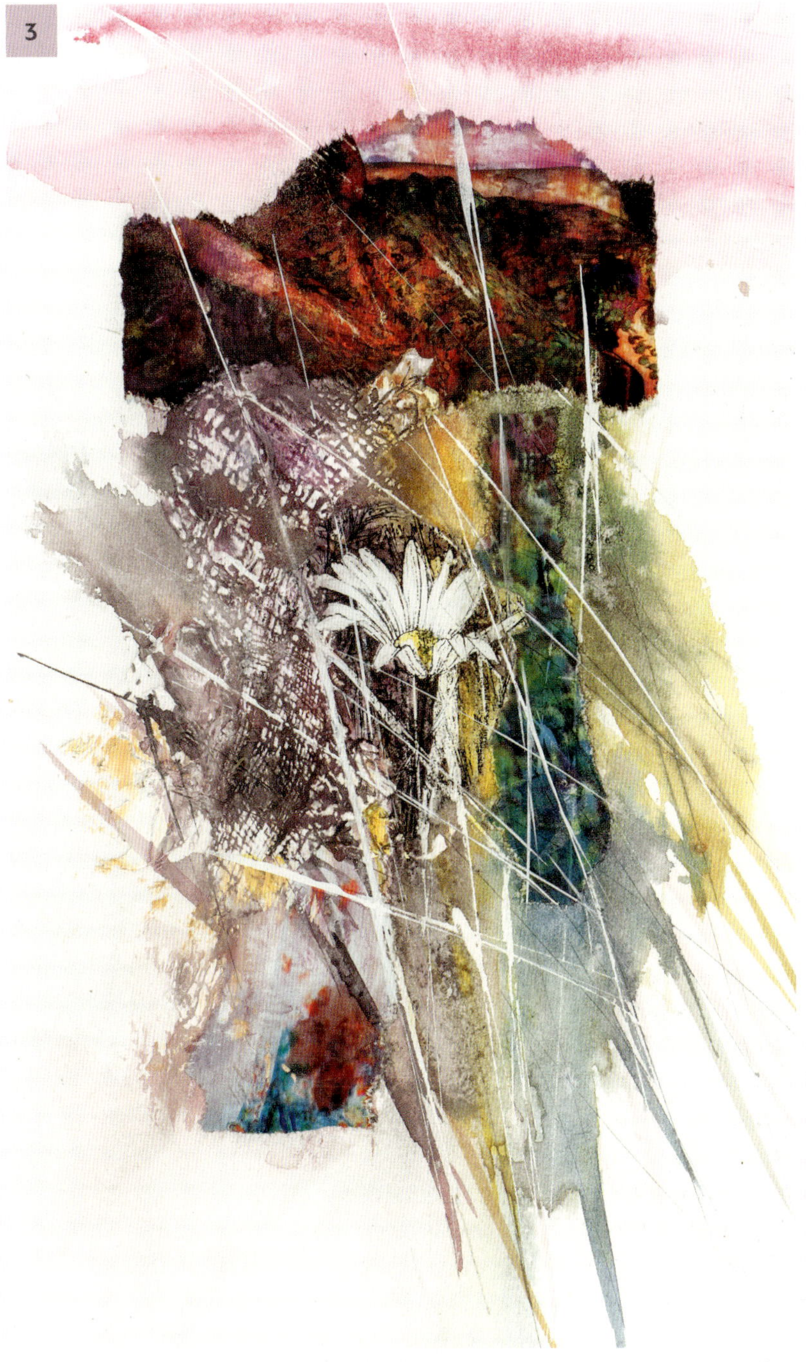

Purely abstract

You may prefer to choose collage pieces that have no suggestion of a subject, but are interesting for their formal elements alone – colour, pattern, texture and so forth. (The collage start on page 104 shows an example.)

Any marks or pattern that such pieces contain could be repeated or developed, perhaps by drawing or mark making with paint, ink or crayon.

Reuse and recycle

There is no need to restrict yourself to using ready-made printed material taken from magazines, newspapers or other printed matter. While these provide a very direct way to create focal points in your artworks, by injecting splashes of colour, texture or areas of contrast, you can use other materials too. In fact, anything light enough to be attached to the surface as described on page 104 can be used in your collages. Used foil and sweet wrappers provide similar eye-catching areas and, like paper, can also be used to cover up and rework unsuccessful areas.

Recycling paintings that, for whatever reason, are unsuccessful is something that I'm always keen to do. It's a shame to waste them and there are usually some parts of a painting that can be saved. I rip these pieces out, trying, as mentioned below, to tear shapes with interesting edges.

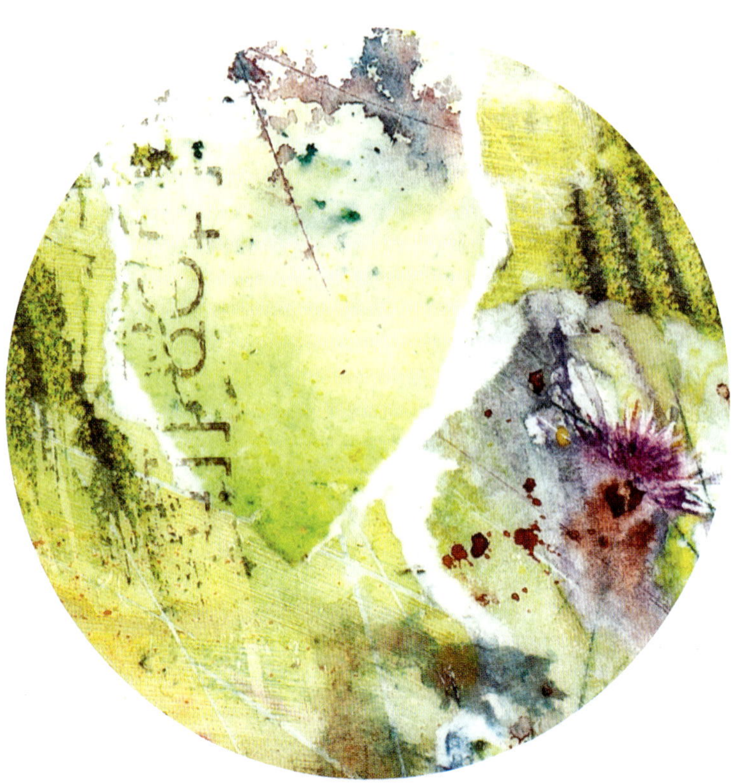

Interesting edges

I like the torn edges of paper collage, and like to combine varied types and thicknesses of paper, each torn in different ways.

I try to tear pieces interestingly. Thick paper, for example, can have wider, more ragged edges that you can choose to celebrate or disguise. A painting might be made up of torn collage or a mixture of uneven and cut or straight edges.

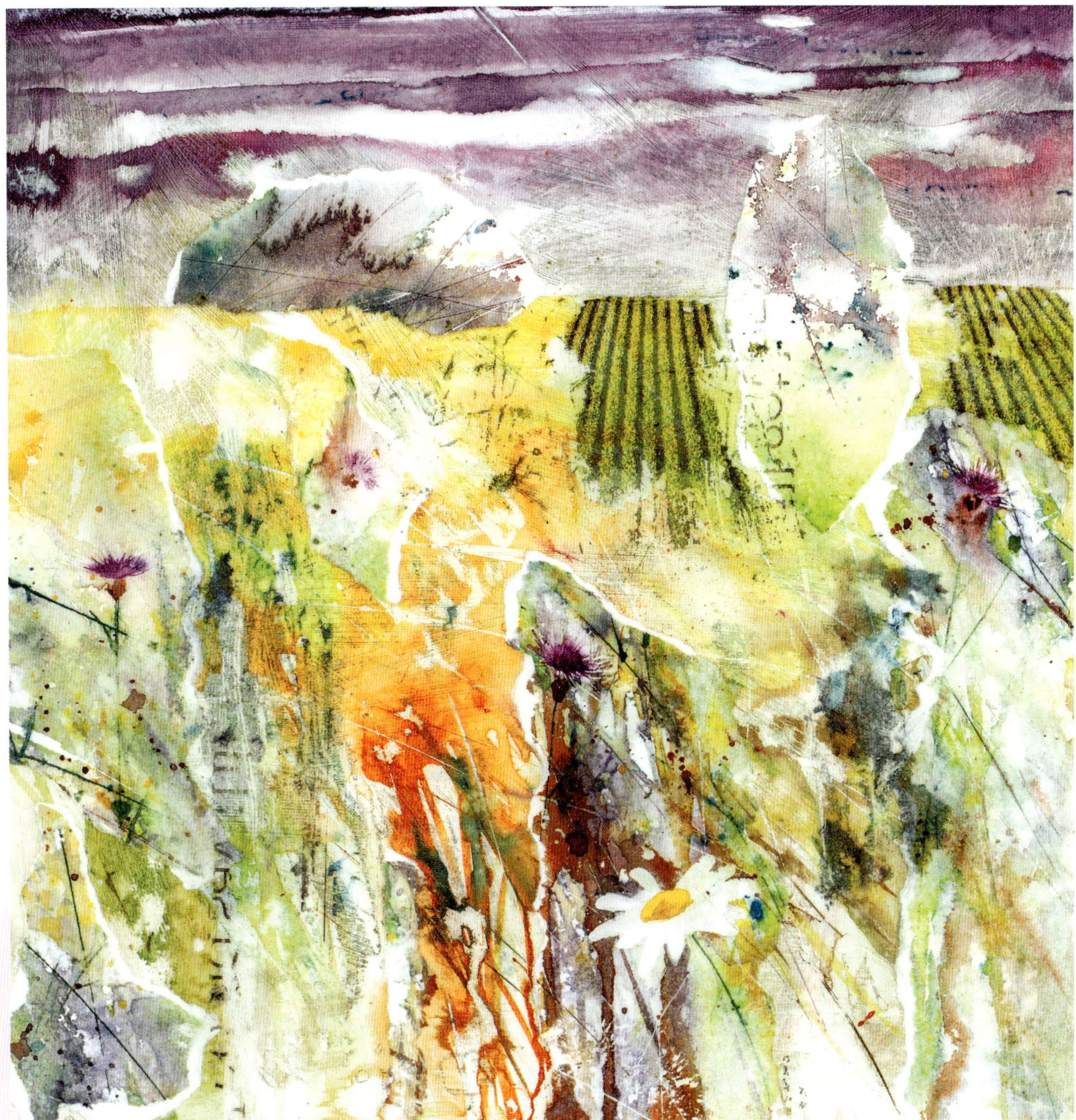

Painting *Green and Pleasant Land*

Every now and then I go through my saved collage pieces and try
placing a few of them onto a support. You may need to move them
around and try out various combinations but it can help to kickstart
a creative process that leads to the birth of a new piece. This painting
started life in just this way.

Green and Pleasant Land
30 × 30cm (11¾ × 11¾in)

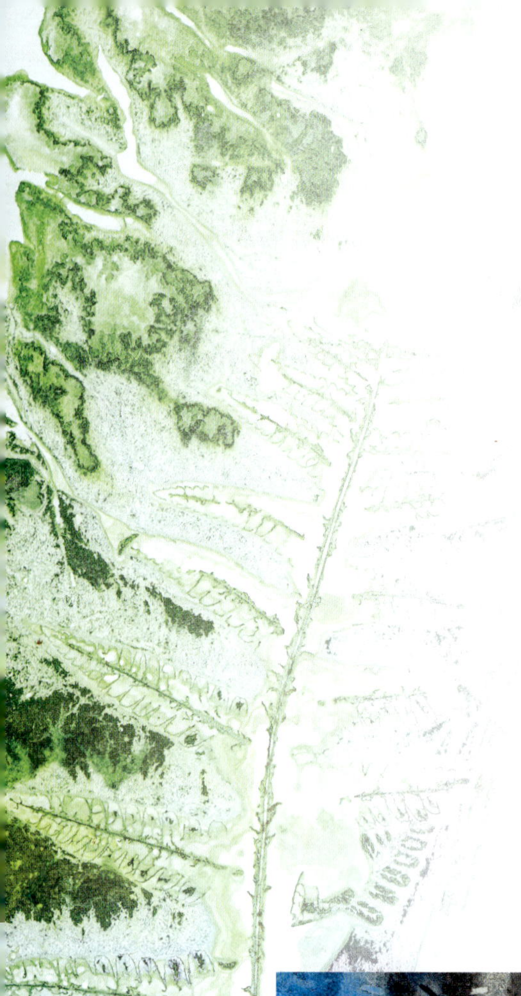

Nature prints

Leaves are a testament to nature's talent for diversity, made evident by the widely varying shapes, patterns, surface textures and veining. Taking prints from leaves can seem magical when you manage to reproduce realistic details. The undersides of leaves and those with a good pattern of raised veins often produce the best prints as do those with softer, rather than leathery leaves, for example: plantain, ferns, sage, geranium, primrose and buttercup.

Taking these prints onto smooth surfaces, like printing paper, cartridge or HP (hot pressed) watercolour paper works a treat, but you can also use a wide range of other papers, such as Not surface watercolour paper, any kind of tissue paper, decorative Japanese papers, etc. Prints can also be successfully taken on canvas that has been sealed with an acrylic primer. (Note that off-the-shelf canvasses are often ready primed.) You could also use mount card or experiment with a support of your choice.

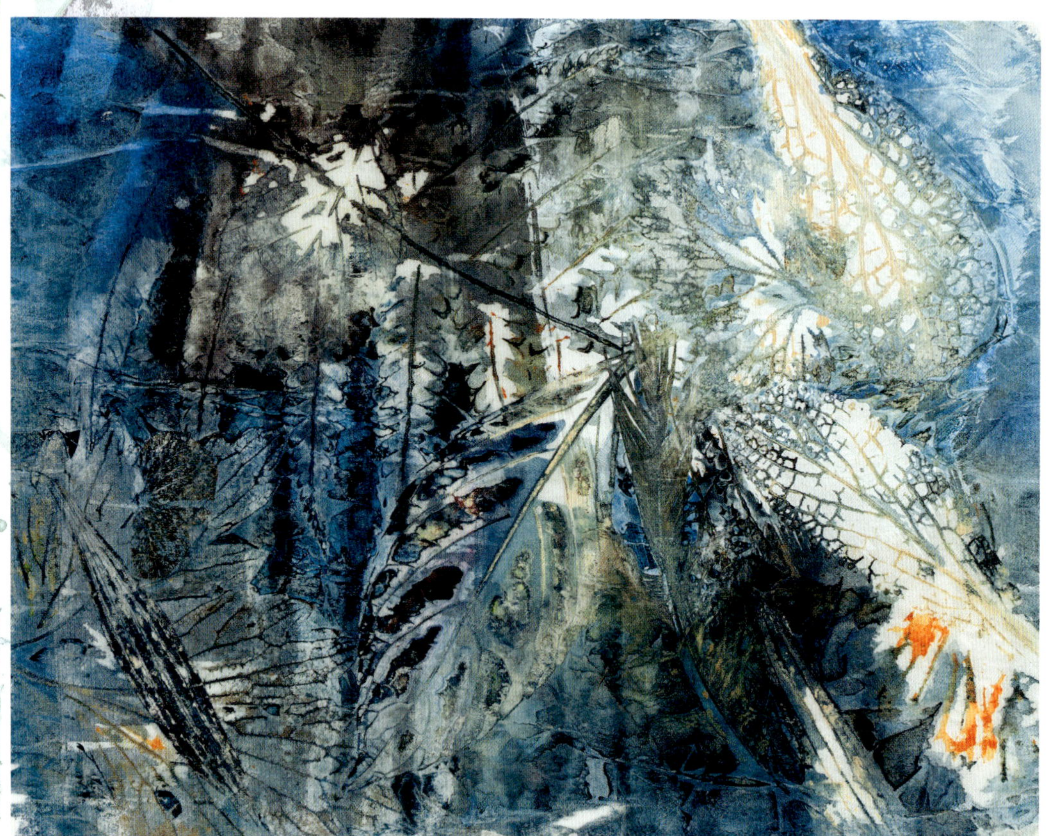

Leaf print experimental study
27 × 21cm (10½ × 8¼in)

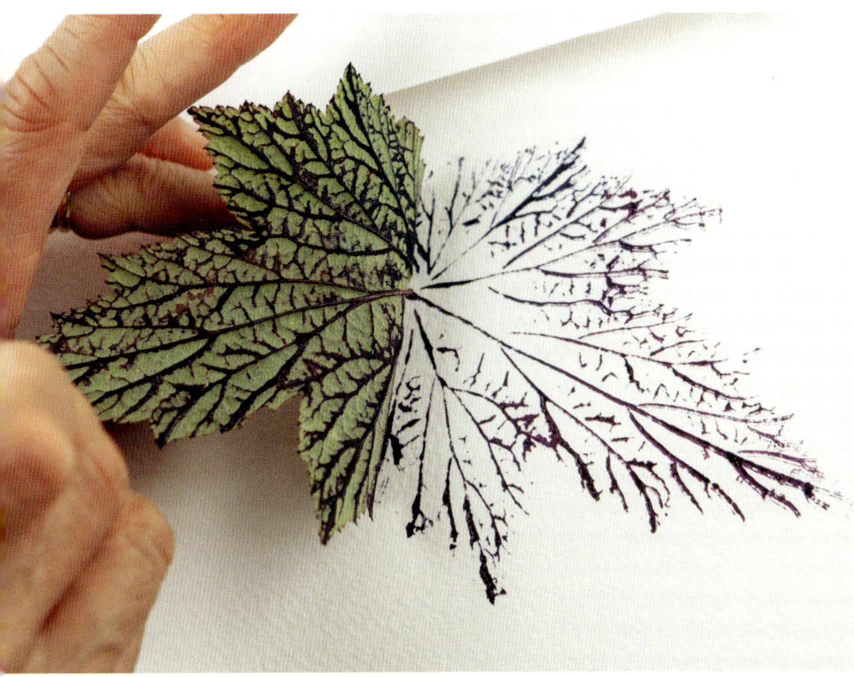

Making leaf prints

The process of making leaf prints is fairly simple but takes a little practice. A brayer is useful when pressing the material down evenly to ensure a clear print.

1 Apply a stiff mixture of paint or ink thinly and evenly to the surface of the object using the side of a brush or a sponge.

2 Carefully lay it, paint side down, onto your support and cover it with a sheet of waxed paper.

3 Press it down carefully but firmly.

4 Lift away the waxed paper and object from the support to reveal the print.

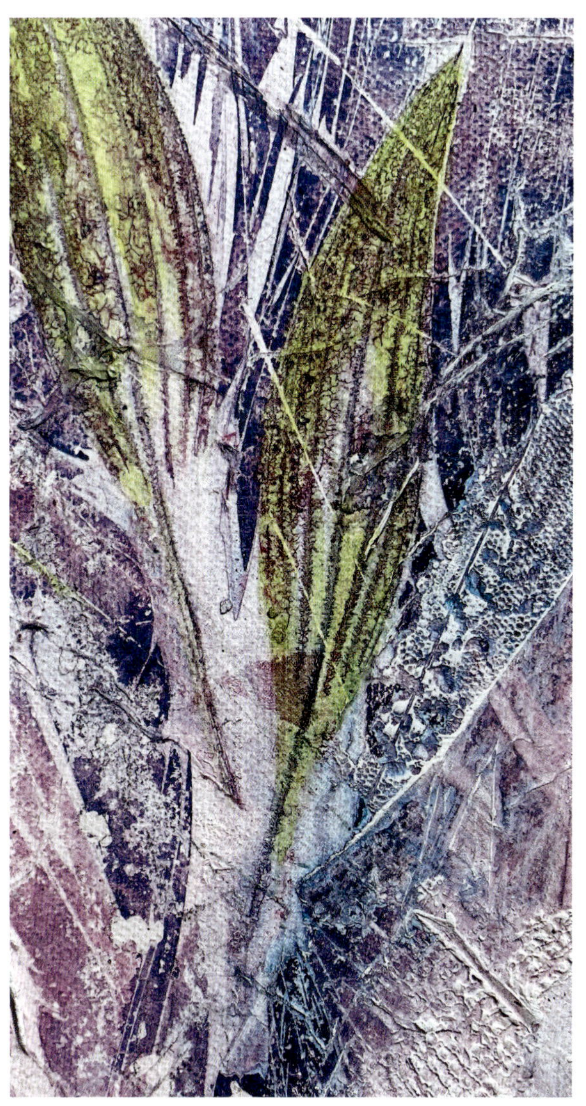

Detail of leaf print on canvas
12 × 18cm (4¾ × 7in)

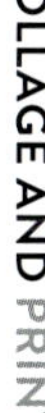

EXERCISE Nature prints through tissue

Painting leaves and other natural materials through tissue paper is an experimental technique that combines the beautiful random shapes and creases of the tissue itself with leaf and plant prints. Like many things, it takes practice and some results will, of course, be better than others – but don't be too hasty in discarding what you think are failures; any pieces that has good colour or interesting texture can be torn up to make useful collage.

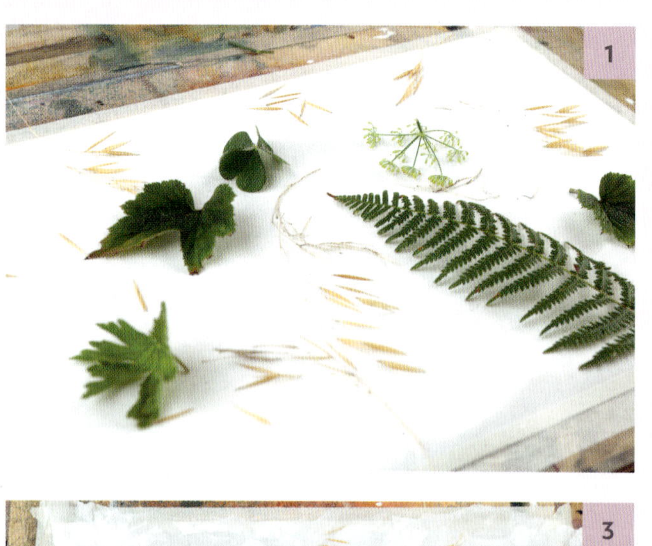

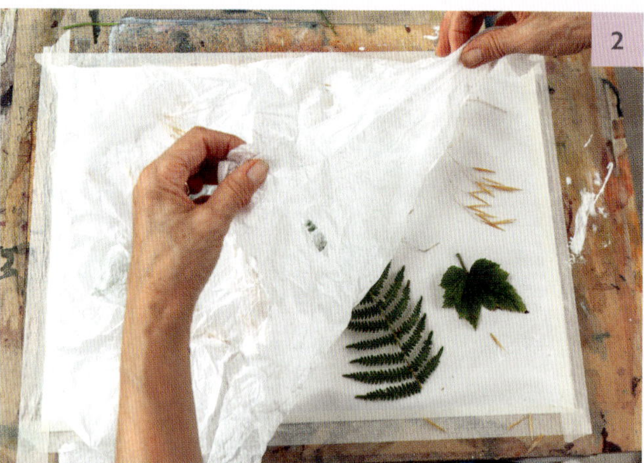

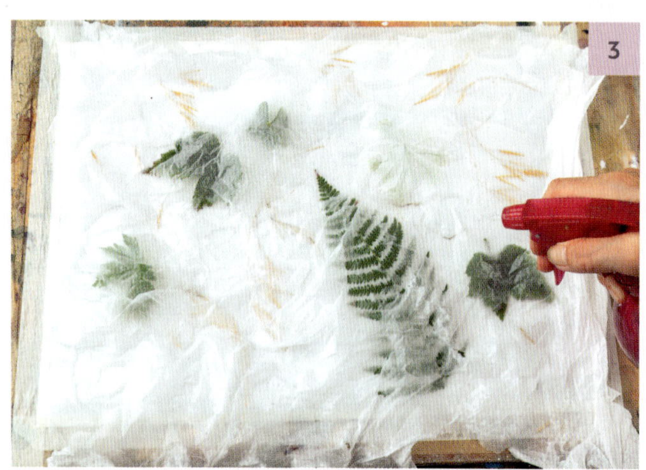

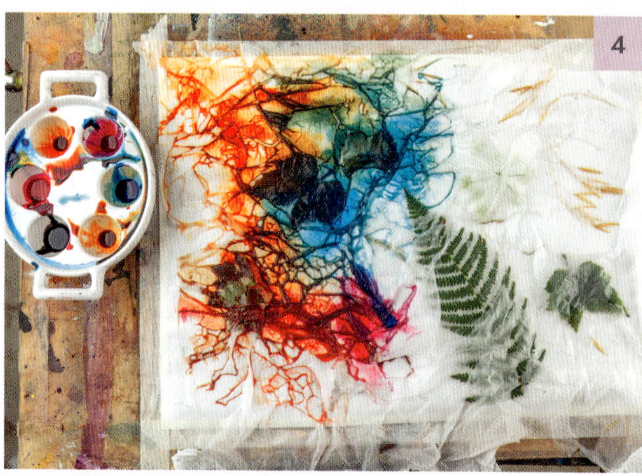

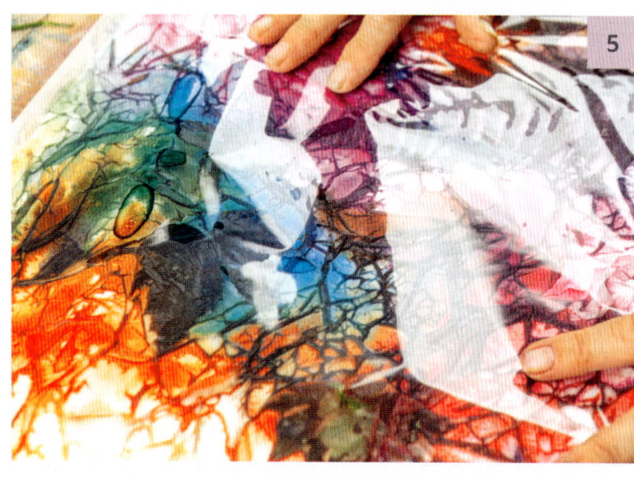

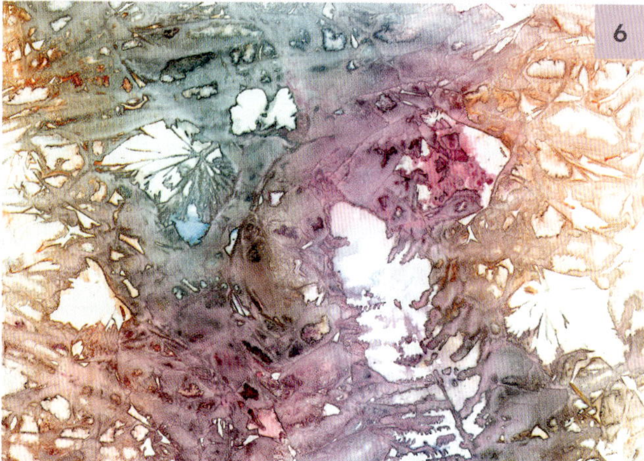

Quick transfer prints

Textures, gestural marks or even asemic writing (that is, marks that look like writing but have no meaning) can be transferred directly onto a painting from a variety of materials.

Apply or make marks with acrylic paint, gouache or printing ink onto scrunched tissue paper, food wrap, other soft plastics or various textured paper or fabrics and then press them directly onto your support.

1 Secure the paper of your choice to a sturdy board using masking tape, then arrange leaves and other subject matter onto the paper.

2 Spray the leaves lightly all over with clean water, which will help to draw the colour down. Lay a sheet of scrunched and opened-out tissue over the top.

3 Spray the tissue lightly with water so that it adheres to the surface.

4 Begin adding colour directly onto the tissue. You can vary the tone and colour, from monochrome to full colour, as you choose.

5 When you have finished painting, cover the piece completely with a sheet of waterproof plastic (you can use cellophane or plastic food wrap). Put a board and some heavy books on top to weight it down and leave overnight until dry.

6 Remove the plastic, tissue and leaves to reveal the result.

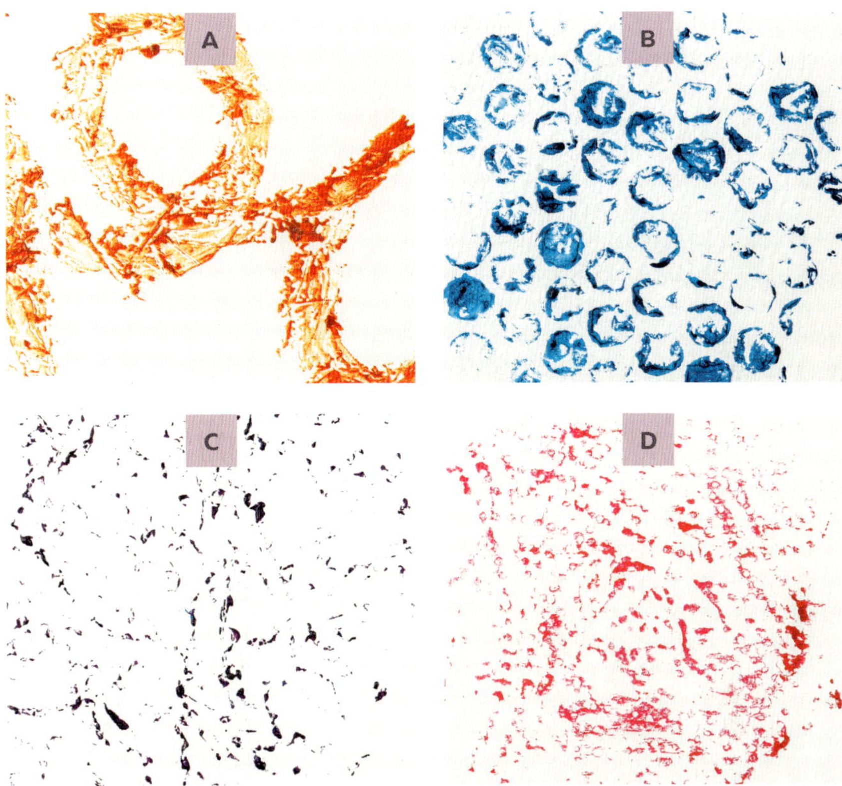

A Print made with plastic food wrap.

B Bubble wrap gives a recognizable and regular print.

C The tips that point out from a ball of aluminium foil make for an interesting random pattern.

D Even kitchen paper can be used for printing – textured but unpatterned is what I favour.

Tips

- Don't add too many leaves – the shapes and creases in the tissue paper will also create interest.

- If the tissue starts to disintegrate at step 3, change it for a stronger sheet.

- Take care when removing the tissue, as acrylic inks are very adhesive and may well be stuck in a few places. I use a palette knife to remove the tissue paper very carefully, much like an archaeologist uncovering treasure!

Prints from scrim

Cotton scrim is a loose weave material that is widely used in printmaking and textile art. I first came across it in printmaking workshops, where it was used for wiping excess ink from etching plates and cleaning up. It is a cheap and seemingly inconsequential fabric that makes beautiful prints with a natural and organic appearance.

Prints from scrim – such as the one below – are beautiful in their own right but details and hints of scrim texture can be effective in a painting. Scrim prints can suggest the texture of sea, as in *Sea of Waves* shown on page 45; or perhaps a vegetative tangle of plants as illustrated opposite in *End of Summer.*

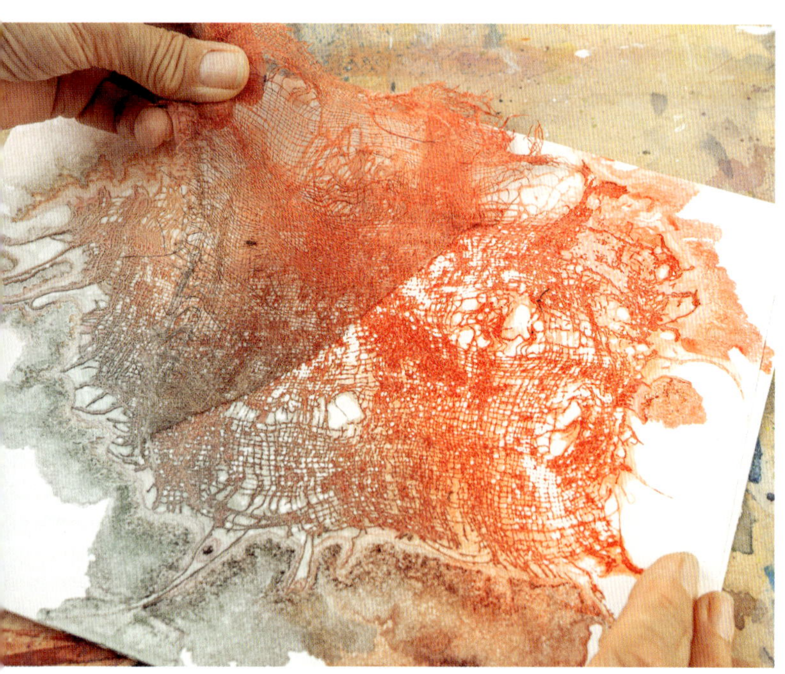

Revealing the result is always a treat.

Making prints from scrim

Before you begin, take some time to rip, open out and generally prepare a piece of scrim to your liking. You can use watercolour, inks or a mixture of both depending how strong a print you want to achieve.

1 Arrange the scrim onto a sheet of cellophane or plastic.

2 Spray the scrim all over with water. This adheres the scrim to the plastic and allows you to paint it wet in wet in the next step.

3 Mix your colours to a milk-like consistency and apply the paint or ink using a large round watercolour brush on its side, a sponge paddle or roller. As the scrim is wet, it will take up the paint without too much pressure.

4 When you are ready to take a print, turn over the cellophane or plastic with the scrim still in place and position it on your support. Weight it down with heavy books and leave it to dry completely.

5 Once it has dried, lift away the books along with the plastic and scrim to reveal the paper with the scrim print.

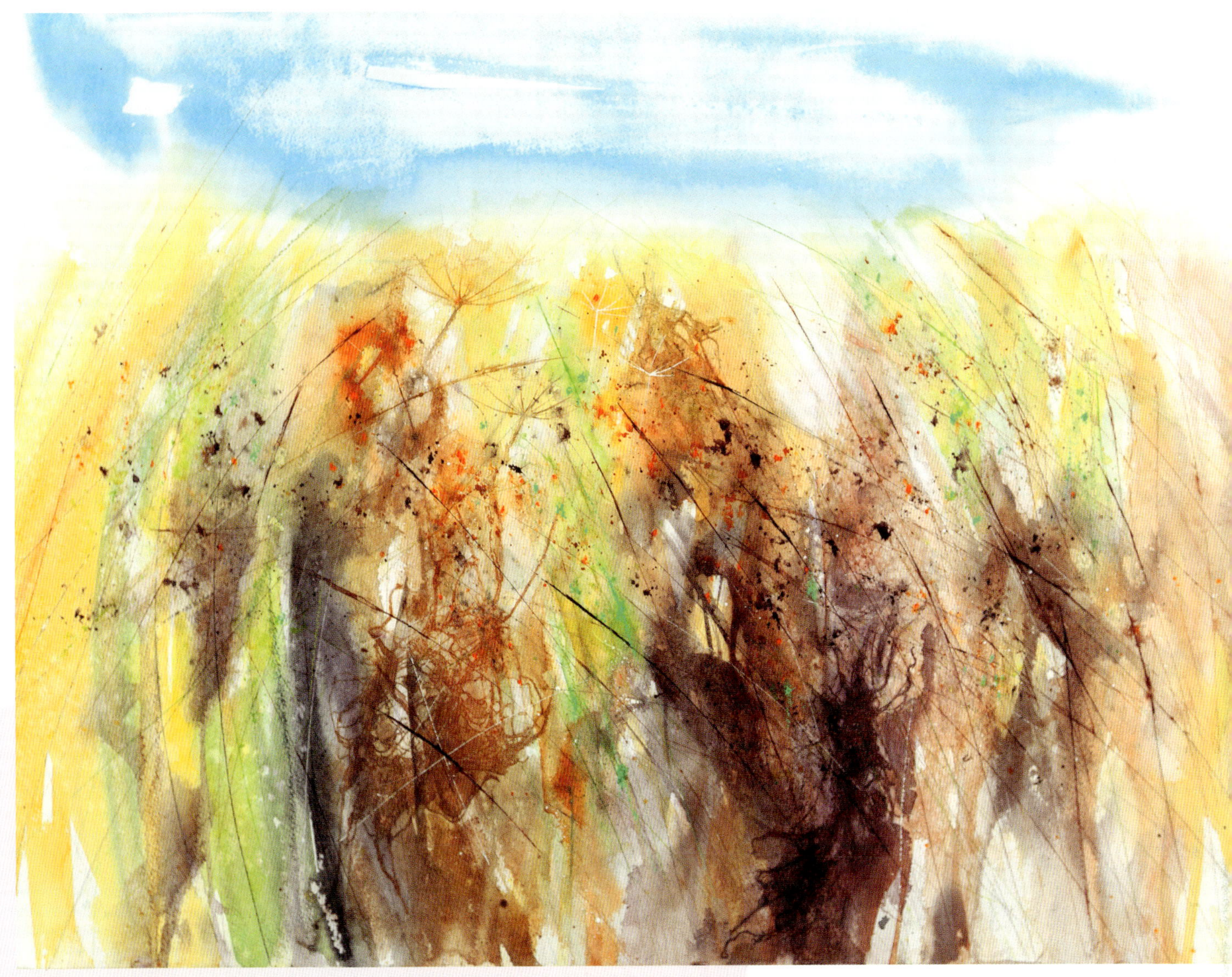

Painting *End of Summer*

This painting demonstrates how scrim prints incorporated into a painting can add interesting textural elements. The pieces of scrim should be prepared in advance, following the instructions on the opposite page, and they can then be added at any stage of the painting. Weigh them down, leaving the cellophane backing in place, until dry. You can then either remove the cellophane and scrim or leave the scrim in place for an even more textural effect.

End of Summer
75 × 50cm (29½ × 19¾in)

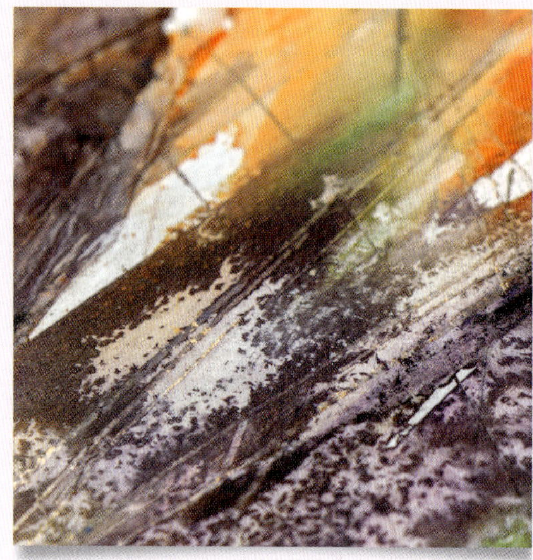

Autumn Seed Heads

This project is an opportunity to combine collage with techniques explored earlier in the book, such as resists. We'll use gouache lift and washing off to create results that are very strong and textural.

I'm keen to encourage you to explore and experiment, so rather than a list of prescriptive instructions, consider how you might adapt the stages and materials to your own ideas and way of working. In particular, choose colours from the collage that you select, and change or expand on the range of tools listed.

You will need

- 35 × 35cm (13¾ × 13¾in) 425gsm (200lb) watercolour paper with a Not surface, secured to a painting board

- Collage materials, acrylic medium and applicator

- Soft pencil, such as a 2B or 4B

- Brushes: size 12 round, 25mm (1in) flat, size 6 round

- Watercolour paints: burnt sienna, Aussie red gold, French ultramarine

- Gouache paint: titanium white

- Masking fluid

- Acrylic inks: burnt sienna, quinacridone magenta, phthalo blue, black

- Deep-welled palette

- Palette knife, ruling pen and toothbrush

- Water sprayer

- Table salt

- Gold bronzing powder – I used Schmincke Aqua-Bronze in rich pale gold

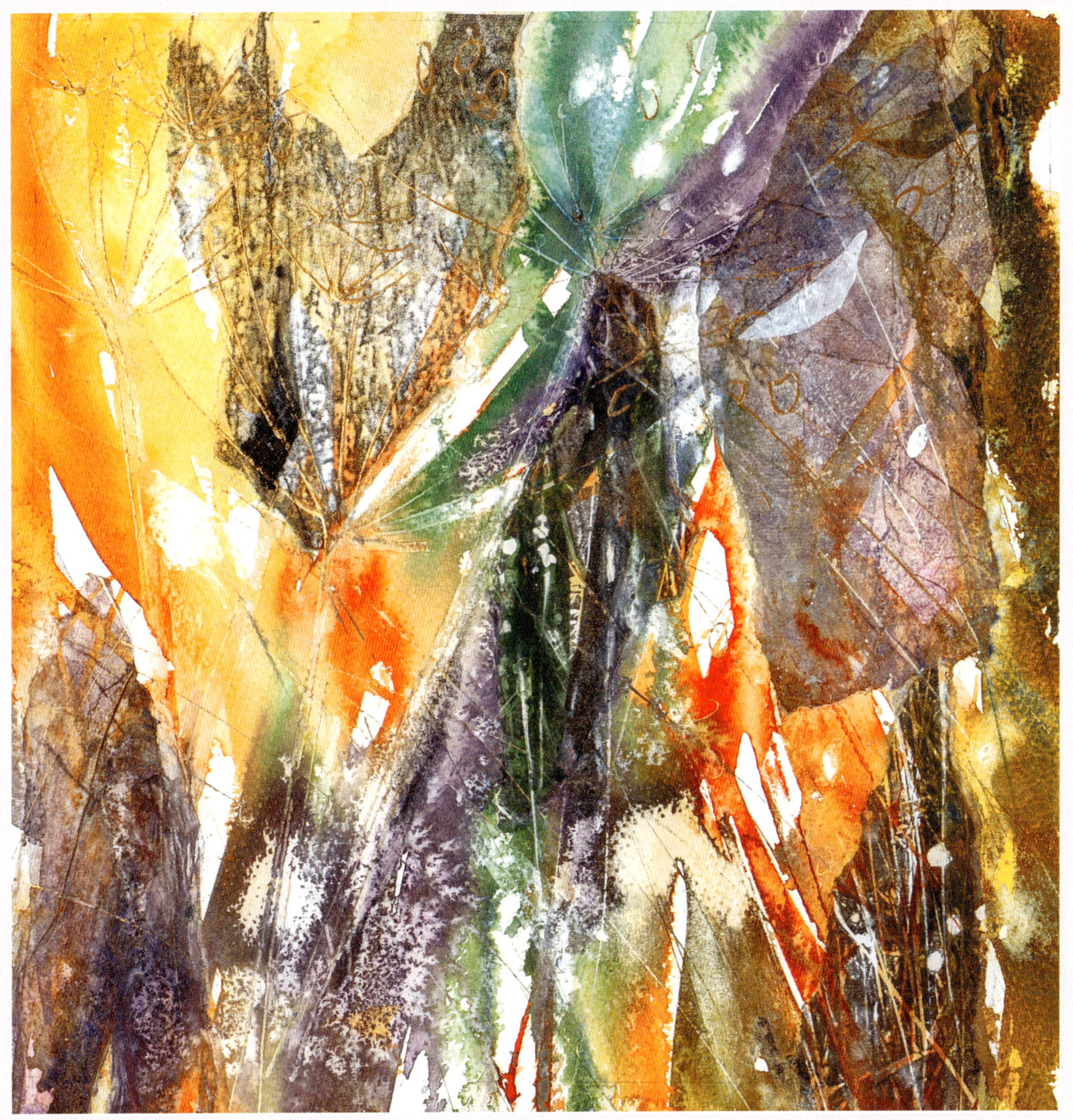

The finished painting
35 × 35cm (13¾ × 13¾in)

1 Composing with collage

This stage is concerned with creating an irregular but balanced composition. In general, you should be focussing on the linear nature of the seed heads and grasses; and how they form geometrical shapes as they intersect.

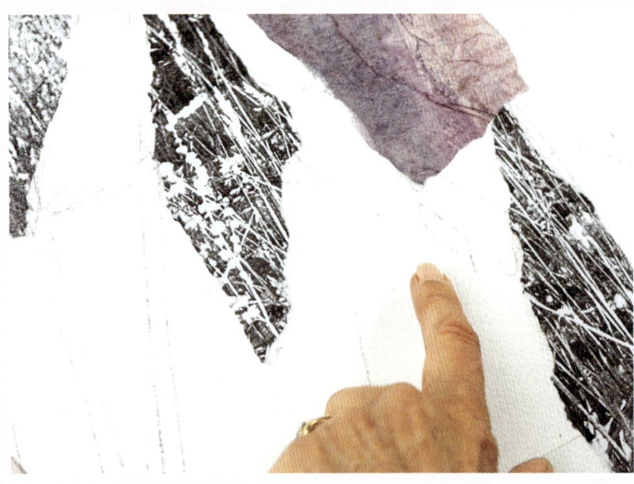

When drawing, look for the opportunity to create interesting geometric shapes through negative drawing.

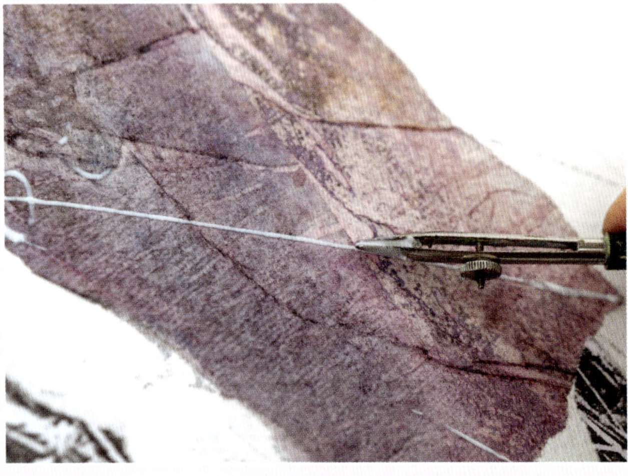

Ensure you have the ruling pen turned on its side as shown to apply clean lines.

- Working freehand, sketch on the design using a soft pencil. Use the rule of thirds (see page 24) to help position the seedheads. I've placed a cluster of seedheads in the top left-hand corner, for example. Use these lines to connect and complement the collage pieces.

- Choose and position a few collage pieces. These could be irregular torn shapes or a mix of cut and torn pieces. I have selected some black and white, as well as some painted-through pieces (see page 112). Use the lines in the drawing to connect and complement the collage pieces. The piece placed near the centre will create a focal point. Secure the collage with acrylic medium and leave to dry.

- Apply masking fluid using the ruling pen or palette knife. Respond to the sketch lines, rather than following them slavishly. These marks will be covered with gold later, so think about how to place them to evoke reflected sunlight.

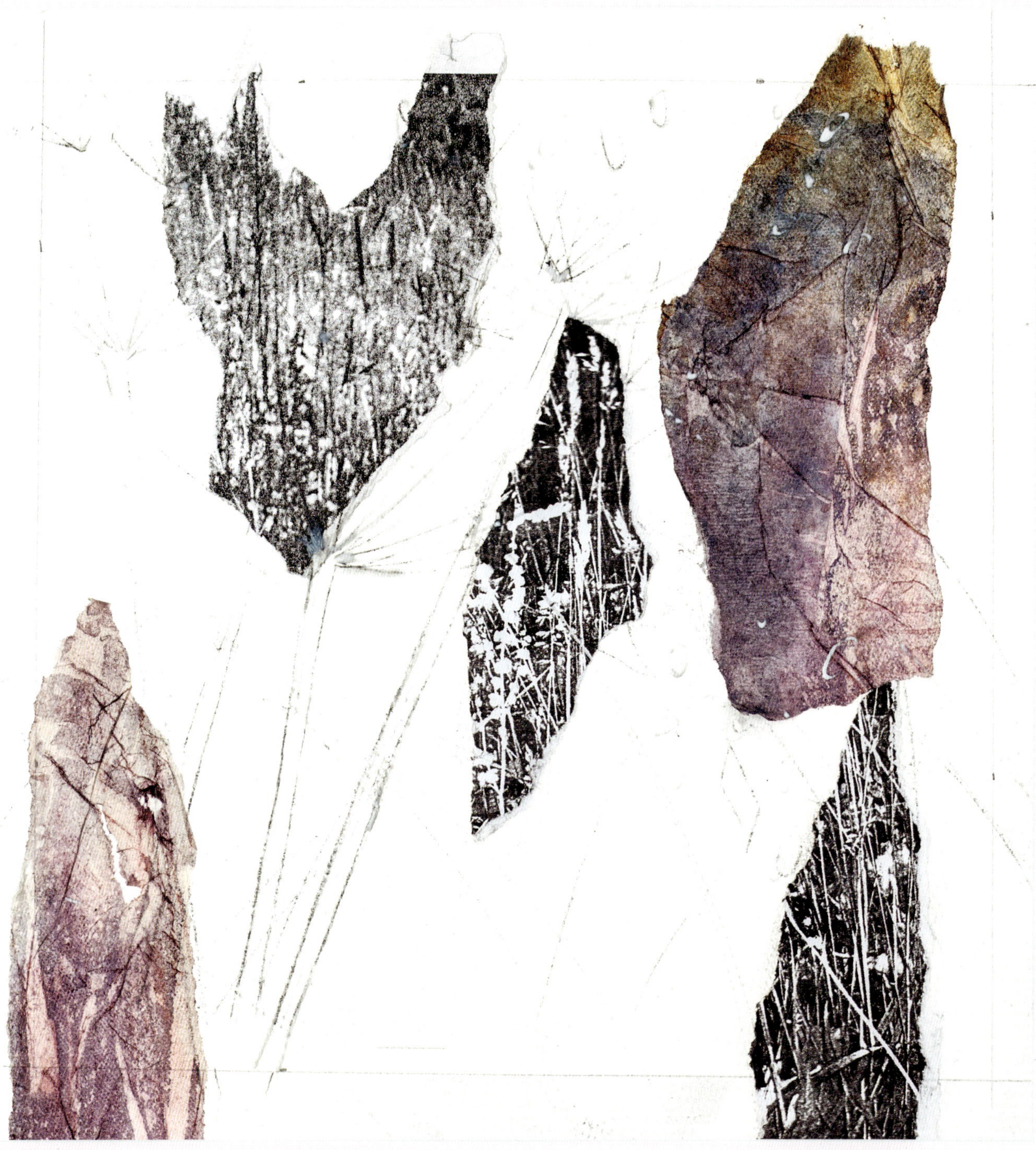

The painting at the end of this stage.

Adding colour and washing off

The key here is to apply the paint and wash it off, leaving random textures and shapes that are impossible to achieve through painting alone. We'll apply gouache as a resist, then paint over with a mix of watercolour and ink. When painting, you're aiming for contrast both in tone and in colour across the composition as a whole.

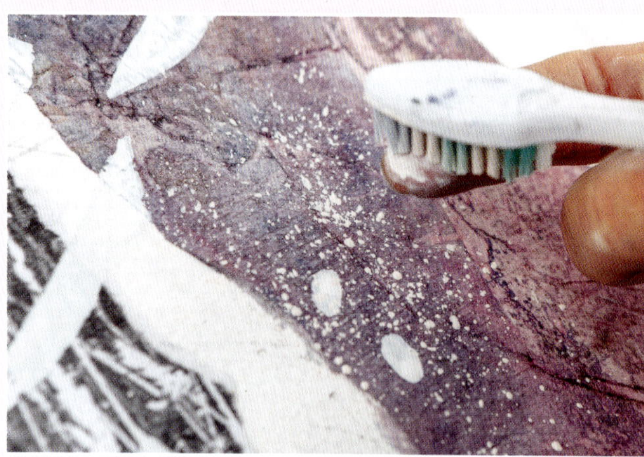

Using a variety of applicators can add interest. I used a size 12 round brush for most of the gouache, but swapped to a palette knife for long fine grasses, and used a toothbrush loaded with gouache to create speckles by drawing my finger over the bristles.

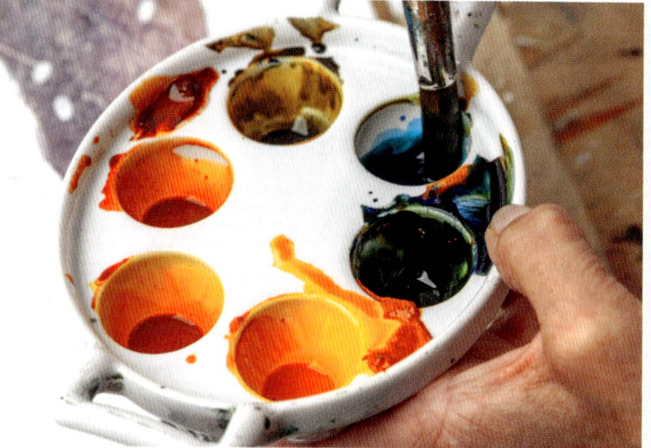

Change to a clean brush, clean palette and clean water when mixing up your watercolour washes, as even a small amount of gouache can resist.

- Apply white gouache in open shapes, both thinly and more generously. Pick out geometric shapes in the negative spaces created by the lines of the umbellifers and the grasses. Work intuitively to help with creating an abstract impression.

- Prepare burnt sienna, Aussie red gold and French ultramarine watercolours in a deep-welled palette. Add drops of burnt sienna, phthalo blue, quinacridone magenta and black acrylic inks. Paint freely using the size 12 round and 25mm (1in) flat brush. Use a light touch to avoid moving the gouache too much – but don't worry that it re-wets a little.

- While the paint and ink are wet, sprinkle in a little table salt in areas you want to create additional texture. Allow the painting to dry a little.

- Before it dries completely, wash areas off; this is done simply by tilting it up and pouring clean water over the painting. This gouache lift technique (see page 78) gives you random textural effects.

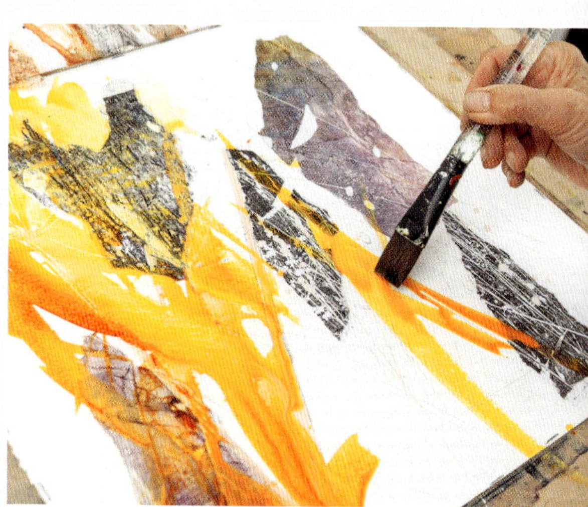

Avoid covering the whole surface with paints and inks; allow some of the collage to show through. Use negative painting to leave some geometric shapes.

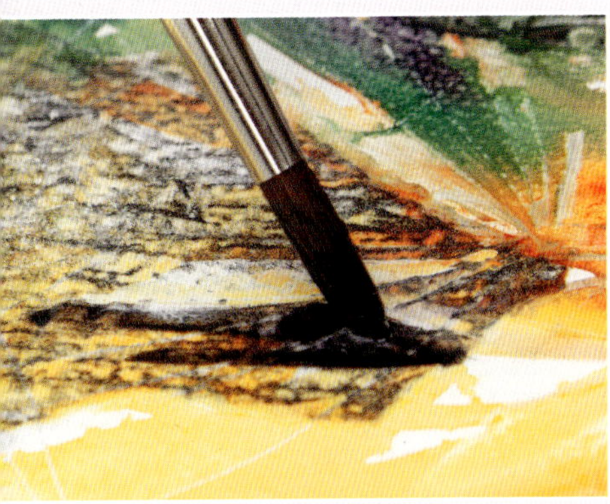

Washing off will soften the colours, so be bold with tones and hues when adding the initial colour.

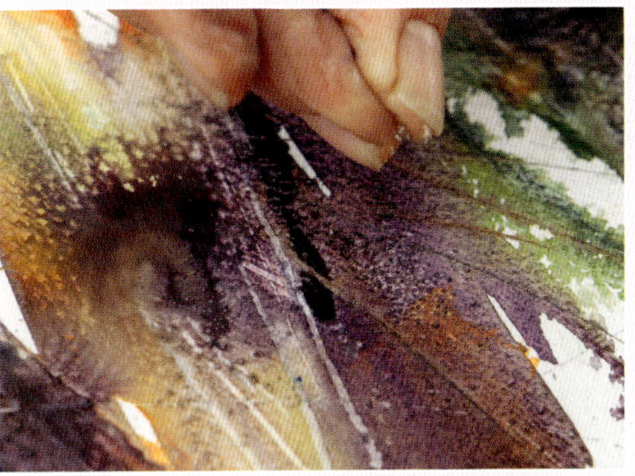

The effects that salt creates will depend on how much you add, so experiment with using a lot or a little. Bear in mind that the effect is not immediate; give it time to work.

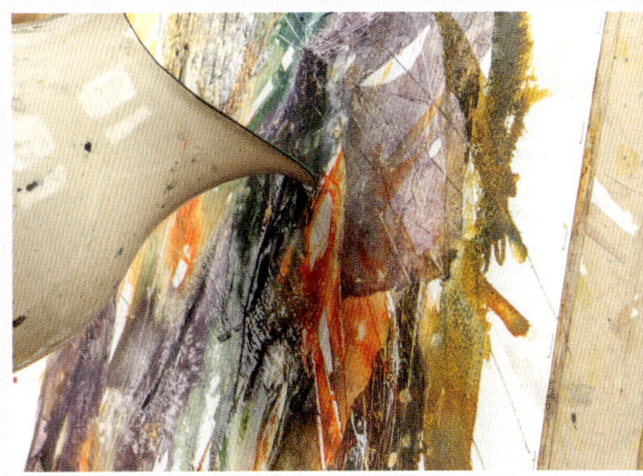

Washing off can be selective, or you can pour the water over the whole painting. If you look closely, you'll see the cloudiness where the gouache is lifting off a little.

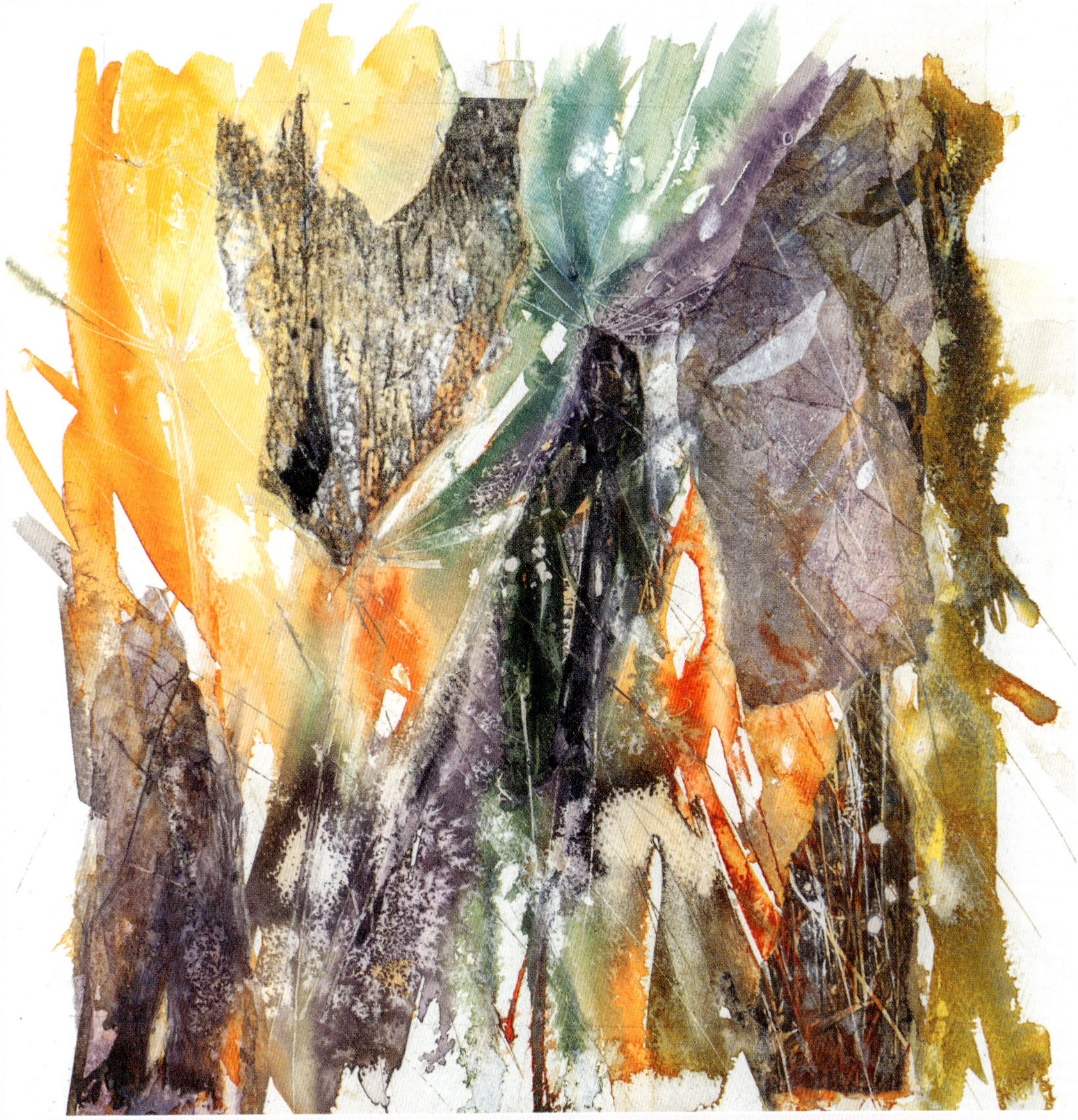

The painting at the end of this stage.

3 Refining and finishing touches

After drying completely, we move on to finishing touches. If you have lost good tonal contrasts, you might want to strengthen the darks and bring up highlights before continuing.

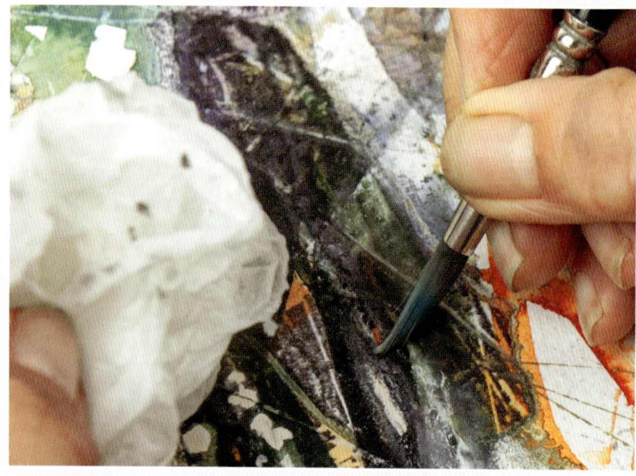

Lifting re-wetted watercolour off gouache areas with kitchen paper will allow you to selectively bring up highlights.

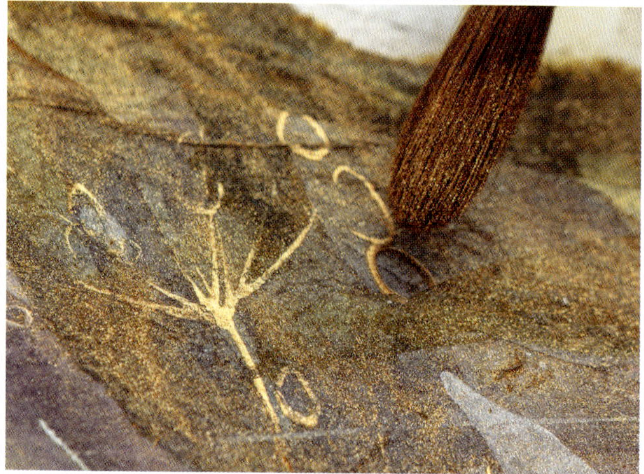

The gold powder will only adhere to the masking fluid. Make sure your brush is completely dry.

- The washing-off technique may miss some areas of gouache, leaving them covered with colour. You can use a damp size 6 round brush to re-wet the paint on any gouache detail, then dab clean kitchen paper on to lift off the paint.

- Once the painting is completely dry, use a dry size 12 round brush to brush gold powder over all the areas of masking fluid. For safety, wear a dust mask to do this. Make sure that all the masking fluid is covered before gently brushing off the excess with a dry brush. The excess powder can be reused on another painting.

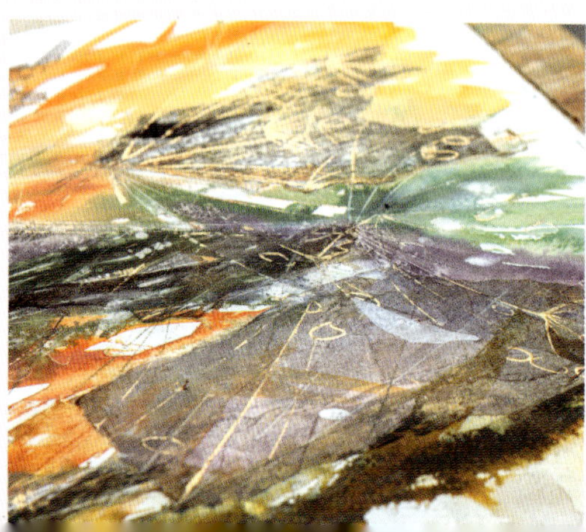

The finished painting can be seen on page 117.

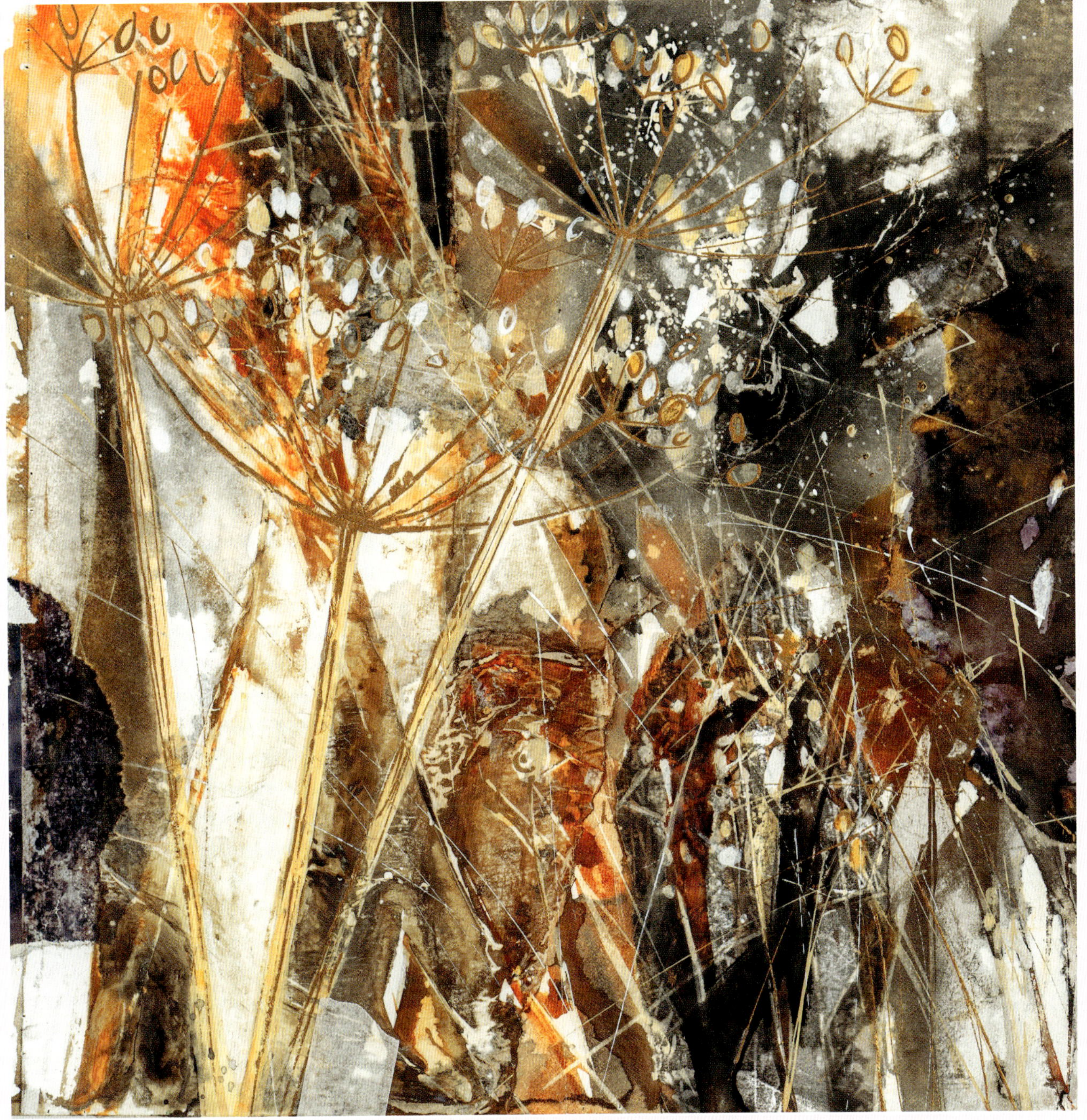

Seed heads study

This study, which uses some of the same techniques as the project, develops the seed head idea further with an almost monochrome colour scheme. Geometric shapes taken from the seed head are echoed around the painting. They form a strong pattern of lights and darks that add contrast and depth to the composition.

ARTISTS WHO INFLUENCE US

Where do we get ideas from and who are our creative influences? The answer, potentially, is anywhere and everyone. They could be friends, family members, the natural world itself and certainly other artists. Nothing in art or life happens in a vacuum; our art is affected by all of these connections. In some way that's not always obvious, they feed into our creativity.

We all accumulate favourite artists, whose work we admire for one reason or another, and these are perhaps the greatest influence on our work. While some lose their appeal as our art moves on, others remain, like friends and helpers to go to when inspiration is low. It's worth trying to analyse what attracts you to particular artists' work, so that you can make the most of their influence. It can be any number of reasons: a style that resonates, striking compositions, use of colour, the marks that are used or the way that paint is applied.

Here are a few of the artists that I admire. Some you will know and some may be less familiar, but I recommend them to you; starting with the master colourist, Henri Matisse (1864–1954) who emerged as a leader of the Fauvist movement in 1905. The Fauves were dubbed 'wild beasts' for the violence of their bold, emotional rather than naturalistic use of colour. I love using colour and so enjoy this aspect of his work, but I also like the way that he abstracted and simplified forms. He often reduced areas of his paintings to line only, flattened, distorted or removed perspective altogether.

Barbara Rae (b. 1943) is one of my favourite British and contemporary artists. A painter and master printmaker, she is also known as an outstanding colourist and cites Matisse as one of her influences. I am mostly inspired by her screen prints, which are vibrantly coloured and worked in tandem with her nature and landscape paintings. Her prints include elements of the history and mythology of a place and the surfaces are activated with a variety of free drawing, marks and layered textures.

Peter Lanyon (1918–1964), also a British artist, was a leading figure of the Cornish, St. Ives school. On the surface, his paintings look completely abstract with drawn or incised lines, gestural marks and areas repainted or scraped away. In fact, they are closely based on his observations of the landscape; they are complex and combine the feeling of a place, together with different angles and variations of light, such are the possibilities of abstraction.

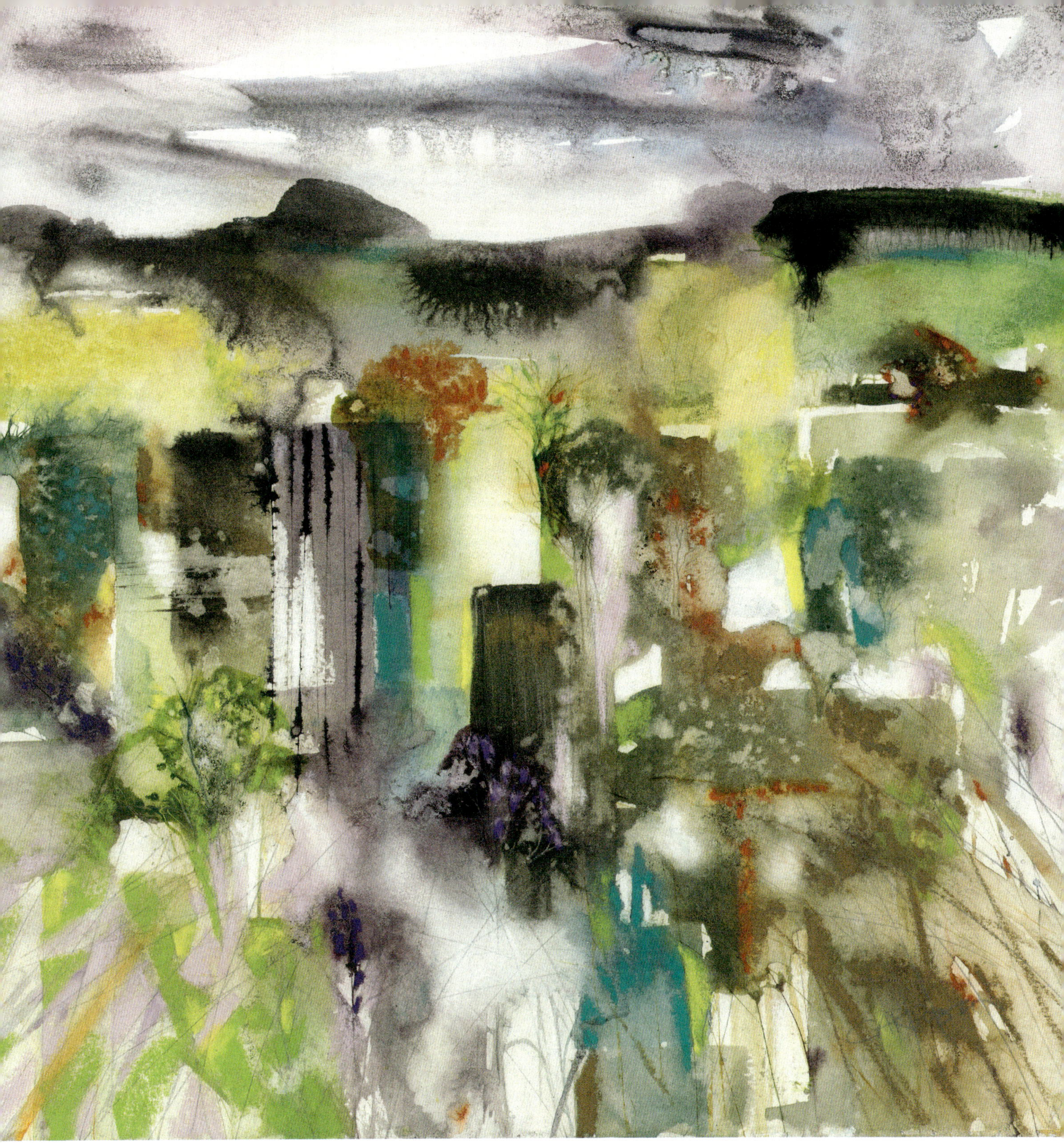

Spring Greens the Winter Gloom
35 × 35cm (13¾ × 13¾in)

Gerhard Richter (b. 1932) is an internationally renowned artist from
Germany. His huge abstract paintings were influenced by the gestural
artist Jackson Pollock, but where Pollock dripped and poured paint, Richter
developed his own distinctive technique. He stood on ladders and used large,
homemade squeegees to drag and layer the paint. He used this skilful and
random process to blend and blur the fluid layers of colour. The humble and
much smaller squeegee has since migrated into most of our artists' toolkits
and his technique is widely emulated.

The best way to discover artists, to find out what drives them and learn
more about their working methods is, of course, to visit art galleries and
exhibitions. It allows you to get close up, to examine the materials and
techniques and answer some very helpful questions. For example: what media
was used, and how was it applied? Was it painted, sprayed, thrown or poured?
Look closely and try to guess what tools were used – what types of brushes?
A palette knife, sticks, pens, crayons? How was the painting built up? What
was the first layer? Was it a wash of colour, texture or perhaps collage, and
what came next? You can often get clues to the process by looking at the
edges of the piece where the layering may be incomplete. Painting labels can
also be very informative.

For me, art exhibitions are part of an enjoyable day out, a treat, as well as
a chance to soak up other artists' influences and I always come away feeling
refreshed and inspired. We don't all have access to galleries, but however
you are able to view art, whether from a book, at a course or online, there is
always lots to learn and enjoy. I believe that the more open we are to ideas
and trends in art and other areas of life, the more that we grow as artists.
The various strands of influence that we absorb, build and weave together are
what adds depth, richness and meaning to our lives and to our art.

Beneath the Ice
35 × 35cm (13¾ × 13¾in)

Acknowledgements

*My grateful thanks go to everyone at Search Press for all of their
various contributions in the production of this book. My special
thanks go to my editor, Edward Ralph for his expertise, guidance
and friendly support. I would also like to thank Mark Davison for his
wonderful photography and the Search Press design team, especially
Emma Sutcliffe for her creative design work.*

*As always, I am eternally grateful to my family and friends for their
feedback, practical help, love and encouragement.*

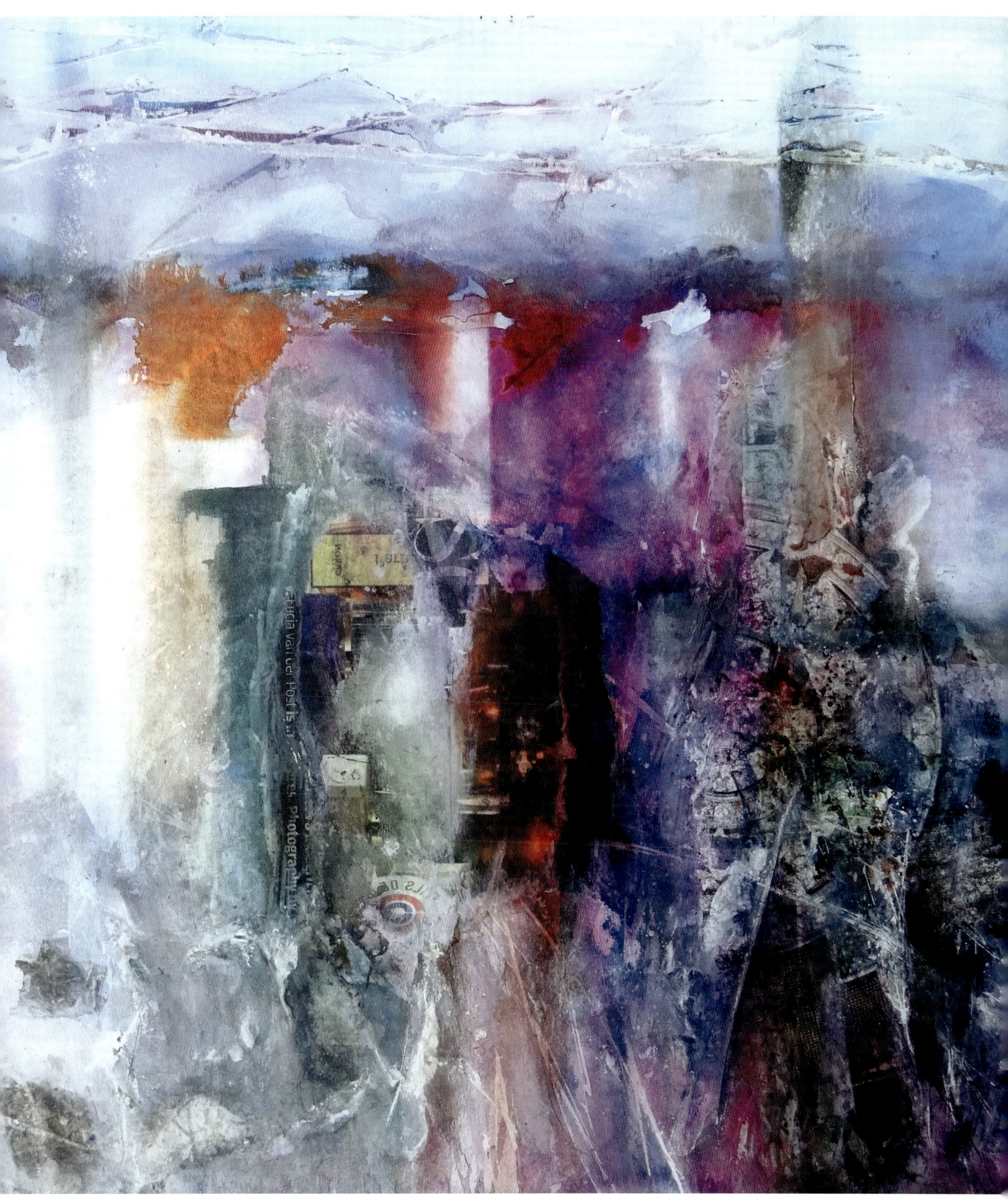

INDEX

acrylic paint 55, 57, 90, 113

balance 15, 28, 29, 118
brushes 58, 80, 94, 116

collage 11, 22, 27, 38, 51, 55, 60, 66, 72, 90, 91, 93, 94, 102, 104, 105, 106, 107, 108, 109, 112, 116, 118, 120, 126
colour
  complementary 12, 14, 15, 43, 59, 92, 100
  emotional 38
  local 38
  mixing 40
  purity 40
  symbolism 36
composing/composition 14, 15, 22, 24, 25, 26, 27, 28, 29, 32, 82, 86, 92, 101, 118, 120, 123
  with collage 118
  with shape 26
  with tone 32

design, principles of 28
digital image-editing 12, 13, 30
dry in wet 18
dry media 59

edges 18, 22, 79, 102, 108, 126
exercises
  collage 106
  colour scheme swatches 41
  creating starts 90
  develop a simple abstract 12
  making and using a tonal scale 31
  nature prints through tissue 112
  swift texture studies 46
  thumbnail sketches 27
  wet in wet 64
experiment 9, 17, 18, 26, 35, 41, 53, 78, 93, 110, 116, 121

form(s) 14, 15, 24, 26, 28, 29, 48, 56, 59, 62, 68, 73, 80, 82, 94, 106, 118, 123, 124
formal elements 14, 15, 29, 62, 107

gesso *see* texture pastes/gels
gestural marks 14, 20, 22, 27, 28, 41, 74, 75, 82, 98, 113, 124, 126
gouache 22, 55, 56, 66, 78, 79, 82, 84, 87, 106, 113, 116, 120, 121, 122
gouache lift 22, 78, 79, 116, 120

inks
  acrylic 13, 35, 57, 65, 71, 73, 75, 76, 77, 78, 79, 80, 91, 94, 100, 116
  Indian 46, 57, 76, 77, 78, 79

layers 48, 57, 72, 88, 90, 93, 94, 104, 126
limited palette 43
line 6, 8, 12, 14, 15, 17, 18, 20, 22, 28, 124

mark making 18
masking fluid 20, 35, 46, 47, 65, 70, 74, 75, 116, 118, 122
mixed media 6, 9, 43, 58, 60, 61, 88, 128
movement 14, 15, 20, 24, 26, 27, 28, 45, 98, 124

Notan 34, 35

paper *see* supports
pastels 43, 59, 72
pattern and repetition 28
pigment 54, 55
print(ing) 22, 45, 50, 70, 102, 110, 111, 113, 114, 128
  leaf 111
  nature 110, 112
  quick transfer 113
  scrim 114

reference 10, 12
rule of thirds 24

scale 28
shape(s) 8, 10, 13, 14, 15, 18, 22, 24, 25, 26, 27, 28, 29, 30, 32, 34, 35, 39, 47, 48, 62, 65, 66, 68, 76, 77, 80, 82, 84, 86, 93, 94, 98, 105, 106, 108, 110, 112, 113, 118, 120, 123
  geometric 8, 15, 24, 28, 29, 66, 84, 118, 120
  mixing organic and geometric shapes 66
  negative shapes 28
  organic shapes 24, 66, 68, 114, 128
source material 10, 12
starts 59, 70, 90, 113
stencils 50, 94, 96
  and texture paste 50
stretching paper 60, 77
supports 60, 61, 76

texture(s) 9, 10, 11, 12, 13, 14, 15, 22, 25, 27, 28, 29, 43, 44, 45, 46, 47, 48, 49, 50, 51, 55, 59, 60, 61, 68, 72, 73, 76, 77, 79, 90, 93, 94, 96, 98, 102, 104, 106, 107, 108, 110, 112, 114, 120, 124, 126
texture pastes/gels 48, 49, 90, 91, 94
  customizing 49
theme 38, 43, 106
thumbnail sketch 27, 32
tonal scale 31
tone(s) 14, 15, 27, 29, 30, 31, 32, 33, 34, 35, 40, 80, 84, 100, 105, 113, 120, 121
tools 13, 14, 17, 35, 48, 55, 58, 62, 74, 86, 93, 116, 126

underpainting 92
unity and harmony 28

value 9, 30, 34
variety 28
viewfinder 11

washes 20, 22, 64, 68, 84, 86, 90, 91, 93, 104, 106, 115, 120
washing off 13, 22, 38, 71, 76, 77, 78, 84, 116, 120, 121
watercolour 13, 18, 20, 33, 41, 46, 54, 55, 56, 58, 59, 60, 61, 64, 65, 66, 68, 70, 71, 72, 73, 76, 77, 80, 88, 90, 93, 100, 110, 114, 116, 120, 122
wax 18, 59, 70, 72, 73
wax resist 72
wet in wet 18, 20, 46, 64, 88, 91, 100, 106

First published in 2024

Search Press Limited
Wellwood, North Farm Road,
Tunbridge Wells, Kent TN2 3DR

Text copyright © Carole Robson, 2024
Photographs by Mark Davison at
Search Press studios.

Photographs and design copyright © Search
Press Ltd. 2024

ISBN: 978-1-80092-016-3
ebook ISBN: 978-1-80093-006-3

Suppliers
For details of suppliers, please visit
the Search Press website:
www.searchpress.com

Publisher's note
All the step-by-step photographs in this
book feature the author, Carole Robson,
demonstrating painting with mixed
media. No models have been used.

For further ideas and inspiration and to join
our free online community, visit
www.bookmarkedhub.com

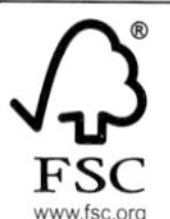